THE WHISTLE
BLOWER

A JOURNEY DEEP INTO THE
HEART OF RUGBY

ALAIN ROLLAND
With
Daragh Ó Conchúir

HEROBOOKS

HEROBOOKS

PUBLISHED BY HERO BOOKS
1 WOODVILLE GREEN
LUCAN
CO. DUBLIN
IRELAND
www.herobooks.ie
Hero Books is an imprint of Umbrella Publishing

First Published 2015

A CIP record for this book is available from the British Library

ISBN: 978-0-9526260-2-2

Printed in Ireland with Print Procedure Ltd
Cover design and typesetting: Jessica Maile
Cover photograph: Inpho
Photographs: Inpho and the Rolland family collection

To my amazing wife, Liz and my wonderful kids,
Mark, Clodagh, Natasha and Amy

ACKNOWLEDGEMENTS

I would like to express my warmest gratitude to all those who helped me in the making of this book.

I would especially like to thank my wife Liz for her unrelenting support. None of this would be possible without her. To my wonderful kids, Mark, Clodagh, Natasha and Amy, thanks for all the sacrifices made without complaint and for being really great kids. I am blessed.

I would also like to express my deepest gratitude to my parents for providing me with a great start in life and to my Mum especially, for keeping us all strong after my Dad's passing.

And, of course, to Daragh Ó Conchúir, a special thanks for the way he captured my life story, for the countless trips to my house to listen to me rabbiting on, and the time and dedication given to bringing this story to life.

To my publisher, Liam Hayes who showed me how there was a story to be told and for his insight in having Daragh as my co-author. Their combined talents have made the task of putting my story into words very easy and seamless for me, and for that I am eternally grateful.

To my teacher, mentor and friend, Owen Doyle for always keeping me focussed on the task at hand and for his unwavering support and friendship. I would never have enjoyed the level of success without him.

To Joel Jutge, who has been a great friend and confidante. His guidance over the last few years of my refereeing career was also invaluable and instrumental to my success on and off the field.

Finally, I would like to thank the referee who failed to turn up at Stradbrook that day in 1995 and left me hurriedly being asked to take charge of my first game, that Third A game between 'Rock and Lansdowne. I'm not sure what your reasons were but they definitely worked in my favour!

Alain Rolland
September, 2015

// As a ref, you know what they're doing across the corridor, but it's your job to make sure that they don't kill one another or die, that they don't cross the line ...

CONTENTS

PROLOGUE

'Oh Jesus. Please Jesus, please Jesus, please Jesus.'

Control has been at the epicentre of my entire adult life but here I am, in a small room of a Paris hotel feeling utterly helpless.

I am happily married with a young family. My professional life is good, I played Test rugby for Ireland and this is my second World Cup as a referee. Confidence is not an issue because of the preparation I have done. I am ready but will I get the chance?

Mr Control is at the mercy of someone else. A quivering mess with head in hands and elbows on knees shaking so much that I must look like one of those bobble-head toys, twitching and convulsing.

'Please Jesus, please Jesus, please Jesus.'

My mind is racing.

'For fuck sake Paddy, get on with it.'

As a player, I was dropped and overlooked, mostly by Ireland. For the guts of a decade, I watched a catalogue of the country's scrum halves leapfrog me to wear the green jersey, while I maintained a regular presence amongst the replacements. On one occasion, Chris Saverimutto was chosen ahead of me even though three of the selectors had never actually seen him play.

Yet I was never reduced to this state. Nothing close to it. I derived tremendous satisfaction in achieving what I did as a player because I had to work so hard for it. Sure, I could have picked up a few more caps but if my best wasn't good enough for the national selectors, I could accept that, for the most part.

Thankfully, it was good enough on one unforgettable day.

October 27, 1990.

The memory of jogging out onto the Lansdowne Road turf made famous by Jack Kyle, Karl Mullen, Syd Millar, Tom Kiernan, Mike Gibson, Willie John McBride and so many other greats, moments away from making my debut for Ireland against Argentina remains vivid and cherished. It was a rickety old ground but I loved the headquarters of Irish rugby and could feel my chest almost bursting with pride that on this day at least, I was considered the best scrum half in the land.

Now, 17 years later, my chest is bursting with a completely different sensation. My heart feels like it might leap right out through my ribcage and onto that patch of carpet I had been staring solidly at for what seems like hours, but is really just a matter of minutes.

No playing experience prompted such emotions and physical reactions. Nothing in refereeing either. Not the inflamed reaction to my dismissal of Wales captain, Sam Warburton early in the World Cup semi-final four years later, nor the silly threats that came subsequently. I had made the right decision then and was in complete control.

Not now though.

My head is going to explode. There is sweat everywhere. Sticky and uncomfortable, tributaries running at various angles and in different directions down my body, t-shirt and shorts clinging to me. Won't someone turn up the air conditioning?

This is torture. If my name isn't the last one called out here now I am going to be devastated. I have never coveted anything so much in my life. I need this, I have worked for it. I am the best man for the job.

'Please Jesus, please Jesus. PLEASSSSSSSSSSE!'

This inner turmoil is a new sensation. Ever since I decided I had enough of being bullied in school and would take matters into my own hands, I have been master of my own destiny for the large part and elected not to waste time on anything beyond that control. Dwelling on the past was pointless too.

Well that principle, which has served me in rugby and life, is well and truly blown out the window here. I want to referee the World Cup final and if I don't I will be inconsolable.

The way they are going about this seems designed to build tension, as if we have an audience of millions around the world. But it's just us 12 referees, seated around this room, waiting for the decision of the Rugby World Cup chief of officials, Paddy O'Brien.

We're kids again, waiting to hear our name on the team. Except there can only be one World Cup final referee. Now I know how the contestants on those reality shows must feel like. This is X-Factor to the power of infinity.

'And the winner is....'

Cue drum roll, with interminable pause to drag it out.

'Get on with it!'

But this isn't even that straightforward. They had decided before the tournament that the top four referees in their pecking order would be given the quarter-finals and the man for the final would come from this group. So it's Joël Jutge, Wayne Barnes, my fellow Irish official Alan Lewis or me.

The semi-finals would go to two other officials. Those announcements are being made too but are irrelevant to the quartet on the precipice of everything and nothing.

'England-France... Jonathan Kaplan.'

'South Africa-Argentina... Steve Walsh.'

This washes over me. In 2003, I had harboured the dream and was close but as a rookie, only refereeing on the international stage four years, it was a tremendous experience to be there at all. Now is my time. I am ready, the man in form. That we are in France, the country of my late father, Henri, only adds to a feeling that the stars are aligned. Having said that, we could be in Timbuktu. This should be mine.

It has been an excellent few weeks. I took the opportunity to visit the Hôtel du Cap-Eden Roc on the Côte d'Azur, where I spent most of my youthful summers. The place is dripping with opulence but the memories that came rushing back were simple enough. A contented boy whiling away his time in a slow pace of swimming, fishing, eating and lazing around.

Most importantly, the tournament had gone well through the group stages and the quarter-final between England and Australia. But this is the prize, the target for all 12 referees at the start of the tournament. If my name is not called out now, it would be a greater blow than any rejection I suffered as a player.

There doesn't seem to be enough air in the room. I am gulping, trying not to hyperventilate or get sick. Just waiting and waiting for Paddy to get through all the bullshit.

Finally.

'And the referee for the final is…'

I swear to God the bastard paused. HE FUCKING PAUSED! Like he's Dermot O'Leary.

'… Alain Rolland.'

YESSSSSSSSSSSSSSSSSSSSSSSSSSSS! Oh my sweet Jesus.

I can't believe it! That sounds strange, given that I felt I deserved it but now that it has actually happened, it is pretty overwhelming. You think of the years of sacrifice, catching up on work in departure lounges, planes and hotels, being away from home so much, foregoing family holidays… it is all for this.

While doing somersaults in my brain, I keep it low key, conscious that Lewy, Barnesy and Joël are as gutted as I would have been. They are colleagues. You don't want to rub it in by going around fist-pumping and high-fiving like Justin Leonard at the 17th in Brookline after sinking that 45-foot tramliner against Jose Maria Olazabal in the 1999 Ryder Cup.

All the guys come over to shake my hand, tap me on the back, offer their congratulations. I'm trying to take the enormity of it all in.

Joël Dumé comes over to give me a hug. That's when I break down, sobbing. I am an emotional wreck for two or three minutes, unable to speak.

I've done it.

PART
ONE

CHAPTER ONE

When you think of the fortune that saw my sports-ignorant parents send me to Willow Park, and later on, the sequence of events that surrounded the beginning of my refereeing career, when an appointed official failed to turn up for a Third A game on a day I just happened to be down at Stradbrook, it may just be that I was destined for a life of rugby.

Go back to the very beginning, when Alain Colm Pierre Rolland was delivered into the world by Dr Karl Mullen at Mount Carmel Hospital on August 22, 1966.

Yes, *that* Karl Mullen. The legend who captained Ireland's first ever Grand Slam-winning team 18 years previously.

Karl and his wife, Doreen had become close friends through the restaurant my parents ran in Killiney for many years, though they certainly wouldn't have discussed rugby. Mum and Dad knew nothing about the game and cared less. Meanwhile, Karl was very unassuming and you would never have known he was guaranteed a place in the annals of Irish rugby.

It seems like a lot of coincidences have brought me from a background involving no sport at all to where I am now, a former Test player and World Cup final referee, using my rugby experiences to earn a living as a consultant within the game and in the business world.

Maybe despite thinking I am, I have never actually been in control at all.

▐▐▐▐

There is a misconception that I was born in France or lived there for a significant period of my life. Apart from holidays, I never have. I am Irish, with a French heritage.

My father, Henri was French but arrived in Ireland as a 13-year-old. It was very difficult for him to have his world turned upside down like that. He was very quiet and introspective, traits I have inherited from him. As a result, he kept a lot of his sadness bottled up.

Without a word of English, he was sent to CUS on Leeson Street. It was a real struggle but a guy called Brian Leonard took him under his wing. Brian could speak French and helped Dad integrate. They would form a strong, enduring friendship.

Dad grew to love Ireland and stayed here the rest of his life. He never lost his accent, and while he was well able to converse fluently, you would never have been in any doubt as to his origins. It wasn't a huge issue because he wasn't a big talker anyway. Mum was happy to pick up the slack in that department!

Helena Dempsey was the love of Dad's life and after getting married, they raised a gang of boys. I was followed by Philippe, André and Gilles. For a while, my parents ran a very successful restaurant but the recession and Dad's ill health ended that venture.

The arrival of the Rolland clan to a rapidly-changing Ireland came by virtue of the world-renowned abilities of my grandfather, Pierre. He was the head chef at the Hôtel du Cap-Eden Roc in Antibes on the Côte d'Azur. This was and still is, one of the most luxurious hotels in the world. In that era, the likes of Marlene Dietrich, Richard Burton and Elizabeth Taylor were regulars. Patrons had to pay by cash until 2006 and nowadays rates rise from €1,000 to €15,000 a night. It is out of this world.

So in 1949, the year Ireland was declared a republic and officially left the British Commonwealth, he accepted an invitation from Ken Besson to take on a role as executive chef of Ireland's first international restaurant in the

Russell Hotel on Harcourt Street. After six months in Dublin on his own, he was joined by his wife, Margerite and three children. My father came in the middle of two girls, Georgette and Mireille.

The appointment was considered a massive coup for the Russell. The *Irish Hotelier* described the new venture as a 'gourmet's paradise', with Monsieur Rolland ranked among the top 10 chefs in France at the time. He was treated like royalty and carried himself in that fashion too.

When my father was 18, he had to do his military service in Algeria, which was compulsory for all French people until 2001. The service lasted three years and I always got the impression it left a very deep imprint on him. He never talked about it and we knew not to bring it up either.

I was to have my own brush with military service many years later thanks to Mamine, which is what we called Margerite as it is the French word for grandmother. My grandfather was Papy.

Mamine was my godmother and unknown to Mum, she registered me with the French Consulate when I was born. We were all in blissful ignorance of this until the day of my 18th birthday in 1984, when my papers arrived in the letter box, informing me that I was to report in Perpignan at 1800 hours on an appointed day.

Unsurprisingly, Mum went ballistic. It did come as a shock but being 18, I didn't dismiss the idea out of hand, thinking it might be worth trying out. At the time, service had been reduced to just nine months, as against the three years my father had done. I kind of fancied it as a bit of an adventure but Mum was having none of it.

So I was marched straight down to the French Embassy where they explained that as I had always resided in Ireland and if I continued to do so until I was 21, military service would not be enforced on me.

It is funny looking back on it now but it left a huge dent on my mother's relationship with Mamine. Mum was furious with her for taking such a liberty behind her back and they didn't speak for a long while after.

All the boys being given French names was Mamine's doing, not that Mum really bothered too much about that. My two middle names were my grandfathers' and Mum did manage to get Colm to be placed before Pierre!

|█|█|

When Dad returned from Algeria, he joined the staff of the Russell. In 1963, the 18-year-old Helena Dempsey began working there as a receptionist. The suave, dapper Frenchman made an instant impression and it seems that the effect was reciprocal.

Mum is from Blackrock initially. Her father, Colm worked in the Irish Tourist Board and he got my gran, Nell onto one of the first flights when Aer Lingus was set up in 1936. Mum has a photo of it. There were only four people on this little plane; my grandparents, the pilot and the co-pilot. Grandad Dempsey died young but Nell lived to the grand age of 99 before passing away in August 2014.

An eight-year age difference was not a stumbling block to any blossoming romance but the seasonal nature of the business they worked in at the time proved an early hurdle. The Russell closed from November to April and during that time, my grandparents went to the Bahamas, as Papy was head chef in the Lyford Cay Club in Nassau. This was another exclusive destination for the rich and famous, more a private, gated community on a 450-acre property than a hotel. A number of scenes in *James Bond* movies were filmed here, and it was most prominent in *Thunderball*.

Dad went with them and in that first year after they met, Mum went to Italy to work as an au pair around the same time. So it was only when they returned from their travels that they started dating. Their romance blossomed quickly and they got married the following year on October 7, 1965 at the Church of the Holy Name on Beachwood Avenue in Ranelagh, with the reception taking place at the Royal Marine Hotel in Dun Laoghaire. I followed very quickly after.

Now that they were married, my parents would travel with Mamine and Papy to work at the Lyford Cay as well. It was a paradise although I remember nothing of that, being just a baby.

Dad and Papy worked as a team with Dad learning at the hands of the master. Close to the greatest testament of their status was that the team at the Russell was chosen to cook at the official State function in the Iveagh House when President John F Kennedy made his historic visit to Ireland in 1963.

Papy, as head chef, was in charge. Ironically, JFK had stayed near Lyford Cay when holding talks with British Prime Minister, Harold Macmillan the previous December, while the president once summered with his family at the Eden-Roc when he was just 21. Indeed the street where the Eden-Roc is located is now called Boulevard JF Kennedy.

The meal took place on June 27 but the preparation began weeks in advance and the whole thing was run with military precision. Speeches and toasts by the President and Taoiseach, Seán Lemass, had to be made at specific times which meant that the food had to arrive punctually to a timetable that was drawn up to the minute. It had to be eaten and cleared by a set time and so on. The coordination of so many moving parts was extraordinary.

My grandfather sent a sample menu first: le foie gras de Strasbourg, consommé double aux profiteroles, Irish lobster timbale, milk-fed Irish lamb. But JFK's aides explained that the president preferred lighter fare and so he settled on Irish smoked salmon, consommé, Irish beef with new potatoes and peas followed by strawberries and cream. The Russell had exclusive Irish rights to certain French wines, thanks to my grandfather's influence. Two were chosen to accompany the meal: a Château le Tuquet 1959 white and a Le Cortin 1959 red.

It was traditional for the head chef to present the food officially to the visiting dignitary. Papy had a pastillage replica made of the patrol torpedo boat commanded by Kennedy in the Pacific during the Second World War. PT-109 earned two battle stars before being sunk and Kennedy's actions in helping to save the majority of his crew made him a war hero.

Unfortunately for my grandfather, he had broken his ankle in a fall and was on crutches, so Dad stepped into the breach. JFK had a custom of presenting PT-109 tie-clasps on occasions such as this and he gave one to my father. It was something he treasured, although not being one to be effusive about anything, he didn't say much about it. Sadly, it was stolen when our home was broken into many years later and like the PT-109 itself, it never surfaced again.

The Russell had revolutionised fine dining in Ireland and Papy and his team, which included Dad, made that happen. Egon Ronay awarded the Russell with three stars when his guide first included Ireland in the early 1960s. When the first Michelin Guide to Great Britain and Ireland was published in 1974, the Russell was the only Dublin restaurant to be awarded a star. It was Papy's second Michelin star.

With two young boys and another on the way, my parents decided that it was time to branch out on their own. When they bought what would be Restaurant Rolland in Killiney, it was actually our first ever home, with the living quarters upstairs.

Because of the seasonal work in the Bahamas, they had felt that buying a house was a waste of time and rented instead when we were back in Ireland. So it was a fairly transient lifestyle, living in one house, going to the Bahamas for five months, coming back to a different house and repeating the cycle.

My father mastered in sauces and pastries – anything made from sugar. He made unbelievable sugar and ice sculptures. For him and chefs of that level, food was art and the aesthetics were hugely important. Presentation wasn't everything, because the flavours and taste were obviously paramount, but it was a key element of the operation and certainly added a wow factor.

Now that he had his own restaurant, he could put all his own philosophies into play. Restaurant Rolland opened for business on February 24, 1972. It was around the beginning of a new wave of chef-proprietor restaurants in Dublin and it went very well for them for many years.

The Russell closed in 1974 so Papy and Mamine left Ireland and returned to the Eden-Roc. That had a significant impact on my life thereafter and I was a couple of months shy of my ninth birthday when I was sent over to Antibes on my own for the first time in June of 1975. There had always been a close connection with Mamine because she was my godmother and made such a fuss of me. So from then until I was 16, my summer holidays were on the French Riviera.

IIIII

It was magnificent and though no-one else in my class could have even imagined the summers I was enjoying in a fantasy environment, it became the most natural thing in the world to me. I don't ever recall feeling lonely or missing home, even at the start.

My parents would bring me to the airport to be met by an air hostess at the check-in desk. I would have a plastic 'Unaccompanied Minor' sign placed around my neck but was never actually out of an adult's sight from the time I was dropped off to when I met my grandparents. It was the same for the return journey.

There were no direct flights to Nice when I first started travelling. That meant I had to go from Dublin to Paris. Somebody would meet me at arrivals and sit with me while we waited for the connecting flight. Then someone else would collect me from the plane in Nice and stay with me until my grandparents arrived.

The final leg of that journey was always funny because while Mamine never drove a car even once, she was never short of instructions for Papy, who was a real connoisseur when it came to cars. I recall that he had a red Alfa Romeo brought over from France when he was in Ireland. My father inherited the love of cars and bought a Sunbeam Alpine convertible around that time too. It was red as well.

I am a chip off the old block in that way. I don't know much about the mechanics of cars but as a young man, I was entranced by the speed. I haven't ever taken anything on the track, though I'd love to, but I pushed it to the limit and beyond a number of times on the open road when I was that foolish age when you think you are indestructible.

I used to go out in the Merrion Inn a lot and it was there I met my future wife, Lizzie McDonald, who was a student in UCD. It was love at first sight when I spotted her across the room and the rest is history. She is my soulmate and I'm as crazy about her today as I was all those years ago when we walked down the aisle together in 1993.

In the good times, my parents were reasonably well off and Dad always had a fancy motor. He had moved on from the Sunbeam Alpine and now owned a Lancia Beta, which could really shift.

I had started driving on the roads at 13 or 14. My mother tells me that when we were in Nassau, she and Dad had a Mini Clubman and at three, I could do the gear shift when I was told to. So I quickly took to driving and when I got older, being a non-drinker, was always trusted to take Dad's car out.

Sometimes a friend and I would decide to have a race on the Stillorgan dual-carriageway. First, we would do a recce up to the Stillorgan Park Hotel to make sure that there were no Gardaí around. Once we had the all-clear, we would cruise back to the lights and then blast it back down the road. A friend had a 205GTi and I would always beat it, doing 120mph by the time I went under the flyover. The buzz was tremendous but of course it was terribly irresponsible, stupid and dangerous.

There was one night when for a split-second, I almost paid the ultimate price for that stupidity. It was a trip down to Cork for a concert and we took the 205GTi. We were on back roads and I nearly lost it. It was the closest thing I got to killing myself. I wasn't used to driving something so light compared to my dad's Lancia, which was a tank.

It was quick though and I was pushing it hard when we hit a bump on the road. For a moment, we were airborne. It felt like an eternity but could only have been a matter of seconds. I was no longer the master of my own destiny on this narrow route with the ditches seemingly closing in.

Somehow, when the car returned to the ground, it was still facing in the right direction and I managed to regain control. To this day, I'm not sure how because I was doing over 100mph when I left *terra firma*. We would have been another road fatality statistic had we hit the ditch, there's no doubt about that.

That slowed me down but only for a little while. It was typical boy-racer stuff with me at that time. You're 19, 20 years of age and you think you're invincible, driving around like a lunatic more often than not. I grew out of it, thankfully.

My grandfather loved his cars but he didn't drive like that – not while we were with him anyway. He would have feared the wrath of my grandmother more than the law or getting killed I would say. Mind you, it would be some thrill going full throttle with the top down on the French Riviera.

▐ ▌ ▐

The speed drug hadn't hit me yet when I began my summer trips to Antibes. The routine in June and July never changed but wasn't boring. After a day amusing myself by the beach, a car would come to bring Mamine and me to the hotel at around 6pm, before the main dinner service started. We'd come in the back door, where a table was set for us to eat with Papy before he had to return to work.

Every night we were served our food and for dessert I would always have a scoop of ice cream in a tuile, which is a French wafer biscuit. When we finished, the car would bring us back down to the house. In those first few years, I was invariably asleep by the time we landed, even though it was only a short distance.

Papy took his holidays in August and we would move down to my grandparents' house in La Croix-Valmer, which is near St Tropez. My grandmother and I went to the beach almost every day. She would buy me an inflatable boat each summer and I would sit in that boat on the water, playing around or just lying there soaking in the rays. Bliss.

The surroundings were so lavish in Antibes and St Tropez. It was wall-to-wall extravagance and unimaginable wealth but honestly, I took no notice. The weather had more of an impact on me than the luxury.

A lot of the time I was on my own, as there weren't always kids around my age but I never minded my own company. That remains true to this day. Maybe that is a result of those solitary summers I had grown accustomed to. I have mates that can't bear to be by themselves for five seconds. If they're in the car, they have to get on the phone to ring somebody. I'm the complete opposite.

In fact I would say that I do not have a best friend, apart from Lizzie. I am aware that to some, that sounds unimaginable and maybe sad. I have made plenty of friends through school, work and rugby. There are plenty of people I socialise with on those somewhat rare occasions I'm actually here to socialise. But I have never felt the need for much more than that. My life has always felt very fulfilled as it is, and probably with so much weekend travel in my life I have not had time for much more.

At school and at home I knocked around with the same three or four guys but I never really kept in contact with them. There was one guy who came into Blackrock as a sixth year from Bray called Billy McVitty and we seemed to click. He was coming in from the outside and I often wonder if that had something to do with it, if I considered myself a bit of an outsider. I don't think I did but there was no doubt my background was a bit different. Billy and I still exchange emails every now and then.

But there would not be anyone I would categorise as a best friend that I talk to regularly. No-one I would tell my deepest, darkest secrets to, other than my wife. That's just not me. I have always been intensely private – until I agreed to do this book anyway! Lizzie and the kids are who I want to spend time with when I'm not working, especially as I have always been away so much travelling for the last 15 years and that has continued now that I am building my consultancy business.

It is probably part of my character too as my father was a quiet man who found small talk torturous. Mind you, my brothers are all much more gregarious so I'm not sure how much of it is nature or nurture. A bit of both perhaps, between my father's genes, those summers on my own in the south of France and having to spend so much time at the restaurant later on, particularly when Dad got sick.

If I was to come down on one side though, I would say that I am just not predisposed to standing on tables singing rebel songs, unlike David Beggy, the former All-Ireland winning Gaelic footballer with Meath who was a long-time team-mate of mine with Blackrock at Stradbrook, as well as Leinster. 'Jinksy' knew how to party and if there was no entertainment, he could provide it. A brilliant guy to be around.

When we are going to a function Lizzie warns me to put my 'social hat' on. She maintains I can be socially lazy. If I am in the mood I can put in a good performance but if I'm not I can leave the other person in my company scrambling for words! But honestly, I can be quite happy sitting in a corner saying nothing.

Being a teetotaller means I have no artificial boost in that regard either. That, very definitely, was down to my father. I made a conscious decision not to drink or smoke because my father did too much of both and it killed him in the end.

Don't get me wrong. I can talk to people, although it is an effort at times. My father actually had a fear of it. He was almost paralysed with terror at the prospect of saying a few words at the reception after my wedding, to such an extent that I told him he didn't have to. In the end, he managed a minute, welcoming Lizzie to the family but it was one of the hardest things he ever did.

I remember when I was named on the Ireland team, a French camera crew came over to Ireland to spend a few days with me in the lead-up to the game. It was big news over there that the son of a Frenchman was being selected to play for another country. I thought it was great *craic* having them around but I remember them trying to record something with Dad and they had to do take-after-take because he kept stuttering and stumbling over his words. And this was in French remember. We tried to get him to feel like he was only talking to the few of us in the room but he knew it was going on television and it scared the daylights out of him.

I do not possess that level of difficulty socially but when it comes to a night out, while I can take it, I can very definitely leave it.

Looking back on it now, I would say that being an independent, mentally strong person helped me as a referee. I wasn't out there to curry favour with anyone. Nor did I crave the spotlight. I was never dictatorial but I would not hesitate for a second to make what I considered the right call and to hell what anyone would think or say afterwards.

When I sent off Wales captain, Sam Warburton in the 18th minute of the 2011 World Cup semi-final against France, it led to supporters and media going apeshit. A commentator described it as 'one of the most controversial decisions in the history of the World Cup'. There were some death threats, though I never paid them much heed.

Warburton did not utter one word of objection when I showed him the red card. Afterwards, he stated publicly that it was the right decision and he did the game of rugby a tremendous service by doing that. It was a measure of the man. It didn't stop his head coach, Warren Gatland moaning about it for a long time afterwards though.

The point is that none of those potential consequences entered my head. The enormity of the occasion, that it was in the early stages of such a big game, what would erupt afterwards. And I was completely unconcerned when it became such a big issue. That remains the case because I made the right decision. I wasn't refereeing to make friends although the thing is, I made plenty.

▌▌▌▌

Of course you were always likely to run into children your own age on a Mediterranean beach and we would have our own adventures, exploring new places or just swimming, fishing and cycling. It was idyllic, a dream for a young boy, lasting three months each year for eight years.

That was how I learned French. It was a matter of necessity if I wanted to converse. People might think I picked it up naturally through my father but that wasn't the case or my brothers would have it too. Philippe has a small bit, but again, that's because he made the summer trip a couple of times. He didn't enjoy it like I did though and preferred to stay at home. André and Gilles wouldn't have a word.

Dad always spoke English to us so whatever grasp of the language I have that was to prove so beneficial later on when refereeing France and French clubs came from my summer holidays. I had to figure it out for myself and have gotten a lot of slagging over the years from French players and officials for my provincial accent and slang. But they appreciated that a referee was able to get the message across and explain decisions to them.

It was like a double life for me in those days because whatever I did there, I didn't do again for another nine months. Fishing was the one exception. In Antibes, you'd make your own bait with dough attached to tiny hooks. The rod was just a big cane that you dropped a line off of with a little float, casting out from the rocks. We would spend hours there, rarely catching anything much bigger than the size of a goldfish. You'd catch them, throw them back in and go again. We did it for hours.

Back home, we would go off Killiney Hill down to Killiney Beach. We rarely caught anything but talked about rugby and girls. The pastime did prompt the nearest to delinquent behaviour I ever indulged in, apart from speeding.

By my teenage days I was Rollers to everyone and most of us had nicknames. I and a few other lads from Killiney used to rob the lead from the roofs of some of the houses to melt and make our own weights, rather than having to buy them. Lizzie says now that I'm a real McGyver but I love working these things out and have done from an early age. Making the weights was just an example of that.

We used to get tops from gin or vodka bottles and coat-hangers. My mother would go mad that the hangers in our house kept disappearing! You'd make a loop from the hangers with pliers and place it in the bottle tops, into which you poured the lead that you melted in an open fire. Sometimes I melted it at home but the smell was rancid. The next morning you'd peel off the bottle tops and *voilá* you have your dead weights.

█▊█▊

Mamine liked to spoil me. I never asked for much but anything I asked for, I got. We were always in La Croix-Valmer for my birthday so I'd have two big presents when I arrived. I'd always get a dinghy or some kind of boat for the beach. That was a gimme.

When it came to the day of my birthday, I could name anything. The best present I ever got was a pair of Nike runners. They were really expensive at the time, costing around 900 francs, which was in the region of £80.

You would think it was the perfect environment for an adolescent boy in other ways too but the whole thing with girls didn't really happen for me. It wasn't just as a player that I was a late developer! I was 18 before I made any sort of progress in that department. While I had kissed a few girls, I did not have a steady girlfriend until I left school. I was only 19 when I met Lizzie and we have been together ever since.

During the 2007 World Cup, when I was based in Marseilles, I took the opportunity to pay a visit to the Hôtel du Cap-Eden Roc. It was my first time in it since my teens. I met a chef, a waiter and a maitre d' who had worked with my grandfather. I showed them where we used to eat every evening and brought them around the back corridor that we used to enter from. They were amazed that I knew the layout of the place so well.

It is incredible how it all came back to me as if it had been the previous week rather than 25 years before. It was all a bit surreal, being reminded of how plush it all was. I was incredibly lucky as a child to have it.

Painted on the wall in the restaurant is a mural of my grandfather standing in front of a buffet he had prepared at the hotel. There is a little boy in the background grabbing something from the table to eat. Apparently it's me.

CHAPTER TWO

With the reputation that my father had established from his time at the Russell, it was no surprise that Restaurant Rolland quickly took off and became a massive success. Located at the top of Killiney Village, right next door to The Druid's Chair pub, it attracted an elite clientele, with high rollers in business, finance and politics amongst the regulars.

Mum was the hostess and perfectly suited to that role given her outgoing nature. Dad did all the cooking and was more than happy to be in the background. They made a perfect team.

When they were open for business we would be upstairs in the living area. The building was laid out in such a way that when you entered through the hall, there was a spiral staircase right in front of you. The restaurant was through a door on the right while there was a reception area on the left where you could have a drink while waiting to be seated. Patrons had to use the toilets upstairs and it wasn't unusual for them to have to pass a bored young Alain sitting on the bottom step in his pyjamas.

The restaurant flourished through the boom when it was full all the time. By the late '70s, Restaurant Rolland was Egon Ronay listed and my parents were making a lot of money but it all changed as a harsh recession crippled the country. Everything collapsed and the restaurant eventually folded, as so many businesses did.

The enterprise weren't helped either by the fact that a stretch of road that brings you down the Ballybrack direction from Killiney Hill subsided. It took nine months to repair and as a result killed passing trade. That accelerated the restaurant's demise and the end result was financial devastation.

As I mentioned earlier, my grandparents were exceedingly wealthy so in the early '80s, when I came home from my holidays, I was like Billy Hayes in *Midnight Express*. The difference was that I had a money pin around my waist and in my underwear while entering the country instead of hash. I was a mule for transporting around £2000-£3000 at a time – significant money in that era. It was a sensible security measure as you wouldn't want to have that sort of cash lying around in your luggage, particularly as a 13-year-old boy. As soon as I got home, I would start stripping to remove the money that was almost stitched to me, so neatly had my grandmother pinned it to my clothing.

Such help was welcome but my grandparents never really knew the extent of the trouble that the restaurant was in and my father was too proud to tell them. He felt like a failure and didn't want to admit that to his parents. That frustrated my mother because she could see the business going down the toilet and my father unwilling to address it because of his pride. At the same time, three boys were at Willow Park and moving on to Blackrock and a fourth would follow. The summer donations were welcome but the restaurant was haemorrhaging money.

Concentrating on the day-to-day running of the business, my parents did not know the extent of the difficulties themselves until it was too late. They had an accountant who ran the finances for them and unfortunately he never raised any red flag for them about the need to cut costs, restructure the business or even cut their losses earlier with a less substantial debt hanging over them.

The struggles left their mark on Dad and he suffered a nervous breakdown. He recovered and came back to the restaurant but his heart wasn't in it any longer. He hadn't the energy and the inevitable occurred in 1985 when Restaurant Rolland closed. It was very sad, the end of 13 years of financial, emotional and spiritual investment. In the end, my parents had to sell the premises to pay off whatever they could and we moved into a house on Brewery Road. I lived there until I got married.

It was sad to see Dad looking a shell of the man he once was. His self-esteem had taken a shattering blow and he would never recover. He was broken. Having only known affirmation and achievement in Lyford Cay, Eden-Roc, the Russell and his own restaurant for the first five or six years, he now considered himself a flop. Having to go work for someone else was the final indignation, as he took on the head chef position at The Graduate on Rochestown Avenue. The family needed the wage.

My plan had always been to follow in his footsteps. I had served an apprenticeship of sorts, helping out in the restaurant, starting off serving in the front of the house but getting more involved in the kitchen as time went by. I really enjoyed that, bringing happiness to people with good food, ensuring they had a night to remember.

When Dad had the breakdown, he spent a few months in St John of God Hospital. I was 18 and had just started a culinary course in Cathal Brugha Street. But we were still hoping against hope that by some miracle, we could keep the business going, so I left college and took Dad's place as chef. Talk about being thrown into the deep end.

It was a huge responsibility but I was willing to sacrifice anything else I had on because my parents had given up so much more for their four boys. I was the oldest so it fell on me to pick up the slack. There wasn't any pressure placed on me to do so. It was just the right thing to do.

It was an eye-opening experience, even though I had seen it all first-hand for more than a decade. There is so much involved before you ever get into the kitchen. I would spend the morning shopping, buying fresh produce for that evening's menu. After lunch, the food had to be prepared. Fish had to be scaled, meat and vegetables trimmed, potatoes peeled and so on. That took two or three hours. Then, after having a bite to eat, I spent the night cooking, taking the place of a master and just doing the best I could.

By this stage, I was playing a lot of rugby and trying to make an impact in my first year with the Blackrock club. With my new schedule in the restaurant however, there wasn't a minute for anything else. Given that I had by this stage built up the type of work ethic that involved doing a lot of training on my own apart from the collective sessions at Stradbrook, this wasn't sustainable.

The realisation set in that I couldn't pursue a career as a chef and continue to play rugby. There was no fucking way. It dawned on me that while I may have liked the idea of being a chef, I didn't want it to take over my life. I wanted to play rugby more.

So when Dad came back, I told my parents that I had to find something else. They were friendly with the McInerneys, so as a stop-gap they organised for me to get a labouring job while I considered my options outside of a life of catering.

A guy called Bill used to pick me up in the morning and we'd trek out to Ballyfermot, where we were building 160 houses. I'd be home at six o'clock in time to go training. I was getting £140 a week and I handed it over. I didn't need it. Mum and Dad did.

Eventually, I began considering the need for something more reliable and long term. I did a sales and marketing course and subsequently secured an interview with TSB Bank. Thankfully, I was taken on and sent to Thomas Street branch for two weeks training. I stayed there for more than four years.

|■■||

I think the only reason I ever considered being a chef was because it was what Dad did. Neither of us was the most talkative but we had a great relationship. Being the eldest and being around him, I would have been living in his pocket quite a bit. I'd go with him when he was buying the produce, and watch him closely in the kitchen. I thought he was amazing. He was amazing.

His expertise with his hands didn't stop at cooking. If something broke, he could fix it. Whatever it was, he seemed to be able to find the solution. So I got my McGyver traits from him. I love that challenge. If somebody says 'That can't be done' I'm thinking 'Let me have a go'. On occasions, when he no longer had a commis chef as the business was being run on a shoestring, Dad would send one of the waiters or waitresses up, looking for me to help out below. I turned it into a competition.

'How many do you need me to make?'

'10.'

'Right, I'll do 15.'

'I need it in 10 minutes.'

'I'll do it in six.'

Dad was a very emotional individual as well, and that rubbed off on me too. The smallest thing can set me off and it was something I had to learn to control on the pitch, both as a player and a referee.

The restaurant closed down not long after Dad came out of hospital and he settled into his new routine. Unfortunately that routine included heavy smoking and drinking a bottle of wine in the evening. I often had a conversation with him in my own mind.

'Jeez Dad, you need to be calming down. Those cigarettes will kill you.'

I never said it out loud because I didn't feel I had the right, given that he and Mum had bust their asses to get us all through Willow Park and Blackrock College. That did not come cheap. So who was I to say 'You need to cool the jets on the cigarettes and the vino'?

Looking back now, I wish I did, although I'm not sure it would have made any difference. You could tell it wasn't going to end well. He was diagnosed with throat cancer late in 1997 and died on October 2, 2000 at the age of 63. He endured a terrible time in between but showed that for all his introspective nature and reserved manner, he was a tough-as-nails fighter.

He had to undergo an operation that had a very high-percentage possibility of killing him, as he spent nearly 16 hours in surgery. They had to cut out part of his tongue because of the cancer, so to replace that, they took a graft from his arm, as well as a vein, and transplanted it. There were two occasions he came close to dying but he got through it.

I still get emotional when I think of that first visit. His face was swollen horribly because they had cut him from the lip down to the throat and peeled the skin back so they could remove all his teeth. He was unrecognisable. I actually passed him twice looking for him.

He had a tube in his throat and could not talk, the swelling was so severe. He did not realise it at first and I could see his eyes widening in panic as he kept trying to say something. He became more and more agitated so I rushed to reception to get a pen and paper. He spelled out one word.

C-H-O-K-E.

He thought he was choking. So I explained that he was okay, that the tube would ensure that he could not choke, that he would be breathing fine. It was heart-wrenching because he was so helpless. I can still see the relief on his face.

He was never able to eat or drink anything orally after that operation. It all went through a bag directly to his stomach. It was another cruel twist for a man who specialised in food and how it tasted. He would never know flavour again.

Being the eldest in the family, everything came back on my shoulders. I had to be there for my Mum and my brothers as well. You take on a certain responsibility and I was doing that from the time the restaurant started to hit the skids and Dad had his breakdown.

There was more to it than that though. When I was 14 or 15, I was pushed around and knocked around a bit. I was small and easy to bully and being in an all-boys school, there were always guys who wouldn't let the opportunity pass.

I remember one occasion in the swimming pool, the fucking bastards dunked me under. They just did it because they could. They weren't big guys. The big guys didn't usually bother with that sort of stuff. They had nothing to prove. These bastards felt inferior, were bigger than me and I was the handy target.

There was absolutely nothing I could do to prevent it. Like the other times I had been the victim of bullying, I was helpless. More than fear or pain, it is the helplessness that got to me most. But this incident sparked something in me. I remember the moment quite clearly, as I brought myself gasping to the side of the pool. I was struggling to breathe but my mind was steeled.

'I am gonna show those bastards. I'm gonna get stronger and fitter and this isn't going to happen again. I am not gonna be a victim anymore. From now on, I take control.'

That changed my life.

I started working out. I stretched a bit the summer just before I turned 17, although these things are relative as I peaked at 1.75m (5'9"). I got into the gym and just loved training. I got into it passionately. At lunch time I'd go for a run. After school, if there wasn't training or a match, I'd do the same. I'd run from Blackrock out to Ringsend, around by Dun Laoghaire and back to the school.

Then I'd hit the gym. I loved doing weights and the results they brought about. I became extremely disciplined about my training, what I ate and what

I drank. Being methodical, once I decided to do it, it was all-in. Those are traits that helped me significantly as a player and a referee and in my career now. They are who and what I am.

Apart from those characteristics though, had I not made that decision to improve myself physically and committed myself to it, I would not be where I am now. I would not have played school rugby, not to mind at Test level. Of course if that had been the case, I would never have ended up refereeing the most important game in the sport, the World Cup final. That was the start of it. I guess I should thank those pricks.

It was this dedication that made me resolve never to drink or smoke. What I saw at home with Dad only reaffirmed that in my mind.

There was one occasion when I was 13 or 14, where my Mum was convinced that I was smoking although it was actually Philippe. She threw the two of us in the closet with a packet of cigarettes.

'Smoke them' she insisted, ushering us into the closet. 'You're not getting out until they're gone.'

My protestations of innocence fell on deaf ears. Meanwhile, Philippe smoked the pack of cigarettes with delight and I almost got sick from the smell. When we got out, Philippe was quite happy to tell Mum that he was the smoker but he wasn't going to do it until he had finished the box.

Mum is an incredible woman, a very tough lady. She had to go through a lot. She got married very young and had us quickly. She helped set up and run what was a successful business for a long while. When it went bust, she had to deal not only with that but with what it did to my father. Then there was his subsequent illness and death. She is a remarkably resilient person, who always seems to bounce back. That is because she is an eternal optimist.

Every day I miss Dad. But every day I am thankful for Mum.

CHAPTER THREE

My sojourns on the French Mediterranean coincided with summer holidays, so I never missed school. My parents' seasonal work abroad only lasted until I was five and I hadn't begun formal education at that stage.

I was sent to a Montessori-type place initially and then spent a year in a French school in Foxrock. But once my parents made a commitment to Ireland, a couple of key things happened.

The first was that we would have a home for a period of longer than six months. The second was that there would be a regular school. Home was the restaurant and it was the restaurant that was largely responsible for where I went to school.

My parents took the task of making this decision for their first-born seriously and they lobbied a number of influential people they knew through work, patrons that frequented the restaurant and some that had been customers in the Russell. The place that received the most glowing testimony was Willow Park, the junior school of Blackrock College.

As I said earlier, they certainly didn't make the decision based on rugby. They were interested only in me getting a good education and felt that a private school was most advantageous in that regard. If it helped later in life in terms of contacts and so on, that would be good too. As a result of their forensic investigations, Willow Park was selected.

Of course it was possibly the single-most influential decision made on my behalf in my life because without it, there would have been no rugby. And I shudder at the very thought of that now given the experiences, the many parts of the world the game has brought me and the path it has brought me in my professional life. It was a big call; and a brilliant one.

Mum used to drive us to Willow Park. She was under 30 when I started going and I'd say she caused consternation amongst the priests with her mini-skirts. On one occasion, we passed a priest on the way in to the school. Mum rolled down the window and leaned her head out to offer a lift. She was wearing only a hastily thrown on dressing gown and I'd say the poor man didn't know where to look. Let's just say she wouldn't have been covered from neck to ankle! Every time I think about it I laugh.

|▮▮▮|

Rugby was compulsory in Willow so I only started playing because I had to. If it had been another school, it would have been hockey, cricket, hurling, soccer or Gaelic football. There was training twice a week and a game on Sunday.

I certainly didn't fall in love with the game immediately. I wasn't captivated by the mud, cold and rain, that's for sure. Neither did I blow my coaches away with any innate spellbinding talent. In fact when I started playing first, I was put in as a prop for Brother Luke's U9s because I was small and chubby. In time, I would be just small but initially, I had the correct body shape for the front row, even if I was fairly soft. Maybe it explains why I earned a reputation for officiating at the scrum pretty well… first-hand experience!

Thankfully the puppy fat disappeared at around 11 or 12 and I found myself relocated to the back division because of my speed. Gradually I worked my way into scrum half and was good enough to play there for the 13s and 14s at Blackrock.

I don't know why that move was made but once it happened, I just started working on the skills over time. At that stage, I hadn't developed my intense hunger for self-improvement, but seeing as I was now playing at 9, it made sense to work on my pass.

I wasn't very robust and could offer no resistance to the physical and mental bullying. This was an instance when being the first child probably didn't help. As my brothers got older, we beat the shit out of each other a bit more and that helped toughen us all up. But early on, I was in no position to offer any resistance.

When I had the Eureka moment in the pool, it all changed and as I stood up for myself, my problems dissolved. Getting better at rugby by virtue of being fitter and stronger also helped because in Blackrock, if you were good at rugby, you earned respect and weren't messed with.

That sense of defiance was inherent in my entire playing career. There were many setbacks with Ireland, Leinster or even at club level with Blackrock, through being overlooked, dropped or played out of position, yet I lived by the mantra of being as good as I could be. I will get better. I will get faster and stronger. I will show them.

Interestingly, refereeing never evolved in the same manner. I had a pretty meteoric rise once I took on the whistle and there weren't too many interruptions. I operated at the highest level until finishing up on my own terms.

The conclusion may have been the one part of my refereeing where previous experiences had an influence. I consciously decided to jump before I may have been pushed. I would have hated to be told my time was up and so took control. That is something I strive for, having hated the experience of helplessness when bullied. It is an integral part of my make-up now. Of course refereeing is all about control and so is playing scrum half.

So too is leadership. I captained a lot of teams after leaving school. It comes naturally to the position. You are the equivalent of a quarterback in American Football, a key playmaker, an onfield general. You have to dictate what happens in the pack but you're the link to what occurs in the back division too.

Funnily enough, I remember asking an Ireland selector once why I had been dropped from the senior squad and he said that there were some concerns about my decision-making. Then they made me captain of the 'A' team to play the following weekend, where I would have to make all the big decisions! I just shook my head in bemusement and carried on.

▮▮▮▮

In Willow, we learned the skills and developed our game sense. There was no real emphasis on structure until you maybe hit Junior Cup level at Blackrock College. It was ramped up significantly once you were fighting for Senior Cup glory.

On the SCT, we would often have a backs' session in the morning before class. Then at lunchtime, you might have lineout practice with the forwards. There was normal team training after school and on a Thursday, we would go down to Stradbrook to scrummage against Blackrock RFC's J1s or seconds. Being a scrum half, you were involved in all those facets so that was a huge commitment.

But this was Blackrock College. There was a tradition to uphold and doing that was taken very seriously. It didn't come as a shock to the system because you had been subconsciously preparing yourself. Winning the Leinster Schools Senior Cup was the only target every year. It still is. The school has won 68 Senior Cups, having been victorious in the first final in 1888. The next nearest winner in relation to numbers is 10 (Belvedere and Terenure).

You are so aware of the enormity of it all. The evidence is around every corner, down every corridor. The halls are lined with photographs of all the Cup-winning teams. The trophy cabinets display the spoils of combat. When you're in Willow, you see these heroes. From a very early age, you look upon them in awe and want to emulate them.

'That's the SCT' you whisper, in the presence of greatness. 'They're playing today.'

I was lucky enough to see the likes of Hugo McNeill, Brendan Mullin and Neil Francis around the place. They were the kings and you were envious of their status. They were the benchmark. Then suddenly, I was a member of the SCT.

Often I strolled down those halls, moving from one to the next and thinking, *Fucking hell, whatever happens, I'm not leaving this place without a senior medal.* I had no other goal in life at that point.

The expectation is huge. That brings pressure but it also brings responsibility and means that the preparation is rarely less than exemplary. There is massive pride too though, even if you don't play. Being a 'Rock boy means something. Being a 'Rock player is a badge of honour.

When 'Rock go to Donnybrook, the support has to be on the left-hand side. It's sacrosanct and the cheerleaders will be there at 5am if needs be to ensure it. There is practice in the hall before the games to make sure the students know all the songs for the Cup campaign.

On game day, you came into school wearing your official blazer. You wouldn't have to go to all your classes because the match took priority. So you walked around, chilling out, cock of the walk. Everywhere you went you had people wishing you good luck, cheering and back-slapping. We were like warriors going into battle, carrying the hopes and dreams of our community; defending the Blackrock honour and representing a glorious tradition.

Afterwards, you returned to the school to be greeted by the rest of the student body. If you won, it was a remarkable feeling, the victorious soldiers returning from war. We would congregate in the cafeteria and the ovation was deafening. Anyone who scored a try or kicked the points would be singled out.

'Congratulations to Alain for his try today.'

You stood up on a chair or table to acknowledge the adulation. It is a heady feeling, being placed on that pedestal as a teenager and you can see how some people might have struggled to cope with being an ordinary individual when it was all over. I certainly got caught up in it all but I enjoyed it thoroughly and wouldn't change a thing apart from losing the final in 1985. That took a while to get over.

I only made the bench on the JCT, which was good preparation for my international career, but at least we won and I progressed to make the SCT my last two years. It was probably a surprise the first time as Johnny Kennedy had been scrum half the previous season. When I got my chances I played really well though and managed to wrestle the position from him. He hasn't forgiven me to this day and it came up again when we had our 30-year reunion recently!

Unfortunately, I missed out on winning the ultimate prize. My decision to repeat the Leaving Cert to have another crack almost paid off. In most places, reaching a final would be considered a good achievement but you won't see any reference to that team in Blackrock. Second isn't good enough when you have 68 titles. You have to win.

Training was very testing but we always had the endgame in mind. We used to do a warm-up run comprising the whole circumference of the school, including Willow Park. I was one of the fittest guys in the squad but I found it very difficult, especially when we had to do it in the snow one Christmas.

You began at the main pitch, running past the changing rooms and along the main road of Williamstown to the Willow Park entrance. From there you'd continue to the very top of the school. There's a big incline going up to the top pitch which was known as Calvary. Running hard up that hill with the snow coming up to your shins left a mark on you to say the least. When you made it up there, you freewheeled down by the soccer pitch and back into the school, concluding with a loop of the rugby pitches. If we were doing fitness training, we would do a number of those laps.

That snowy Christmas, I remember not being able to shake off the cold despite having run so hard that it was the closest I ever got to puking. It was physically and mentally demanding but by that stage, I was in the mode of pushing myself to my very limit and refusing to give in. I wouldn't let it beat me. I would be lying if I said I enjoyed that though. It was agony.

We had two coaches. Fr Malachy Kilbride put the fear of God into you. He was deadly serious at all times and had a command over the players. You either bought into it or you despised it. For those involved with the rugby, and who understood what it was he was trying to do in terms of instilling discipline, he was deserving of some respect. But some of the guys in the school that weren't within the rugby fraternity couldn't hack it and hated him.

He wasn't just about laying down the law though. He was a good coach, very knowledgeable, and we enjoyed playing under him.

One of the lay teachers, Vincent Costello took over from Fr Malachy in my last campaign. He was excellent too. Like Fr Kilbride, the time he gave to it was amazing, given he must have had a life outside of the college. He knew his stuff and almost brought us all the way.

There was a specific playing kit for the Cup campaign. It was a special Sky Blue. We never wore that particular jersey and socks in League games or friendlies. It was another 'Rock tradition.

When I got picked to play for the Barbarians against Leicester in the early '90s, I was so proud to wear my 'Rock SCT socks. The Baa-Baas tradition is that you wear your club socks but I recalled Brendan Mullin, Neil Francis and Hugo McNeill wearing their SCT socks. So when I got called up, I knew I would do the same. The boys had established another 'Rock tradition and I was going to carry it on. I was representing the Williamstown realm once again and that was a wonderful feeling.

▐ ■ ■ ▌

In my first year on the SCT we won the League but lost to Clongowes in the quarter-final of the Cup. So I decided to repeat my Leaving and give it another crack.

We began our campaign against Cistercian College Roscrea in Portlaoise at the end of January. CCR had future Irish international, Ben Cronin in their ranks but we made heavy enough weather of it. Lock Steven Ross bulldozed over for an early try and crucially, Michael O'Brien followed up just before the interval when I fed him on the blind side of a 22 metre scrum. My mate, Billy McVitty kicked the conversion and we led 10-0 at half time.

We were playing into a strong wind though and future TD Barry Cowen, a brother of former Taoiseach Brian Cowen, kicked two penalties in the second half to ensure a nailbiting finish.

With seven minutes remaining, we had a scrum in our own half but Roscrea won the heel against the head. Luckily, I just managed to nip in and kick the ball clear before my counterpart, Stephen Crehan could gather possession and threaten our try-line.

It was more comfortable next time out in Donnybrook, when we beat Newbridge 18-6. The highlight for me was scoring a try and the photos appearing in the paper the next day. Most of the talk though was about what one headline described as 'unpleasant incidents'.

The match was refereed by the Australian official, Kerry Fitzgerald. He had been appointed to the Ireland-France Five Nations Test in Dublin 12 days later and requested a domestic game to acclimatise to the conditions.

Who would have guessed that there were two future World Cup final referees on the pitch that day? Kerry took charge of the inaugural decider two years later in Auckland but unfortunately passed away in 1991.

If he thought this schools' game would be a gentle affair, he was mistaken as he had to deal with a spectator coming onto the pitch during the game to object about some of the touch judge's decisions. The spectator came back for more afterwards. It wasn't something you saw that often in rugby, particularly at schools level.

It emerged afterwards that Newbridge had been forced to field without a player who was injured in an attack in Dublin, so there was no absence of incident surrounding the game. My try was a typical scrum half effort off the base of a five-metre scrum. Michael and our captain, Dara O'Flaherty followed up with four-pointers to confirm our position in the last eight.

There was more drama in the quarter-final when we rescued the situation in injury time. We were hot favourites to beat High School but they made it really difficult for us after we failed to turn an early dominance into scores.

It looked like curtains for us as we trailed by two points but the pack got us into a good position one last time. From the ruck, I whipped the ball out to our out half, Niall Eyre and he beat the cover defence to gallop over. Billy kicked the extras and we were through to a semi-final against Clongowes by virtue of a 13-9 scoreline.

There was an interesting postscript to that game. It was the week before the aforementioned Ireland-France game and *L'Equipe*, the French daily national sports paper, always sent a team of journalists abroad to cover the build-up to major events. The eagle-eyed Henri Bru noted the French surname on the Blackrock College team and got in touch with the family. He wrote a piece on us, detailing Ireland's French connection. It was the start of an excellent relationship with the French media and rugby public in general, who have always treated me as one of their own.

Thankfully, the semi-final was easier, as we scored five tries in a 28-9 win over Clongowes at Lansdowne Road. I provided Billy with an assist for his score and went over for our second off a scrum. Norman McInerney, Niall and Dara also crossed the whitewash. Ciaran Gleeson, who only started on the right wing due to Michael's injury having been out half the previous year, kicked four conversions.

The build-up to the final at Lansdowne on March 18 was incredible. We were treated like royalty and prepared almost like full-time athletes. Nothing else mattered. Not to me anyway. We knew De La Salle would present a stern challenge but dreamed of entering the annals as 'Rock heroes. We were favourites to do so but there was no storybook ending. De La Salle prevailed by scoring the only try in the game, edging it 10-6.

I have seen it written somewhere that Mick Doyle, who was the national coach at the time, came into our dressing room beforehand to give us a motivational talk. His son, Andrew was our openside flanker. It can't have been one of his inspirational 'Give it a lash' orations that worked so well with Ireland though, as I have no recollection of it at all.

The game itself was a bit of an arm wrestle. We had a strong wind in the first half and dominated possession but while we got away with not being clinical against High School, we were punished this time around.

Our superiority in the set-piece was almost complete. We won five scrums against the head in the first half alone and had the upper hand out of touch as well. Yet we only went in level at half time. De La Salle scrum half, David O'Connor kicked a brilliant drop goal into the teeth of the gale to put them in front and though James Patterson levelled in similar fashion, we were in trouble.

Brian Glennon, who was one of two survivors along with Stephen Hayes from the DLS team that had won the Cup two years previously, scored a good try in the second half and we just couldn't escape the shackles as they tackled fervently, no matter how hard we tried to get things going. Brian had the honour of being presented the trophy by his mother as the victorious captain and went on to be a team-mate of mine with Leinster. A Lansdowne favourite for more than a decade, he earned one Ireland cap as a replacement against France in 1993.

The Churchtown team had an out half by the name of David Harmon, who was a really big, strong, scary-looking guy. He made a phenomenal tackle with two minutes remaining to deny Niall a try. It turned out that he was a freestyle wrestler and he went on to represent Ireland at the Seoul Olympics three years later.

Towards the end of the game, we had a scrum on their five-yard line and David Burnett gave a penalty against us. I was gutted because from that close I fancied myself and could see my name in lights.

The feeling of desolation at the final whistle was total. It was absolute devastation and I have rarely felt as low after a game. I was inconsolable. I suppose the thing about how much the Cup is built up in Blackrock, with the expectation and weight of meaning, is that the fall on the other side is so steep if it goes wrong. I had repeated my Leaving to win a Senior Cup. So much for best laid plans.

If a 'Rock team wins the Senior Cup, the players are carried all the way from the back gate to the entrance of the hall, where the captain presents the trophy to the president of the school. I wanted that experience badly. I wanted the damned medal, to be up there on the winning wall.

Of course I have more context now. At 18, it was the end of the world and now I know it isn't. Indeed I rarely allowed defeat to have the same effect on me, although I always fought hard to win. It's just that I know it's a game. Still, there are times, in moments of solitude, when that Cup final crawls out of the recesses of my mind. That scrum at the end especially.

Bloody ref.

PART
TWO

CHAPTER FOUR

There is a well-trodden route if you want to continue with rugby after leaving Blackrock College. UCD or Trinity are potential first clubs if you go there but the majority of the guys from my era ended up at Blackrock College RFC.

I felt comfortable in Stradbrook straight away and the disappointment of the Cup final wore off quickly.

Fergus Slattery was the big legend on the team at that time, while Neil Francis was establishing himself. When I joined Hugo MacNeill was playing with London Irish and Brendan Mullin was at Oxford University but both would return to Stradbrook. When you think of it, Slatts, Hugo and Brenny each won a Triple Crown and toured with the British and Irish Lions. Hugo and Brenny were still a huge part of the national side.

I had no such aspirations at the time. Realising any potential I might have was the extent of my ambition. In fact my only goal was to make it at Stradbrook.

There were about 10 teams at Blackrock but the tradition was to start with the U20s no matter who you were. That gave you one more season with your peers, some of the guys you played with and against in secondary school. That campaign finished in February and it was only then that you went to one of the senior teams.

We got to the final of the McCorry Cup with the U20s at the end of 1985 but UCD beat us in Donnybrook. It was disappointing but my first rugby medal earned on the field of play was just around the corner.

I started with the third As, which was the fourth team. It was the first introduction of playing against adults and a real eye-opener. We were used to playing a very clean, fast style of rugby. Suddenly, you were thrown into a situation where lads were often boxing the heads off each other, using different 'skills' to gain the upper hand. When you are the wrong side of 30 and going toe-to-toe with some quick, cocky kid, intimidation is an obvious tactic. You learned from it.

We had a great experience though as we won the Moran Cup that year, beating Lansdowne 19-15 at Donnybrook on April 30, 1986. It was great to finally be on the pitch in a winning side. I had a medal from the JCT at school but not having been on the team, it wasn't something I treasured. This was undoubtedly better and scoring the winning try with time almost up gave it an added resonance.

My progress was fairly quick after that. Having failed to trouble any representative selection committees throughout school, I quickly made the Leinster U19s. This was a brilliant experience as we travelled with the seniors, playing on the undercard to their games. You were in an exalted circle, sharing the bus with Tony Ward, Paul Dean, Brendan Mullin, Dessie Fitzgerald, Nicky Popplewell... icons of the game.

It wasn't long before people recognised my work ethic and the extra hours of training I did. I was always practicing my pass and it was to become one of my greatest weapons.

There was no great science to that practice. Often, I would just throw a medicine ball against the wall over and over again. I also did a drill after team training designed to speed up my pass, looking to gain even a millisecond. That millisecond can make all the difference out wide.

I wasn't doing anything new. I was just doing more than anyone else. In that era, it was all about quantity rather than quality. At 5'9" I needed to get as strong as possible and I did but there was only so much meat you could put on those bones. I needed to get the ball away quickly.

Endurance was important too. I cycled to work and played a lot of tennis for a while. I found that excellent for the reflexes.

Being a non-smoker and teetotaller meant getting fit was easier for me than for many of my colleagues. When I broke through to the seniors initially, the lads could not get their heads around the fact that I didn't drink alcohol. It was such a part of the game at that time that not partaking made you stick out like a sore thumb. In those days, you beat the daylights out of one another out on the pitch and once the final whistle was over, you got drunk together.

A regular scene played itself out when I broke through first.

'Have a pint Rollers.'

'No, I don't drink.'

In that grand Irish way, my wishes were ignored because sure I didn't really mean it. A pint would land in front of me.

'No, no, no, I don't drink.'

'Have a fucking drink Rollers, for fuck's sake,' came the oft-exasperated response.

'No, I don't fucking drink!' was my equally exasperated riposte.

So when I wouldn't take a drink, they'd slip a Mickey Finn into whatever I was having. They were never going to catch me out though. I rarely even took a sip as I could smell alcohol a mile off. After a while, they got smart to that and went with vodka, which doesn't have an obvious smell of alcohol. But one sip would prompt a simultaneous grimace and 'Jesus!', as the combination of rank taste and burning throat had its way with me.

In fairness to the lads, it wasn't bullying or anything like that. They just couldn't understand it and were trying to help me learn the error of my ways. They'd get me to realise that drinking was great *craic* and sure I could thank them later by getting a few rounds.

They were wasting their money but persisted for the first three or four away trips. After that, the realisation dawned that I was, in fact, hell-bent on actually not drinking alcohol. They thought this type of behaviour was odd as fuck but they were live-and-let-live guys and there was no more about it after that, apart from the odd prank, just for the laugh and to piss me off.

They didn't treat me any differently. I was still one of the lads, who worked hard with them on the pitch and went out with them after. I just didn't drink pints and get off my head. They accepted that this was Rollers' way.

Later on, when I was in the Irish set-up, I got the nickname Cinderella or Cinders, because I was always back in the hotel before midnight. They would be giving it socks down in Tiger Tiger in Cardiff and I'd be tucked up in my bed sound asleep.

Before long, the lads realised that having a sober guy with them was in fact a huge positive. I became responsible for getting them all home, whether I liked it or not.

You got to see some crazy carry-on, particularly when they got into the drinking games. Lads would get destroyed, especially the younger crew. And it would be up to me to get them to bed or even to make sure everyone was on the bus home the following morning.

On many occasions we were without the full complement departing hotels. You'd find the missing person buckled in his bed, having been abandoned by his room-mate. You'd drag him to the shower, put his stuff in his bag and carry him down to the bus. I was an unpaid baby-sitter a lot of the time but smiled at the suffering that the rest of gang were enduring on the journey.

There were a variety of games the lads would play when the session got into full swing. Most of them were stupid and simple. They were all designed to get people blind drunk. Quickly.

Being a non-drinker didn't excuse me. I had my own penalty and to be honest, it was much worse than knocking back a pint of lager or shot. I would have a pint glass with a variety of concoctions including tomato sauce, brown sauce, tabasco sauce, egg, flour and anything else the boys could get their hands on.

I would have to take a drink out of this sludge as my forfeit. It was disgusting. So I got very good at these games quickly. The lads wanted to mess up so they could take a drink. I didn't want to touch what was in my glass.

▌ ▌ ▌ ▌

Conor Sparks took me under his wing when I stepped up to the first team initially. It can be daunting going from playing guys your own age to taking on hardened pros, not to mind internationals who knew every trick. It was a whole new ball game.

Unlike a lot of older players who forget their own introduction, Sparky understood and recognised that he could be a real guide being my half back partner, and looked after me.

We had a natural affinity with one another. He was a lovely footballer, with a fantastic step. He had a calming influence and possessed a deep reservoir of knowledge and expertise. He just looked out for me. I think he saw something in me and wanted to nurture me. He told me if I was in trouble, to just shift the ball out to him and he would look after it. He wanted me to find my feet and not take too much responsibility on until I had become comfortable with the increased tempo and physicality of the game. I will never forget that.

Mind you, I settled in fairly quickly. I wasn't in awe of moving up a level, of playing with or against Test players. I wasn't cocky but if there was something to say, I'd say it. That just came from being a scrum half.

You cannot be timid as a 9. It is a bossy position. You need to dictate. You have to order the pack around. Whether they take it in and maul; move to the left, move to the right. It's the job. You are the eyes so you are the driving force.

So it doesn't matter if it's Slattery there. If you need him to go somewhere or do something, you bawl at him to do it. And he expects it of you. I thrived on the responsibility that went with that leadership role.

I never modelled myself on anyone but Gareth Edwards was my hero. Simply because he is the best scrum half the game of rugby has ever seen.

In 2009, I was in Edinburgh to referee Scotland-Wales and I had my son Mark with me. On the morning of the game I spotted Gareth having breakfast with JPR Williams in our hotel. Mark was only nine at the time and wouldn't have known that these were two of the greatest players ever to lace a pair of boots. So I brought him over to them.

'Are you proud of your Daddy?' asked Gareth of Mark at one stage.

I cannot recall the answer but what I do remember is considering the ridiculousness of the statement coming from the mouth of such an icon.

They signed their autographs for Mark but I got a much bigger thrill out of that than he did.

❙❙ ■ ❙❙

We got to the semi-final of the Leinster Senior League in my first season but Lansdowne just got the better of us, 16-13. Still, I was buzzing and making ground at an extraordinary rate.

The inaugural World Cup was coming up in 1987. It is such a staple part of the calendar now but there was some uncertainty about its value initially. It wasn't even on my radar but then, in March, I was selected on a Combined Provinces team to play The Rest Of Ireland in a national trial for players that had not played in the Five Nations.

It was bizarre as I had never even had a trial with Leinster. It wasn't the first time national and provincial selection committees were at odds with one another when it came to my abilities. For most of my career, it would be the other way around, as I got chosen for Leinster ahead of Fergus Aherne or Niall Hogan, but they would get the start in green.

An injury to Gus got me the call-up for the trial day before but given my inexperience, it was still scarcely believable.

Adding to my excitement was that I was partnering Tony Ward, a true star of the game in Ireland, even if he had fallen out of favour at Test level by that juncture, with Paul Dean the preferred 10 for Mick Doyle and his selectors.

The rugby fraternity and media continued to debate the merits of picking one or the other, just as they had done at the height of the Ward-Campbell era. In both cases, Leinster tended to try one or other of them at centre. While everyone seemed to have an opinion, I don't recall the situation ever coming up amongst the squad. We just got on with it.

It certainly was a thrill to be supplying the bullets for Wardy and overall, the game went well. Tony Doyle was my direct opponent. He was a very experienced and reliable operator, having served as understudy to Michael Bradley for many years without getting on the pitch too often. I was to get to know that situation all too well.

It was in Doyler's stead that I was selected for my Leinster senior debut in October against Llanelli and I followed up with two tries for Blackrock against Old Wesley. Things were happening quickly now and Jim Davidson called me up to the Ireland training panel as cover, because of a doubt to Ulster's Rab Brady.

The momentum slowed in 1988 when Blackrock brought in Sean O'Beirne from UCD to play in my position. Sean had played for Leinster and was a very good place-kicker into the bargain. What's more, he had won a Leinster Schools' Senior Cup alongside Brenny and Frano in 1982. That was the day Mullin changed the entire impetus of the game when switched to out half.

It came as a bit of a shock to me, given that I had caught the eye of the national selectors. Clearly it was felt that Sean had a better pedigree. My misgivings only worsened when I was picked on the wing on a wet, shitty day against Cork Con.

The life of a winger in that era was a lonely one. You could go through a game without getting a pass and the only danger was that I might get pneumonia. Apart from chasing the odd welly forward, there was nothing to do.

For someone accustomed to being at the very hub of activities, it was horrific. This was not what I played the game for. So I said as much.

'I'm not playing on the wing anymore. It's scrum half or nothing.'

For a little while, it looked like Door No 2. I was dropped for the next game and didn't play the one after that either. But I held firm.

If it had been the national team, I would have played prop had they wanted but that was different. Who knew if you would ever get another game at Test level? But this was me, having started off at 'Rock and seeking to establish myself. If I spread myself thin, that might never happen.

Being seen as versatile isn't always beneficial as players of that ilk never seem to get a run in one position. I was a scrum half. If I was going to make it at Stradbrook, it would be in the No 9 jersey. If I wasn't deemed good enough to claim it, I would fight hard to change that view. But I would not play in any other role.

At the foundation of that mindset was a burgeoning confidence arising out of my improvement in the previous four years. Deep down, I knew I was at least as good as my competition, if not better. That included Sean.

In the end, my stance paid off. After those two games on the sidelines, I was brought back in and scored a try as we beat Skerries 11-7. Slatts made his seasonal debut in that game at 39, for it was a case of all hands to the pump by now in a struggling season. I played the majority of the remaining games and Sean moved on to St Mary's at the end of the season.

It was a bittersweet campaign though. There was the significant satisfaction of seeing off the O'Beirne challenge and then playing a major part in winning the Leinster Senior Cup. We should have lost in the first round against Monkstown but snatched it with a late try and had to stage a second-half rally to see off Wanderers in the quarter-final. Two tries from Brenny got us over the line against Old Wesley and we were into the final.

Star power did the trick in the decider too as we beat Trinity 12-6 in a physical affair at Lansdowne Road in May. Hugo was the hero this time, coming up with a stupendous drop goal that remains one of the greatest scores ever seen at the old ground.

My memory could be playing tricks on me but Hugo was close to the half-way line and tight to the right-hand touchline. The distance has increased and the angle more acute as the years elapsed. In truth, I don't know what possessed Hugo but it was a monstrous kick and a pivotal moment.

This was the first of two Senior Cups I won with Blackrock. In the amateur era, the Senior Cup was tremendously prestigious. That applied in all the provinces. It was why the Leinster decider was played in Lansdowne Road and attracted large attendances.

The second Cup victory arrived in 1992. There was an incredible turnover of players and Frano and I were the only survivors from four years previously. I was captain and relished the extra accountability, scoring two tries in the quarter-final win over Skerries. We overcame Terenure in the penultimate round and beat Old Wesley 12-6 in the final, David Brophy taking my pass to score the match-sealing try.

To join a select group of men that lifted the famous old trophy was a wonderful feeling. Winning anything was hard and you had to enjoy it when it came around. It was even more noteworthy because eight of the 20 on the match-day panel were under 21. There was no Brendan Mullin or Steve Bachop. It was a brilliant achievement and a career highlight.

The first one was special too though. At 21, it represented a major milestone for me. It was so important for the club as well. When I came into the team, it was as part of a massive overhaul. We were in such a transitional phase that there were only four survivors from the side that had completed the League and Cup double in an unforgettable Centenary campaign, five years previously in 1983.

There was a pretty serious downside to that season though. Inconsistency was a by-product of fielding so many inexperienced players. As well as that, Brenny and Frano were unavailable for much of the League campaign, having stayed on in Australia after the World Cup.

As a result we lost far too many games and our hopes of remaining in Division 1 of the Leinster Senior League came down to a winner-takes-all tie against Wanderers in Stradbrook, three months before our brilliant Cup win.

I didn't play in that game, with Sean getting picked and to his credit, scoring a try. We led through the entire game until the final minute, when Neil Metchette galloped through for a try under the posts to give John Doyle an easy conversion. They snatched it 18-16 and we were relegated.

That was a devastating blow but once we reflected upon it, there was a feeling that we could make a quick return, given our age profile. The manner in which we picked it up to go on that Cup-winning run only served to bolster this belief and we did make it back the following year.

▏▐▊▐▏

My position at 'Rock was threatened on one other occasion. Eddie O'Sullivan is the best coach I have ever worked with, a man who was ahead of his time, but I wasn't impressed when he decided to rotate his scrum halves.

Nicky Assaf was a prodigious talent that everyone was predicting great things about. He was an Ireland U21 international who had already forced himself onto the Leinster senior squad but when Eddie told us he would be giving us every second game I reckoned it was bullshit. How can you build any form if you're not in regularly? Eddie argued that it would keep us fresh but I was fit enough to play every week.

In addition, I was the club captain and felt I should be leading from the front. It was a role I took very seriously. Not playing would dilute the position. You don't provide leadership in the shadows. You charge from the front.

The situation attracted a lot of attention and St Mary's approached me in the summer of 1993, promising that I would be their undisputed first choice scrum half. It was an offer I considered quite seriously because I wanted to play and if my contribution wasn't valued enough to be a regular, it was best for all parties that I move on.

It was flattering because Mary's were one of the top teams in the country at the time and had gotten agonisingly close to winning the AIL Division 1 title on a couple of occasions. Approaching my 27th birthday, it would have been perceived in many circles as a great move if I wanted to achieve more success at the top level and add to my one Ireland cap at that stage.

In the end, I chose to fight for the spot once more. Jimmy Smyth was probably responsible for me making that call. He was a great clubman and I had a good chat with him. He persuaded me to stand my ground. Talking to him also reminded me of my ties to Stradbrook, the many friends I had at the club. Could I play with the same passion for any other club? That was doubtful. This was where my friends were.

The last serious consideration was the knowledge we were building something and I wanted to be a part of it. Over time, my form persuaded Eddie to go with me as his primary No 9, with Nicky togging out on the wing most of the time. He was willing to do it and had the skills to pull it off. As well as that, we were beginning to spin the ball wider than the one time I was banished to the wing, so he got involved a lot more.

▮▮▮▮

The debate around an All-Ireland League started gaining real traction and the embryonic competition began in the 1990-91 season. The timing was bad for us as we weren't eligible, having been relegated from the top division of the LSL.

The AIL was so welcome because it gave you more games and introduced a freshness, with some really unique pairings. In that inaugural season, Malone and Shannon played each other for the first time ever in a history that spanned more than 100 years of rugby in Ireland. So there was a big appetite for the competition amongst players.

The club game was second only to international rugby in that era. The interprovincial team was bottom of the ladder and remained that way until the advent of professionalism. Even when the European Cup started, it was a curiosity approached with caution and a little suspicion. But once it became properly established, the province became a club in itself, with the AIL suffering a dilution of its prestige as a result.

For the first decade of its existence though, it was the place to be, with games televised live and habitually attracting attendances of 10,000. Indeed there were 20,000 people at Lansdowne Road in 1993 when Ger Earls, father of Keith, scored an intercept try as Young Munster stunned hot favourites St Mary's to win the title.

We got ourselves involved very quickly although it was a circuitous route to get the job done. I scored the first try as we beat Clontarf 13-3 in a play-off at Anglesea Road on January 26, 1991 to claim the LSL title.

The club distributed leaflets immediately after the final whistle advertising the subsequent AIL play-off game with Dungannon in Ravenhill. There was some furore around that, with the club being accused of taking the win for granted but it had nothing to do with the players. We were focussed on the job at hand, as the performance and result indicated.

The leaflets were the work of Mervyn Dalton and Des Hutchinson of the Blackrock Social Club. They were just making sure they were prepared I guess! There must have been a bit of concern though about whether the expense might be for naught as it wasn't until George Roche came on and ran in a try nine minutes from the end that we finally broke the stubborn Clontarf resistance. As it happened, the Dungannon game was postponed due to snow.

The play-off was a round-robin affair involving the four provincial League champions and the Dungannon tie wasn't the only one to fall foul of the weather's inclemency. The Dolphin game didn't make it first-time around either, while the Galwegians clash was a dour affair that finished 3-3.

Brenny Mullin was taking the kicks at The Sportsground that day and had a nightmare, managing one from six attempts. A spectator ran onto the field the same day to break up a scrap between opposing props, Job Langbroek and Pat Leahy.

Future Ireland, Wales and Lions coach, Warren Gatland was playing for Galwegians. I don't recall him in that game but in the future, he was to have plenty to say about my refereeing. But then Warren always has plenty to say.

Crucially, we secured AIL status and just about managed to hold our place in the League the following season.

Promotion to Division 1 was achieved in February 1993 when we beat Terenure at Templeogue with tries from Woody, Frano and Brenny. There was controversy right at the end as they were camped on our line on two separate occasions in the closing minutes. In all, there were eight scrums and four penalties given against us but we avoided the concession of a penalty try.

Terenure were incensed that Alan Watson didn't see fit to head for the posts, especially as Owen Doyle had done so in Young Munster's favour against Garryowen the previous week after just one collapsed scrum.

Their mood wasn't helped when, after finally deciding to run the ball, Tom Darcy appeared to have touched down but again, the referee remained unmoved. I don't know if it was a try or not but the papers seemed to think so.

I didn't care. We had finally reached the top tier of club rugby and if it took a bit of luck along the way to get there, I wasn't going to apologise for it.

We had a couple of shots at winning the League in the next couple of seasons. Under Eddie, we improved gradually. He recruited astutely to give us a hard-working, tough pack. Dean Oswald was a durable New Zealander who provided leadership and a bit of mongrel up front. John Etheridge did likewise.

Frano was a casualty of this process. It was a little divisive in the club because he was such a popular individual around Stradbrook and was Blackrock through and through. But you could see why it came down to this.

For Eddie, workrate and preparation were paramount. That is why I relished dealing with him. It is also why he and Frano were never going to get on. Neil is a good guy, who possessed the most amazing athleticism but he was, by his own admission, a lazy fucker.

It frustrated everybody because when he was in the zone, you could not compete with him. Not just in the lineout at 2 or 4, but he could cover the ground in a ridiculous fashion for a man of his size. I have a picture of him in my mind running 40 metres down the touchline against Terenure in Lansdowne Road. He was tall, quick and agile.

I wanted to get him into the Sevens and he played when we won the illustrious Melrose event in 1991 but he was just too unfit for that format. I would doubt if he was ever at more than 70% and when he did get there, he was brilliant. Had his attitude to training been better, he would have been untouchable, one of the all-time greats. He never realised his potential.

So in the end, he moved on. It was sad but Frano was not going to turn over a new leaf and did not respond well to Eddie's prodding and poking. It was the best move for everyone.

We were a better team for having a pack that enjoyed the nitty-gritty of their responsibilities, were willing to employ a few dark arts and had the capacity to do so for 80 minutes. They gave us the platform to unleash what was definitely the best back division in club rugby at the time. Alan McGowan and I dictated from the halfback positions and Brenny was the play-making wizard in the centre. He was surrounded by the likes of Martin 'Trigger' Ridge, Nicky, Niall Woods and David Beggy.

'Jinksy', as David was known because of his mesmerising feet and body swerve, was a brilliant player, who made his name initially as a key member of the Meath football team that won a couple of All-Irelands in 1987 and 1988. He was just as good in rugby, with a similar unpredictability, going on to be a regular for Leinster. Eddie described him in his autobiography as 'the real rabbit in the hat'.

We were primed for an all-out assault.

▌▌ ■ ▌▌

The extent of the travelling involved in the AIL competition was a completely new development for us and the alickadoos didn't like it because of the increased expense. Often, you would spend the night before a game in a hotel. That was completely new for anyone who wasn't involved at international level.

We had a huge support for away games and would travel on chartered trains with them after games in Cork. That was an incredible experience, especially when you were winning. The singing and chanting would start as you pulled out of Kent Station and didn't cease until arrival at Heuston. *Rock Boys Are We* got many an airing on the good days.

The battles in Limerick were the ones that stood out. The posh boys down from Dublin were always a scalp for them. They looked on us as cannon-fodder. All style, no substance. Give it to us hard and we'd fold.

That's why from a club point of view, one of my fondest memories is of beating Shannon in Thomond Park in February of 1994. We didn't just beat them, we kicked their arses, 18-6. That was probably our best game in my era with 'Rock. Everything we did worked.

Fergal O'Beirne, Dean Oswald and Danny Casey led the way in the back row, facing off against Anthony Foley and Eddie Halvey. They smashed everything that moved in a Shannon jersey that day and made so much ground with ball in hand. We beat them at their own style of game.

They say packs decide who wins a game and backs decree by how much. As the game wore on, we opened up and they had no answer. Brenny was imperious, while Woody and Nicky scored the tries. To be honest, we were very smug leaving Thomond Park that day. It was an unbelievable feeling of satisfaction. No doubt, they stored the memory of that loss and our happy, smiling faces after the final whistle for our next clash but this was our day.

We were entitled to enjoy it because you didn't have too many fond memories of playing in Limerick generally. Being dropped into the molten lava of Tom Clifford Park was probably the most intimidating experience and Young Munster brought us back down to earth very quickly in front of 7,000 people the following month.

Being a visiting scrum half in that environment was challenging to say the least, with Peter Clohessy, Ger Earls and John 'Paco' Fitzgerald staring wild-eyed at you like breakfast. The verbals were incessant. Instilling fear was such a huge part of what they were about and they would try to do that with word and deed. One way or another, they would leave something on you.

'Who the fuck do you think you are, pretty boy? Swanning down here from Donnybrook with your fancy hair like you own the place. We'll fucking show you. Wait 'til I get you on the ground. I'll rip you to fucking pieces.'

Usually, you don't take much notice of talk because invariably it's just that. The thing about these guys is that the threats weren't idle. If you were at the bottom of a ruck, you knew what was coming.

That's what you expected down there. That was part of the game and it was a great eclectic mix of cultures. They were representing their passionate people, who were baying for some Fancy Dan Dublin blood. They invariably got it.

They beat us 10-3 but after we edged out Cork Con in Stradbrook, when

I set up Paul Wallace for a try, we were still in with a chance of annexing the League title. In the end, it came down to another trip to the Treaty City. It was winner-takes-all as we rolled into Dooradoyle to take on Garryowen.

It has been claimed that there were 10,000 in attendance that day. I don't know if that's true but they could not have squeezed another body in. Maybe that is why the game was played but it shouldn't have been because the pitch was unplayable.

The conspiracy theorists insist that Garryowen watered the pitch to make it as unsuitable to creativity as possible. Club officials claimed they had helicopters hovering over the pitch to try and dry it off just a little.

They would have been desperate for the game to go ahead because those conditions would suit them while also handicapping us severely. Our back division revelled in top-of-the-ground turf. When it was soft, they literally got bogged down. What we know for sure is that it rained heavily and the pitch was a quagmire.

It was billed as a battle of the packs. Garryowen had Keith Wood, Paul Hogan and Ben Cronin and afterwards, Eddie admitted that they had gotten the better of us up front. In particular, Cronin got the upper hand on Dean on this occasion, which wasn't something that happened too often. We couldn't get going at all and lost 9-3. It was one of my worst days as a player. I was crestfallen.

We challenged strongly the following season too but again just fell short. Shannon would have loved the fact that they nicked it from us. What's more, they did it by beating us in Stradbrook. Sweet revenge for what had happened in Thomond the previous year.

Again, the weather gods went against us as it poured all day. While we had the pack to operate, the speed, skill and trickery behind the scrum made us stand out. The boys could not impose themselves with a greasy ball and soggy paddock. Shannon went on to garner the first of four AIL crowns on the trot, an incredible achievement for The Parish.

That was as close as we got but it was a magnificent time. Eddie was absolutely essential to it all. He was far ahead of his time in relation to how he prepared. The norm in that time was to practice moves without any opposition. When you think of it now, it makes no sense and explains why so many of them never came off. Opponents tend not to be accommodating to your wishes. Eddie changed that in Stradbrook.

He recruited cleverly, identifying our weaknesses and making the necessary alterations. His analysis was at a different level. For the first time, we watched videos of games.

Then there was the concept of playing to patterns. It will horrify the modern player to learn that we had never encountered that. The notion of taking the ball up a number of phases before then carrying out a rehearsed move was revolutionary. We were thinking three moves ahead. That would be nothing now but it was completely alien at the time.

Generally, fitness had been left to yourself, unless we were playing Murderball, picking and driving and tackling. Knocking the shit out of each other in other words. Eddie wanted more sport-specific fitness training so he got Jim Burns in. Jim was an athletics coach at Blackrock College who also worked with Brenny – an international hurdler as well, lest anyone forget.

Jim taught us about running techniques. We did drills that doubled as fitness training but were primarily about how you ran. Emphasis was placed on shortening the stride so you could put your foot down to change your pace and your direction. It was radical and I lapped it up.

It was no surprise that Eddie went on to coach at the very highest level. It might not have ended as he would have liked with Ireland but that should never cloud his magnificent achievements. I might not have agreed with him on everything – and definitely not on rotating his scrum halves – but he was the most enlightened, visionary coach I ever had.

CHAPTER FIVE

The provincial scene was pretty nondescript for the majority of my playing career. You rarely played more than five or six times a season. There were three games in the interprovincial series and then a couple against visiting teams. Sometimes, you travelled to England or Wales for a game. That was it. That only changed with the advent of the European Cup and subsequently, the Celtic League, which is now the PRO12. Initially, nobody was too sure about European competition. Games were midweek and the competition was over by January. Slowly it morphed into the Heineken Cup, a behemoth widely considered the greatest club rugby tournament in the world, so important that clubs are willing to invest millions to try to win it. That money played a huge part in the unfortunate butting of heads that led to the hasty restructuring and establishment of the Champions Cup

I played five European Cup games towards the end of my career and we had a great run when getting to the semi-final in the 1995-96 campaign.

We were finally getting our act together by then, having endured a very fallow period. When Leinster completed the Grand Slam in 1984, they were claiming the interprovincial championship for the fifth successive time. It was another 10 years before we returned to the winner's enclosure.

It was great to be involved in that. The regular defeats, at the hands of Ulster in particular, gave it real value. In 1995, I scored the winning try when we recorded what would be our last victory at Thomond Park until 2010. We were successful in the interprovincial championship again in 1996 and it was nice to pick up some silverware towards the end of a decade in the famous blue jersey.

Competition was almost as stiff for Leinster as with Ireland. I seemed to have more support from the provincial selectors than their national counterparts however, as I played fairly regularly from 1987 to 1997. Often, I got the nod for Leinster over Gus Aherne and Niall Hogan, when they were playing for Ireland. I was keeping Hogie out of the side when he was Ireland captain.

That led to a tally of 40 provincial caps, which stands up pretty well given the competition at the time, and the dearth of games. It is safe to say that I played more often than I didn't for Leinster over a decade.

Making the Leinster U19s straight out of school was my first representative call-up. Good form with Blackrock led to my senior debut against Llanelli in November 1987 in place of Tony Doyle, who had been captain. It went well as we beat the Welshmen in Donnybrook 27-10. Paul Dean was at out half and Tony Ward in the centre for that game as the bid to find the best use of their talents continued.

I kept my place for the interprovincial game against Munster the following week but that was a horror show, as we lost to them for the first time in five years. Amazingly, given how Munster sides liked to beat up on their Leinster brethren in Limerick, it was Leinster's first loss to them in Thomond Park since 1975.

Initially, the big rivalry was with Gus. He was captain for a while but one of us would get a run of games and then the other would get in. The province just wasn't very good at that time and lost a lot of games. It was a pretty disorganised set-up, reflective really of a group of players rarely training or playing together. Not winning games led to a lot of chopping and changing, which wasn't helpful either.

That situation improved significantly when Jim Glennon took over and brought in Ciaran Callan and Paul Dean with him. They oversaw the implementation of a proper structure and plan. The two interprovincial titles and reaching the semi-final of the inaugural European Cup came as a result of that.

Even then, Jim was nicknamed 'The Politician' because of the way he talked. He would become a TD the following decade and was a natural for the role. He made you believe in what he was trying to do. Cally and Deano provided the coaching and the improvement was radical.

Newspaper reports described the Heineken Cup as being viewed with an 'understandable level of apprehension'. Because the games were scheduled for the middle of the week, you had to get time off work for away trips. There was a concern that there were now too many games, particularly in a calendar that had absolutely no conceivable configuration as it was.

Imagine this scenario if you can. The build-up to the semi-final was dominated by issues of whether or not any member of the Ireland squad would be available to play in the final if we made it through. The problem was that Ireland were playing USA in Atlanta the day before the European Cup final was fixed and were leaving the previous week.

After negotiations with Ireland manager Pat Whelan, it was agreed that any player not selected on the Ireland team could fly back but that would have been some ordeal, having flown out in the first place. In the end, it proved a moot point but it illustrates the prevailing issues.

We got our campaign off to a win in Milan. We got out of jail big time there as Diego Dominguez missed seven kicks at goal. He was one of the great out halves but thankfully chose that day to suffer a dose of the yips. We staggered over the line thanks to tries from Conor O'Shea and Niall Woods.

Along with Paul Wallace and Victor Costello, Conor was one of the real pros of the Leinster set-up. We called him 'Caesar' because he had one of those bowl-type haircuts so beloved by the Romans. It is absolutely no surprise to see him doing so well as director of rugby at Harlequins and in his work on RTÉ as an analyst.

As a player, he had a wonderful understanding of the game. Not many of his contemporaries thought about it like he did or had his knowledge. He had the drive and enthusiasm to go with it, as he couldn't envisage not getting the very best out of himself.

He was a team man rather than an individual and was extremely popular as a result. Of course he is very engaging anyway and what makes him so good about what he does now, both as a coach and pundit, is that he doesn't just understand what is going on, he can communicate it.

Niall Hogan was the Leinster captain by now but I was holding him off for the European run. And we managed to just about do the same against Pontypridd at a floodlit Lansdowne Road in a thriller, edging it 23-22. In a three-team group, a draw would have sufficed for the visitors as they had beaten Milan by more.

When Crispin Cormack crossed the whitewash in the 72nd minute it looked like we were toast but my 'Rock clubmate, Alan McGowan was nerveless as he kicked a winning penalty three minute from time. It was some show of balls because he had missed three penalties in the first six minutes. Conor was wide with another attempt.

A try settled Alan down and Kurt McQuilkin also went over for what was now a five-pointer to give us an 11-point lead. Pontypridd threw the kitchen sink at us to hit the front themselves. Then, after Alan wrestled back the advantage with the three points that saw him eclipse Ollie Campbell as Leinster's leading scorer of all time, there was even more drama.

Pontypridd were awarded a penalty from 33 yards out on the left. If the kicking machine, Neil Jenkins had been playing, we would have gone out in the most sickening circumstances. He wasn't on the pitch that day though.

To be fair, Lee Jarvis had a 100% record and never looked like missing all day. But the pressure was immense now and Jenkins would have been more comfortable in that type of situation. Jarvis' attempt drifted across the face of goal and we survived. Having gone off injured after 31 minutes, I had to watch it all unfold from the line.

Mention semi-finals nowadays and you think of searing sun and bright, blue skies. Especially if they are taking place on the Mediterranean, as has been the case for quite a few of the most recent ones. Regardless of the venue, the final run-in around April allows for the games to be generally played in improved weather.

Back then, it was a less congested affair fixtures-wise and our semi-final took place the day before New Year's Eve. Frost presented a serious threat and Cardiff Arms Park had to survive a pitch inspection before being deemed fit for action.

It wasn't to be our day. In truth, pushing Cardiff to 23-14 on their home turf was a monumental effort as they fielded a team with 14 internationals. We were well in touch at the interval but the second half turned into a bit of an arm-wrestle and the only score was a drop-goal from their scrum half, Andy Moore.

It took a team as great as Toulouse to beat Cardiff in the Arms Park, and it needed extra time to do so. Guy Noves' all-singing, all-dancing men of many talents always held the upper hand. The mercurial Thomas Castaignède scored a try and a drop goal but Adrian Davies kicked six penalties to ensure that the teams were still level, with a penalty shootout looming.

With seconds remaining in extra time, David McHugh spotted Cardiff hands in the ruck though and Christophe Deylaud broke Welsh hearts from the tee. I was the man in the middle nine years later when Toulouse would suffer their own last-minute anguish with Robert Howley's try for Wasps in the 2004 final.

When you look at how the Heineken Cup has grown into such a mammoth sporting and commercial enterprise, evolving now to the Champions' Cup, it is nice to have been there at the start. That is especially the case given that my European odyssey continued and while I never got to play in the final, I did referee three of them, which was the next best thing.

▮▮▮▮

That season did conclude successfully as we beat Ulster to claim the interprovincial championship outright, having shared it with them two years previously.

I continued to play for the next couple of seasons, even during my spell with Moseley in England, and was picked to play the touring Aussies in 1996 but the game was a victim of the never-accommodating Irish weather.

There were a couple of more Heineken Cup appearances, including one away encounter in Toulouse on October 11, 1997. The game ended in a 38-19 loss at Les Sept Deniers, as the Stade Ernest-Wallon is called by the locals, but that isn't what it's remembered for now.

It was a tough build-up as Victor Costello's father had died. I stayed behind as the rest of the team flew over and travelled with Victor on the

Tuesday. I would have known him well from his Blackrock days and being a senior player at the time, felt it was the right thing to do. It was a tough time for Victor but he was anxious to play the game, which says a lot about him.

Toulouse were on a different level to us in terms of skill, fitness and conditioning but nobody was too downhearted and the party quickly got under way. After a quick drink, I let them at it and as was my custom, went back to my hotel.

I was out cold when woken up by some pretty frantic knocking at 2am. It was Paul Flavin and Shane Byrne, practically blowing the door off its hinges.

'Rollers! Rollers!'

Fuck off, I thought to myself. Drunken bastards.

'Rollers! Rollers!'

'What' I groaned.

'You've got to get up and come with us. There's a taxi outside.'

'It's two o'clock in the morning. What's going on?'

'We'll explain on the way.'

'Where are we going?'

'To the police station. A few of the lads have been arrested.'

'Whaaaat? Jesus!'

So the lads filled me in. Trevor Brennan, Reggie Corrigan, Victor and Denis Hickie had gotten involved in some sort of fracas outside a bar. They were quickly rounded up, packed into a Black Maria and taken down to the police station. The lads high-tailed it to me because A) I was sober and B) I could speak French.

I sent Shane and Flav back to the hotel to tell Jim and Cally. There was no hiding this from them. They had to be brought into the loop.

The whole thing was fairly harmless but my understanding of the French law is that the police could not question the boys until they were under the alcohol limit. That would mean waiting until the morning. The problem was, we were scheduled to fly back to Dublin at 9am. Missing that would lead to a serious shit storm.

I pleaded with them but to little effect. They explained that the only way they could let the lads go was if a judge gave them permission to do so.

'Can you ring the judge?' I begged.

Again, no luck. Under no circumstances were they going to rouse a judge from his slumber at 4am.

Eventually I wore them down, emphasising the early flight. The fact that the lads didn't cause them one iota of trouble was noted too. So they rang the judge, who was a rugby man fortunately. Maybe if we had beaten Toulouse we would be there still. But he gave the go-ahead to leave. We got back to the hotel about 6.30am, with the bus ready to go to the airport at 7.

We had a quick meeting at the airport and made it clear that nobody was to speak about it. What happens in Toulouse... But it got out, probably thanks to some alickadoo.

Trevor wrote about it subsequently in his autobiography. Of course he moved to Toulouse and had a wonderful career there, winning two Heineken Cups. He is still living there, immersed in the culture and his son, Daniel is now part of the French development system.

The pub where he had the hassle with the natives?

He bought it.

▯ ▮ ▮ ▯

Professionalism brought my Leinster career to an end. I had been on a part-time contract but by now, there was a real drive to turn the provinces into club teams capable of competing at European level. The IRFU had been slow to the party when it came to professionalism but they now recognised that it could help the national team too and were on the way to establishing the model that is now the envy of all the other northern hemisphere federations.

I had established a very good career in the financial sector and was now with Cornmarket, dealing primarily as a mortgage broker. There wasn't much point in me throwing all that away in my 30s for the sake of one more year or two at the most. I wouldn't earn enough to make having to start all over again worthwhile.

So it was time to call it quits.

CHAPTER SIX

Tactical substitutions were introduced on November 4, 1996.

It was about six years too late for me.

Had I been starting out instead of finishing up when the International Board introduced the new law to eradicate the increasing tactic of feigning injury to get replacements on, I might have accumulated 20 caps for Ireland.

As it was, I wound up with three. That's three more than I ever dreamt of when I first laced boots. I played one full game and came on twice as an injury replacement. The sense of pride in getting those opportunities is overwhelming and I still feel it today.

There is some frustration that there could have been more over a nine-year period of being called into Ireland squads, and around five or six years of being right in the mix. But not much. Because I can look myself in the mirror and know that there wasn't any more I could have done to make that happen.

Why did I not win more caps? I don't know. Obviously, there was some really good competition at the time. Michael Bradley was the main man but the likes of Gus Aherne and Niall Hogan were tough opponents.

Rob Saunders and Chris Saverimutto were parachuted in from nowhere and returned to nowhere pretty quickly afterwards. David O'Mahony came in for one game ahead of me and never played again, although he had some back luck with injuries.

My perceived weaknesses? I was only 5'9" but I never considered being short as any handicap. I concentrated on using my speed but I was physical. I got stuck in. I did a lot of gym work and was strong.

Thankfully, I didn't break many bones but I got split an awful lot and must have had 50 stitches around my eyes. That might not be a lot to a forward, but you didn't see too many behind the scrum picking up that sort of scar tissue.

Just patch me up and get me back out there.

I only had to be carted into hospital once, after a club game in Stradbrook against Old Crescent. I don't remember anything about the incident but saw it on the video afterwards when we were doing match analysis.

This guy led with his head like a Scud missile. I was in and out of consciousness and have a hazy memory of going into the ambulance. Doc Cummiskey absolutely destroyed his cashmere coat with the flow of blood. Apparently the split was so big it was like I had a third eye.

They kept me in hospital overnight because I was displaying the usual symptoms of a pretty bad concussion, throwing up a lot. But I recovered and it had no impact in how I approached physicality subsequently.

Apart from that, I was pretty lucky with injuries. You always picked up knocks. I broke my arm once and what should have been a six- or seven-week absence turned to 13 as it was very slow to heal. Apart from that, I tweaked hamstrings, had some knee ligament damage, bust my thumbs a couple of times. You would take that at the start of a rugby career.

Ultimately, I had a good pass, had gotten myself very strong, was quick, extremely fit and possessed a reasonable understanding for what it is we were trying to do out on the pitch. I could take things on board quite quickly. I could read a game well and manage it.

That is a matter of opinion of course. Clearly, there was some issue or doubt about me when it came to international rugby.

I would look for an explanation when I was left out of the Ireland team. Not because I felt I should be there and was throwing a hissy fit, but because it was in my DNA to identify an area of weakness and improve it.

You're not picking me? Tell me why, I will go away and make sure it is no longer a problem. And then you won't have a reason not to give me the jersey.

'Sometimes we're not quite sure about your decision-making.'

That was the only message I ever got. It was at odds with how I felt about my game but then I was probably biased.

Here's the thing though. I was captain of Blackrock and Leinster at various times. Even when I wasn't, I was a leader. When we won the interprovincial championship with Leinster and got to the semi-final of the Heineken Cup, Shane Byrne spoke about my leadership in the media. I was making decisions all the time. It goes with being a scrum half.

What made you question the given reason the most is that the guys who told me my decision-making might not be 100% reliable, made me captain of the Ireland B team. Figure that one out!

'I'm not good enough to make the senior team because of my decision-making but you're going to make me chief decision-maker for the second team?'

I don't dwell on things but that always got to me a little because it just made no sense. So the obvious conclusion then is that there must be some other reason. I don't know if my face didn't fit or what. Maybe they couldn't put their finger on it themselves.

They just formed a perception of me as a good guy to have around the squad, one of the highest scorers on the bleep test at 14.5, when some of the guys could not make 10, but they didn't fancy me. They always seemed to look at me and think that there must be somebody else.

If I had just been given maybe a run of a couple of games it could have been all different but that's the way it is. I had splinters on my backside from the number of times I sat on the bench but when it came to the big tours or World Cups, I didn't make the cut. The one exception was Australia in 1994 and that was cut short through injury. It was like having a glimpse of paradise and being turned back at the entrance.

I've always believed that you can only control the controllables. You do your best and that's either good enough or it isn't. When you know deep down that you have put every effort into ensuring you are the best you can be, that's fine, even if it doesn't get you to the Promised Land.

On October 27, 1990, when I got my first cap, I was the proudest man in the world and nobody can take that away from me. I have always drawn from that, rather than be somebody who was pissed off about getting three caps.

I treasure those appearances and especially that day in Lansdowne when I started against Argentina to make my debut.

Playing and being involved with Ireland was a resoundingly positive experience for me. I loved being part of it. Even when I wasn't getting on, I was thinking, *I have a sniff. I'm being given an opportunity to train with these guys. Maybe I can learn something.*

It is the highest honour that can be bestowed on a player and there are many good ones that didn't get a chance.

That'll do me.

▮▮▮▮

There were early indications that I might be destined for more. Having been a slow-burner, I made very quick strides once I got into adult rugby. The first national training session call-up arrived in my debut season on Blackrock's firsts, little more than two years after playing in the Leinster Senior Cup Schools' final.

I got selected to play in a Combined Provinces side against The Rest in a national trial at Ravenhill in March 1987. It was exclusively for players that had played no part in the Five Nations but I did very well against Tony Doyle, who was the reserve scrum half to Mickey Bradley and was providing the service to Tony Ward as we won 17-3.

It was unbelievable really. I hadn't even had a trial for Leinster.

There were some newspaper reports that John Robbie might return from South Africa to play in the inaugural World Cup. It didn't happen but even without that, there were too many good and experienced 9s around for me to be considered. Not making it for any of the next two was disappointing but I never considered myself a contender for the first one in New Zealand and Australia. Just knowing they were aware of my existence was a huge boost.

Jim Davidson took over from Mick Doyle as coach after the World Cup and he called me in as cover to a training squad, with Ulster's Rab Brady an injury doubt. I was on the edge of things and invariably got the call when additional players were required so they could have full training games.

When Italy came to Ireland on a three-match tour and beat a Combined

Provinces team, as well as an Ireland U25s, the IRFU recognised that not enough players were being exposed to a higher level of competition, leaving them ill-prepared for the step-up.

So they reintroduced the Ireland B side and with no full internationals eligible, I was picked. Edmund Van Esbeck called my selection ahead of Shannon's Oliver Kiely 'the most contentious decision the selectors have made'. Ned didn't appear to be my biggest supporter when I was playing but I can't complain, as he showered praise on me when I took up the whistle.

It was a strong team chosen to play Scotland, with Peter Clohessy, Mick Galwey, Jim Staples, Brian Robinson, Brian Rigney and Kenny Murphy joining me in the starting line-up. Future full internationals Paddy Johns, Gary Halpin and Ken O'Connell were named in the replacements.

It meant so much to put on a green jersey for the first time in Murrayfield on December 9, 1989. We drew 22-22 but I obviously didn't do enough to impress as I was one of only four in that team not to be named in the full squad a few days later for a training camp.

I was on the bench for an Ireland U25 team that played USA to mark the official opening of the new Thomond Park the following March but was selected when the U25s took on Spain at the same venue in September.

This was a fantastic opportunity. There was a certainty in my mind that this was the dress rehearsal. The opposition might not have been established but they would be enthusiastic and physical. If I wanted to step up to the next level I needed to make an impact.

It couldn't have gone any better. One report described me as the architect of a 36-17 demolition, though I certainly benefited from being behind a dominant scrum. We flew out of the traps and I had a try after a few minutes, setting up another for the brilliant Simon Geoghegan before half time. Apart from that, I just felt really good, flying around the park and flinging out quick and accurate passes.

Three of the national selectors were in attendance and when the first squad of the Ciaran Fitzgerald era was selected for the Autumn programme, I was preferred to Gus.

At 24, the high point of my playing life was just around the corner.

CHAPTER SEVEN

'Hi Alain, I just wanted to let you know that you have been selected on the team to play Argentina. Congratulations.'

'I can't believe it. Is it official?'

'It is.'

'Thank you very much.'

Forgive me. I have the memory of a sieve, which has made this exercise a challenging one to say the least. I cannot recall if it was Johnny Moloney or Ciaran Fitzgerald who rang me with the news.

It wasn't the individual that made the impact though, with all due respect to him. It was the message. So many thoughts were whirring through my head but the prevailing sense was one of immense gratification.

I was walking on air.

To say playing for my country at the highest level was the realisation of a childhood dream would be inaccurate because I never thought it might be possible until getting the call-up to the national training squad three years earlier, and then establishing myself with Leinster.

It doesn't get any better than this. And it never did.

Later on, I would reach the pinnacle of refereeing when taking charge of the 2007 World Cup final. That was something I wanted so badly but nothing beats playing for your country. Absolutely nothing.

There were similarities between the two situations. I knew I had done well for Leinster and Ireland U25s and probably should be selected. But when it actually happened, I was still overwhelmed by the enormity of it.

There was always a suspicion that that the press had some influence on selection at that time and the claim was persistently denied by the IRFU bigwigs. Clearly my form put me in the shop window but there was a real momentum behind me as the papers were talking up the speed of my distribution and general game.

After that, the whole thing took on a life of its own. There was a lot of focus on my background and the phone started hopping with journalists calling round the clock.

Then there were the TV crews. RTÉ came into the bank. It was all very strange given that I was just a guy playing rugby. The previous week, nobody outside of my immediate circle had a clue who I was. Now I was on the news.

I can't quite explain it because I am shy, but I really enjoyed that experience. It certainly wasn't a distraction. Or maybe it was but in a good sense. I wasn't worrying about the game. Anyway, I loved it.

A crew arrived over from France to follow me around for three days because apparently, it was a big deal over there that Ireland were giving a debut to a man of French descent (*Le Franco-Irlandais* as one headline over there had it). Since then, they have always had a fascination about me. To this day, I would have a much bigger profile in France than I do in Ireland.

That was great *craic* altogether as they followed me everywhere. They came into the bank and brought me down to Seapoint beach for some of those moody, elemental, atmospheric shots of me walking along the concrete wall by the sea and down the boardwalk, in deep, contemplative mode. I was just trying not to burst out laughing.

My father didn't enjoy that experience so much. He was very proud of me but having to do an interview was a heavy price for him to pay. He wasn't able. They did so many takes and we tried to put him at ease but it crippled him, looking into that camera.

They filmed me at home, at training with 'Rock, training on my own.

There were plenty of interviews. It was my 15 minutes of fame and I milked it for all it was worth.

Once, I had to go into a sports shop in the Stillorgan Shopping Centre to buy a pair of blue shorts for 'Rock – in those days you bought your own gear. I could see the attendant looking at me.

'Are you Alain Rolland?'

That was a first. He congratulated me and gave me the shorts on the house. I was thinking that this was something I could get used to! But it didn't last.

▌▌▌▌

A notable aspect of this particular team was that both half backs had dual citizenship. I have a French social security number thanks to Mamine registering me when I was born and nearly having me carted off to Perpignan to do my national service.

The out half for my debut was Brian Smith, the Australian who actually played against Ireland as a scrum half in the 1987 World Cup quarter-final, before using the Granny Rule to hook up with us two years later.

He divided opinions from people who didn't like the idea of recruiting players ahead of those born in Ireland. Others felt he didn't produce enough, though my suspicion is that he was judged at a higher level to others because of the nature of his arrival.

I was a huge fan. I had played with Tony Ward and Paul Dean and I felt he compared very favourably with them.

Brian Smith was completely ahead of his time. Well, ahead of his time in Ireland anyway. He was a product of his southern hemisphere grounding. There was no-one in Ireland preparing like he was for rugby internationals. He was a professional in an amateur era.

This was a time when you might play an AIL game on a Saturday and then hook up with the international squad that night for a squad session on the back pitch in Lansdowne the following morning. There were no sessions in the pool, no isotonic drinks, no chicken and pasta.

There was plenty of drink though. Most of the lads would just drop their gear in the Berkeley Court Hotel before strolling down the road to Leeson

Street for some rehydration of a different kind.

You would be flogged on the pitch the next morning, with particularly heavy contact work coming less than 24 hours after a massively competitive game that was followed by a lengthy trip for the guys not based in Dublin. Throw in the fact that half of them were dying of a hangover and it was crazy.

You didn't see Brian Smith involved in anything detrimental to his performance if he could avoid it. He trained hard and conscientiously but it wasn't just that. It was evident in his diet, how he stretched, the importance he placed on rest and getting plenty of sleep. It was a considerable eye-opener for all of us, even someone like me.

I thought I had all the bases covered when it came to looking after my body but Brian was on a different level. He was a man after my own heart in that fashion and I loved having him around. That was the environment I coveted because it was how you got the best out of yourself.

The man was in an unbelievable shape. Again, I thought I was in good condition but seeing him togged off for the first time, all I could think to myself was, *Fucking hell, what would you need to do be ripped like that?* There wasn't an ounce of fat on him.

You'd swear I fancied him but he was a really good looking guy too, and the girls were hanging out of him. That blond, Queensland surfer look went down well with them, if not his detractors, who used the flash exterior as another stick to beat him with, as if it were evidence of a softness that to be fair, didn't exist.

In truth, his ultra-professional approach didn't help his cause in gaining acceptance. That's a poor reflection of where the game was here. He was greeted with suspicion and considered a threat. People wanted the days of the piss-ups and fucking around to last forever. It's a pity as they could have learned so much from him. That was my attitude and I must have driven him to distraction quizzing him about drills, gym work and what I should be eating.

There was no escape for Brian because the custom then was for the partnerships to room together. But I don't think he minded too much. We had a good relationship and still get on very well now. I just had a thirst for knowledge and he was a fountain of it.

Through life, you can hang around negative people and you become one of those. The alternative is to surround yourself with high achievers. I always sought out the positive people. I have no time for moaners. I don't even want to know them.

Brian Smith was someone who knew how to do things better. That was good enough for me.

❙❙❙❙

People presume that you are going to be very nervous playing Test rugby for the first time but I wasn't. I had been to a funeral the day before and that placed what was ahead of me firmly in perspective.

John McDonnell was a clubmate at Stradbrook and as I sat next to Brenny Mullin in the church and looked at Joan, John's Mum, I thought, *What the fuck do I have to be nervous about?*

A son of Joe Mac, who was a great clubman, John was only a year or two older than me and was very popular in 'Rock. I had been talking to him the previous week and he was in great form. He had had a big win in the Lottery and was planning on getting married to his girlfriend. In a flash, everything was gone as he was killed in a car crash.

All I was doing was playing a fucking rugby match.

❙❙❙❙

I still had butterflies, of course. I would imagine the other debutants, Paddy Johns and Phil Lawlor were the same. We were fortunate in that it was the first time full caps were being awarded for a game against Argentina.

Paddy had been close the previous year in a bizarre set of circumstances that encapsulated the amateur era. A dental student in Trinity, he was representing the Irish Universities in Paris on the same weekend of a Five Nations game involving France and Ireland.

Willie Anderson became ill overnight so the carrier pigeons were sent out across the French capital in search of the tall Dungannon lock who would be needed to sit on the bench. He was located in a bistro and much to his chagrin, carted off to bed.

He had been out long enough mind you and it was to his eternal relief that the two starting second rows lasted the 80 minutes!

There were no such scares this time around, although having to sing a song on the team bus wasn't exactly a walk in the park. It was a tradition that all new caps would have to belt out a tune of their choosing coming back from training and it frightened the shit out of me.

I had been captain of a number of squads and you said your few words before and after a game but that was it. Very straightforward. At general public gatherings, you wouldn't even know I was there. I had never done anything like this before.

It was probably one of the most nerve-wracking experiences of my life. I wasn't quite as bad as Dad when it came to public displays of any sort but I was no exhibitionist. I have always been an Elvis fan so I went for *In The Ghetto*.

I think it was Paddy that went before me. I couldn't tell you if he was good or bad but it took a bit of the pressure off not having to be the first to make an eejit of myself. I had to learn the words, sang two verses and got away with it.

Emboldened by the experience, I decided to repeat it at my wedding reception three years later. Lizzie was, and still is, a big Tom Cruise fan. She only agreed to marry me when she finally accepted that nothing was going to happen between the two of them.

So in honour of the scene from Top Gun, where Tom Cruise serenades Kelly McGillis really badly I decided to surprise her with a rendition of *You've Lost that Loving Feeling*. Knowing me better than anyone, she would be stunned and she was.

Fortunately, the rest of the guests joined in for the chorus and I like to think I did a better job than Maverick anyway.

There was one more bit of singing associated with my first cap. That surrounded *Amhrán na bhFiann*, the national anthem. I had to learn the words for that as well and it was a real struggle because I am useless at Irish.

That probably seems strange given that my command of French, while not brilliant, is functional. But then I was exposed to that all my life. I never heard the Irish language until I went to school. Anything the kids have to ask about Irish, I direct to Mark. After two stints in Irish college, he knows more than anyone else in the family.

I could easily have gotten away with not knowing the anthem. Nobody would have taken any notice really had I not been singing it. It was important to me though. This was a huge day in my life and I wanted to embrace everything about being Irish before I went into battle for my country.

▌▐▌▌

There was no ceremony in terms of having your jersey presented to you or anything like that on your debut. You just walked into the dressing room and it was hanging up waiting for you.

It was a very different jersey to the ones they have now, hanging loosely off you in a one-size-fits-all model that sort of went for the average and wasn't very flattering for props or scrum halves. Nowadays, they are skin-tight on the backs, while they are just the tiniest bit looser for the pack so that they can bind. And everyone has the conditioning to look good in them.

When I walked into the dressing room at Lansdowne Road on October 27, that heavy, cotton, long-sleeved garment with the number '9' on the back was the most beautiful thing I had ever seen.

Fucking hell.

I was 24 years old, winning my first cap. I wasn't so presumptuous that there would be many more but it felt good to be the man in possession and I did think I would get a few more chances than ultimately proved the case.

Match day went by in a bit of a blur. I tried to enjoy it as best I could. The game itself wasn't very good but I did okay despite the fact that the pack struggled. In particular, I was happy with the grubber for Kenny Hooks to touch down in the corner.

It was an eight-nine move around the corner and with the cover pushing up, I just felt there was a little space in behind to dink it into. Kenny won the race to register the four-pointer. I played a part in Michael Kiernan's try later on so I could certainly say I had a positive impact.

We scraped the victory, 20-18 without having gelled at all. We were expected to win more comprehensively than that as despite having the great Hugo Porta as captain and out half, Argentina were still a developing nation.

They had their own debutant that day. Federico 'Freddie' Mendez was just 18 as he packed down opposite Dessie Fitzgerald, father of Luke. He fared better than me for the remainder of his career, finishing up with 75 caps.

If he was disappointed to lose on his debut, his second senior appearance against England a week later was even less enjoyable, as he was sent off for landing a haymaker on English lock, Paul Ackford 11 minutes from time at Twickenham.

The manner of the loss in Lansdowne really angered the Pumas though. There was a lot of controversy about the decision of New Zealand referee, Colin Hawke to play almost nine minutes of injury time. Nobody really knew where he got it from.

We were already in the added period when Agustin Macome, the Argentina No 8 went over for a try after a succession of scrums. Porta added the extras to give them an 18-17 lead. We all waited for Hawke to blow his whistle but he didn't.

So we played on. And on. About two minutes after the try, the Argentina backs were penalised for going offside. I remember Mick Kiernan asking Hawke what time was left and he was told it was the last kick. I thought it was crazy of Mick to put that sort of pressure on himself. He knew he had to kick it anyway.

Either way, like he did so often, he hit the target and we squeezed home.

It would be four years before I won another cap. I never started another game for Ireland again.

But I'll always have Argentina.

CHAPTER EIGHT

Everything pointed to the notion that I was timing my run to perfection with the second World Cup around the corner. Fitzy and chairman of selectors, Ken Reid watched a couple of Leinster Senior League games but though I thought I was doing okay, I lost my place for the Five Nations.

That was so hard to take. With Mick Bradley injured, it was between me and Gus Aherne as far as I was concerned for the Championship opener against France. When I got the phone call to say I hadn't made the match-day panel, I was shocked to say the least.

So I asked who was in?

'We've selected Rob Saunders and he's going to captain the team.'

Who? Who the fuck is this bloke? was my immediate internal reaction.

He had done well for the Bs against Scotland and was brought on the training camp in Algarve on the back of it. Clearly, he created an impression there and got the nod.

Rob was born in Nottingham to Irish parents, who had moved to Belfast when he was four. He played for Ireland Schools and captained the national U21 team. He was back in England now but eligible for Ulster. He had still to play for them at senior level and spent the season as reserve to Andrew Matchett.

Yet he was deemed good enough to become only the fifth man ever to captain Ireland on his debut and only the second of the 20th century, after another London Irish player, Jim Ritchie in 1956. His inexperience showed at times but despite that, and Ireland managing only one draw against Wales from the four games, he retained the slot for the World Cup.

It would get worse for me though as having been named among the replacements for all the Five Nations games, I was getting no actual minutes on the pitch and unable to create any sort of impression. Gussy was the one who benefited, having a big campaign as Lansdowne won the Leinster Senior Cup.

My fate was sealed with the selection of a 26-man squad for a tour of Namibia in July. Rob and Gus were the scrum halves and I was out, without having played any rugby. I had done nothing wrong but was given no chance to do anything right. I was on an initial extended panel of 44 named for the World Cup but the composition of the group for the ill-fated Namibian odyssey – Ireland lost both tests embarrassingly in Windhoek – informed everyone that this was only a cosmetic exercise.

There were three World Cups spanning my career and to miss out on making even one of them is a major regret. In 1987, I was just starting out and it would have been a massive gamble to pick me ahead of someone as experienced as Tony Doyle to be back-up for Mick Bradley.

This time though, I had been the man in possession going into the Five Nations. What's more, Ireland were co-hosting the tournament and the team was based in Dublin. It would have meant so much to be a part of such a special event, 12 months after the country came to a standstill with the soccer team's progression to the last eight of Italia '90.

With Mick injured for the long term, I was in the box seat. Or so I thought. Instead, this guy comes in from nowhere. The London Irish contingent were in fashion then, but while it was only a matter of time before Simon Geoghegan and Jim Staples were called up, Rob Saunders and Dave Curtis came from left-field.

Unfortunately for Rob, he is best known now for failing to find touch from Michael Lynagh's restart in the dying minutes of the World Cup quarter-final at Lansdowne Road, after Gordon Hamilton's try had given Ireland a one-point lead. Ironically, there seems to be no footage of it as there were so many replays of the Hamilton try shown.

As a result of that error, the Wallabies got themselves a lineout deep inside Irish territory and Lynagh got over in the other corner to break Irish hearts. Rob paid a heavy price for that and though he picked up a few more caps in the next three years – anything to avoid giving me a game – he was rarely in favour again.

I ▮ ▮ I

Nor was I for that matter. I was invited to plenty of training camps but I had fallen down the pecking order sufficiently to be back playing for the B team. There was one forgettable occasion in Richmond when England ran in nine tries to beat us 47-12. It was the highest score ever conceded by an Irish side from Schools level upwards.

Mind you, it was a cracking England team. Tony Underwood scored three tries, while Phil de Glanville and Neil Back also played. They would be World Cup winners in 1995.

Ireland toured New Zealand in 1992 but despite Saunders' unavailability, I didn't make the cut. Instead it was Gus and Brads. I know Brads was stunned himself, as he hadn't been involved for a long while either.

A lot was made of the fact that the manager, Noel Murphy was his father-in-law but I never read too much into that. What Brads lacked in his passing skills he more than made up for in every other area including his leadership, toughness and organisational ability. He was a very good game manager, very astute tactically. The pass could never be called crisp but he tended to be one step ahead out on the pitch. You knew he would be hard to replace but when the selectors did replace him, they tended to look elsewhere.

There was a lot of politics around at the time and you would be surprised by some of the players that indulged in brown-nosing. That wasn't for me. I could never do it and I wouldn't do it to play for Ireland. I believed that if I continued to work hard, the rewards would come. Or maybe they wouldn't? But I could be comfortable and happy with myself that I gave it my all.

But there was no issue with Mick Bradley and politics. The only time I had any problem with Brads was when he played with a bad wrist injury against USA in November 1995. Despite being crocked he played for 72 minutes, while I got on for the last eight. That really hurt. I just felt that there was no way I was going to get a fair shake at dislodging him. I wasn't wanted or trusted.

Tony Ward had transitioned into the media by that stage and he certainly thought I should have been in New Zealand.

'I felt before the tour began that Peter Russell and Michael Bradley would push hard for their Test places and that could still prove to be the case,' wrote Ward.

'However, the best half back pairing and the lads who will wear the green next season, remain here at home clicking their heels.

'I refer to Alain Rolland and Paul Hennebry. Hennebry blows hot and cold but has the skills that (Derek) McAleese can only dream about while Rolland is now the complete scrum half and a representative leader in the making. Their day will come. And soon.'

Those are lovely words to read even now but Tony got it wrong. Neither of us were selected the following season but at least I got a couple more run-ons to bring my tally of caps to three. Poor Paul never experienced the joy of playing for Ireland at senior level.

You wanted to make the big tours and New Zealand would have been such an experience. I was picked in countless squads but missed out on most of the big gigs. The only tour of real significance I was picked for was Australia in 1994, when Gerry Murphy was coach and Frank Sowman manager. With Brads named as captain, I was most definitely the back-up option but having been banished to the wastelands for the previous three years, I was happy just to be back in the mix.

It was startling to see the Australians up close. Even the provincial sides were on a different level, committed as they were to professional lifestyles. We were a bunch of amateurs and got beaten up all over the country. They were just too good for us.

We started off with a facile victory over Western Australia and managed one other win against New South Wales Country. After that it was very difficult indeed, with a number of heavy defeats and plenty of injuries.

I had to wait until the third game to make my first start on the tour. We had shipped a heavy beating at the hands of New South Wales in Sydney and next up were ACT at the Manuka Oval in Canberra. I was part of an all-Blackrock half back pairing completed by Alan McGowan, while Martin Ridge, Niall Woods and Shane Byrne were also selected.

Shane hadn't been on the initial party flying out but got called up after Keith Wood suffered a severe cut around his eye that needed 17 stitches. I was delighted for Munch. We got on really well because we spent a lot of time together. In that era, the hooker was still actually hooking so we would work to get our timing right.

He would endure his own agonies with the national set-up and had given up on ever nailing down a place. He was very much an individual, his own man, who wasn't one for conforming. With his long mullet hairdo, he definitely didn't fit the mould of a clean-cut rugby player.

It was 2001 before he made his Test debut but he made the most of his Indian summer, playing for the Lions in New Zealand, a full 11 years after his southern hemisphere introduction with Ireland. I was thrilled for him.

The build-up to the game was dominated by the comments of Australia captain Phil Kearns, who was predicting 'some x-certificate stuff' in the Tests. He meant dirty play but the manner in which the Wallabies put us to the sword was pretty gory.

I was looking forward to getting some serious action and though we lost 22-9 to ACT, I did okay. Much of my work was defensive but there was going to be a premium placed on those qualities on this trip. It was the only time I went toe-to-toe with George Gregan. He was just getting started and would go on to become a legend in the game with his 139 caps. That was the world record until Brian O'Driscoll supplanted him at the top of that particular tree.

My efforts earned me a spot in the Saturday team against an Australia XV. This was a real chance as the Saturday team was invariably close to the Test side. A good performance here and I would be pushing very hard to start against Australia in Brisbane seven days later.

Those hopes were dashed pretty ruthlessly though. It was an absolute disaster. We conceded nine tries in Mount Isa, losing 57-9, but I was out of the game and out of the tour before half time, picking up a knee ligament injury.

The desolation as I boarded the plane back to Dublin alongside fellow crocks, Roger Wilson and Paul Hogan was in pretty stark contrast to the optimism with which I had run out onto the Kruttschnitt Oval. But I was on first name terms with the slings and arrows of this sport and life in general by now. The disappointment dissipated and I got on with things.

⁞ ▮ ⁞

The trip to America in '95 was nowhere near as glamorous and the organisation reflected that. It was a dog of a trip, poorly planned and poorly executed. Shambolic. The horrendous weather just accentuated that. It became known as the Four Seasons Tour.

As I mentioned already, this trip highlighted the utter mess that was the rugby calendar. Had Leinster won the Heineken Cup semi-final, anyone selected for Ireland would have had to miss out on the final.

Cardiff made sure it wasn't an issue and the day after losing at the Arms Park, we flew to Atlanta with the rest of the Irish squad.

The scrum half picture was so muddled that it had become a bit of a joke. While the Saunders selection for the Five Nations in 1991 hurt me more than any other rejection and was my lowest point ever as a player, when Chris Saverimutto was called up by Murray Kidd for the Test against Fiji in November four years later, it was just laughable.

If Saunders was parachuted in out of nowhere, Saverimutto appeared suddenly like an optical illusion. All that was missing was the puff of smoke and David Copperfield going 'Shazaam!' According to Edmund Van Esbeck, who would have been very well connected within the IRFU, three of the five selectors had never seen him play. It was that much of a farce.

Murray appeared to have more influence than any previous Ireland head coach. He was the first non-native to take charge and the blazers clearly deferred to him because he was a Kiwi.

Like me, Saverimutto played three times for Ireland. But I was around Irish squads for nine years and the timeframe between my first and last appearances was five years. I was always there or thereabouts, desperate to play, committed to the cause and at least good enough to be in the reckoning.

Saverimutto made his debut for Ireland on November 18, 1994. He played for the last time on January 20, 1995 against Scotland. It was an absolute massive error of judgement and painted the clearest picture yet of a scenario in which my face didn't fit. You could even see the reaction of some of the other guys.

Who the fuck is this guy?

It was written all over their faces, similar to my reaction when Rob Saunders catapulted to the front of the queue. For my part, I never considered throwing my hat at it. I had that tenacity. It went back to that day of being dunked in the pool. Every time someone threw a spanner in the works I thought, *Fuck you, I'm going to show you.* That was the thing that kept driving me on, that absolute desire to prove the point that I could do it. It's an essential part of my fabric.

But it fucking well hurt.

The US tour was supposed to provide us with warm-weather training before the Five Nations. The only problem about this plan was that it was bitterly cold and pissing rain. Whoever was in charge of the logistics got it totally arseways and failed to check the climate. They didn't check the facilities either.

I was on the bench once more for the Test against USA, with Hogie being preferred despite the fact that I was keeping him out of the Leinster team that had gotten to the last four in Europe.

It poured down as we chiselled out the victory in a dour game. There were no dressing rooms at the stadium so we had to go straight back to the hotel to get changed. I don't recall anyone making a big deal of it. We were accustomed to the preposterous nature of preparations.

Sky were just starting to become players in the coverage of international sport. They claimed that Murray and the manager, Pat Whelan had beaten a hasty retreat to avoid being interviewed, such was their dissatisfaction with the performance.

To be fair, we weren't good but the decision to go straight back to the hotel had already been taken. It was freezing cold and we were soaked to the skin. It was not a time for hanging around. It was one of the few decisions made surrounding that entire useless trip that I agreed with.

The journey home did not bring any relief either. Not until we landed anyway. It took 24 hours with so many delays caused by the weather. We had to divert to Copenhagen from Atlanta and remain there for a few hours before finally getting into Dublin late Monday night.

It is fair to say that the IRFU have bucked up their ideas a good bit in the intervening 20 years.

▌ ▐ ▌

Sponsorship deals and player contracts were becoming talking points at this stage as the IRFU staggered their way through the maze of professionalism. They had hoped it would go away and made no plans at all.

The national team was struggling badly. I was named on a provisional squad for the 1995 World Cup and made the bench once more when the USA came to Dublin the previous November.

This was the game Brads should never have played. He had a very bad wrist injury and you could see that he was struggling with it. I don't know why it was so important for a man of his experience to play a game of that stature with that injury. I was champing at the bit for the opportunity and would have treasured the memory of playing in it.

Again, it felt like that they did not want me on the pitch if at all possible. I don't think they had anything against me personally. They just didn't believe in me enough. Brads wasn't even close to being fit for that game but they taped him up and shoved him out there nonetheless.

He got himself a handy try straight after half time when he flopped on the ball after the scrum drove it over the line. He finally yielded to his discomfort in the 72nd minute. I was delighted to get a run and win a second cap but eight minutes gave me no time to create an impression. Even if I would have had 20 I might have had a chance. The back line had stuttered the entire game and I would like to think I could have gotten them moving with my pass. Certainly, most of the newspaper analysts said as much subsequently.

We won 26-15 in front of 25,000 people at a sunny Lansdowne Road. It should have been much more but we missed five kicks in the first half alone. Still, it maintained my 100% record when playing for Ireland.

At the end of the month I was on a Combined Provinces side that shipped eight tries against South Africa in a 54-19 beating. That wasn't a result to feel too badly about though as the Springboks rode a tide of emotion built up by Nelson Mandela to win the World Cup on home turf seven months later.

Having said that, this wasn't a first-string 'Boks selection but the likes of Joel Stransky and Gary Teichmann were playing. Kevin Putt, whose wife was from Dublin, was my direct opponent at scrum half and he would return to Ireland around six years later to line out for Terenure and Leinster.

Leinster got hammered by Munster the following week and I subsequently lost the captaincy and my place in the team to Hogie, who then got in to the national team for the Five Nations after the tragic death of Brads' infant son, David the previous week. I was due to be on the bench for the As but got called up to be replacement for the Test side. I wasn't to play at any cost!

I was to revert to my replacement berth for the As when Brads returned for the Scotland tie but Hogie got injured and so it was back to the Test squad once more. Again, I was getting no opportunity to actually get on the park.

My apparent weakness in decision-making didn't prevent me being named captain of an Ireland A team that included former All Black John Gallagher, who was making a late bid for the World Cup squad with the land of his ancestors, after giving up a dominant career with the Kiwis to try rugby league. He made no impact though in our seven-point win.

I did get one final run in green on May 6, in a World Cup warm-up against Italy at Treviso. This time, it was David O'Mahony who started in front of me for his debut, with me fulfilling my customary spot on the bench.

By now, I knew my World Cup dream was over because the only reason I was here was that Hogie was doing his exams and Brads had pulled a hamstring. David was actually carrying a painful leg injury himself, after picking up a knock playing for Cork Con against Garryowen in the Munster Senior Cup. But he wasn't going to pass on winning a first cap and I certainly cannot blame him for that.

He played with a big strapping though and had to come off at half time. So it was that I got my third and final cap. We were losing 12-9 at the time but I was unable to impose myself in any way in front of the 10,000 capacity attendance. Alessandro Troncon flourished behind a dominant pack, Diego

Dominguez kicked penalties for fun and Paolo Vaccari scored a try.

Paul Burke, who I would cross swords with a few times in his role as assistant to Richard Cockerill at Leicester in my refereeing days, slotted four penalties overall as we fell to a fairly tame 22-12 defeat.

I did swap jerseys with Troncon and presented my prize to David in the dressing room after. He deserved it as a memento for his special day. I knew what it meant and understood that he would be so disappointed to have only lasted 40 minutes.

He never played again for Ireland either, so I'm glad I did that.

There was one amusing postscript to that game. The typical no-holds-barred session took place afterwards and it was even more raucous than normal as the lads were drowning their sorrows after a fairly embarrassing defeat.

Things got out of hand a little though and the next morning, after we had all boarded the bus, Noel Murphy marched us all off it again and lined us up outside our hotel like schoolchildren.

It seemed that some laundry bags had gone missing and a large bottle of booze had been swiped from behind the bar. There were many potential culprits, though I'm not sure if the perpetrator came clean.

It was on that note that my international career as a rugby player ended. The tally of caps ended on three and I was fiercely proud of them. There is no doubt that starting and playing the 80 minutes against Argentina in 1990 was the absolute highlight. Nothing I have achieved beats that. Refereeing the World Cup final gets close but you cannot do better than playing for your country, being the number one.

It will be in the history books forever.

CHAPTER NINE

Professionalism has been hugely positive for rugby and I would have embraced it with every fibre of my being. I craved organisation and knowledge, thirsted for it. I train harder in the gym now than when I did as a player and would be stronger as a result. But we just didn't have a clue back then.

The one thing I would have missed was being available to play in invitational tournaments and especially Sevens. If I had a choice between the shortened version of the game or the traditional 15-a-side, I would have plumped for the former.

It was a format that was designed with me in mind. I was the fittest player out there and the sweeping role suited me to a tee. Tackling a guy heading for the corner flag became my speciality.

For me, this was rugby in its purest form. Having space and the freedom to play the way the pioneers had originally envisioned. Open. Invigorating. Entertaining.

I got picked in the first ever Wolfhounds squad that competed in the Monte Carlo Sevens in May, 1987. It was a great thrill to be brought to Monaco as a 20-year-old with the likes of Ralph Keyes, Donal Spring and Michael Gibson, who were full internationals. My Blackrock teammate, Fergus Slattery was manager.

People joke that these were nothing but jolly-ups. They were right. I had plenty of experience of being around rich people living lavish lifestyles from my childhood holidays with Mamine and Papy but as a young man away on a trip with the lads, Monte Carlo nearly blew my mind.

I scored three tries against Wanderers of England. Slatts had to play against a Monaco selection because a few of the lads had cried off. Everybody deemed the trip a success. Especially the lads who were on it.

I played Sevens on an annual basis from then until the end of my career. That sometimes meant you missed Leinster Senior League and Cup games, or later on AIL games for Blackrock. As an amateur, the call was yours of course and it was part of the Corinthian aspect of the game. You weren't likely to be dropped for missing one weekend.

We won the Melrose 7s in Scotland in 1991. That was a huge tournament. Generally, the squad would arrive a few days before things kicked off to have a training session or two. This time, we had a run out on a warm-up pitch behind the main stadium and we could not complete a series of play.

But we won our first game and the quality gradually improved. We emerged from our group and all of a sudden were in the quarter-finals. After winning that, we came up against Randwick, the famous Sydney club who were red-hot favourites. The running game was second nature to them.

They brought that habitual Aussie arrogance with them and as a consequence, the locals cheered for every team they played against. Of course everybody loves the Irish anyway, so the vast majority of the 16,000 people jammed into the ground cheered even more lustily for us.

We played really well. It just clicked. Frano scored a try to put us in the driving seat and as the conversion was being taken, the crowd broke into song.

'Always look on the bright side of life. Do, do. Do, do, do, do, do, do.'

It was fantastic. The Randwick lads were getting a full dose of *Monty Python*. That was typical of Sevens. Everything about it was different. We went on to win that game and the tournament. It was the first time the Wolfhounds won anything as far as I know and this was one of the most illustrious Sevens tournaments in the world.

The Hong Kong Sevens was an incredible event that we participated in a few times, initially as the Wolfhounds and on two subsequent occasions as

As you can see, at age one I was a natural for the front row (above) but with brothers about the place it was time to get into shape; here I am being too kind to Philippe in the Bahamas in 1971.

Myself and Philippe (above) all suited out for the big game in front of Restaurant Rolland, my Dad's place in Killiney in 1975. And with Philippe, Andre and Gilles enjoying the beach at La Croix Valmer in 1981.

The whole family at my grandparent's house in France (above) and my Dad in his army days.

Lizzie and I on our wedding day, and our beautiful family that is growing up all too fast (below) Mark, Clodagh, Natasha and Amy.

A proud moment as I hold Mark on the field shortly after blowing the final whistle on the World Cup final in Paris in 2007.

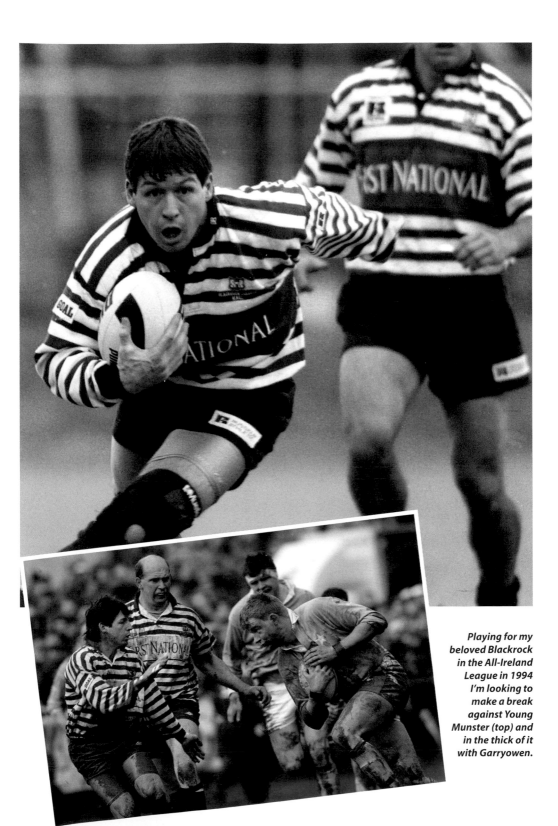

Playing for my beloved Blackrock in the All-Ireland League in 1994 I'm looking to make a break against Young Munster (top) and in the thick of it with Garryowen.

Getting the ball away in my early days with Leinster (top) and on the run in the European Cup in 1995.

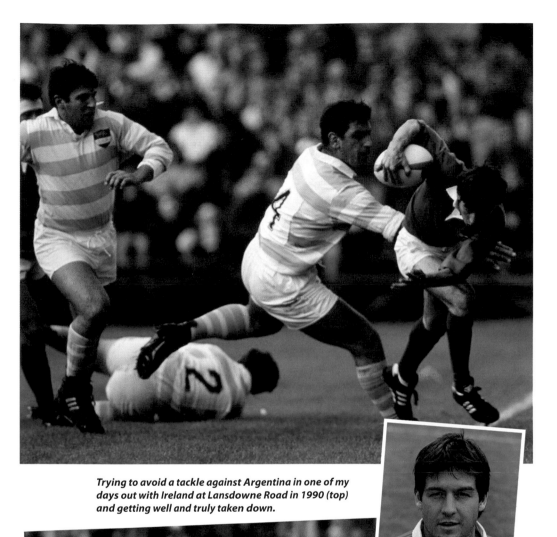

Trying to avoid a tackle against Argentina in one of my days out with Ireland at Lansdowne Road in 1990 (top) and getting well and truly taken down.

I did not get many Ireland caps but each one was an honour.

The early days of my refereeing career, on duty for an All Ireland League game in 2000.

In my final year refereeing in 2014, I got to take charge of Leinster and Munster in the Pro12 in the Aviva Stadium, and keep a close eye on Peter O'Mahony and Jamie Heaslip for the coin toss.

It was also special to be chosen to take charge of the 2014 Heineken Cup final in Cardiff's Millennium Stadium, and watch the classic style of Jonny Wilkinson (right) as he kicked Toulon to victory over Saracens. I also had to muscle up in the same game when tempers flared.

The highest point of my refereeing career was taking charge of the 2007 World Cup final between South Africa and England in the Stade de France, which celebrates the deciding game (above). However the tournament was a big disappointment for Brian O'Driscoll and every other Irishman.

Things did not go to plan in the final for England and Mark Regan, as John Smit lifted the Webb Ellis Trophy for the Springboks.

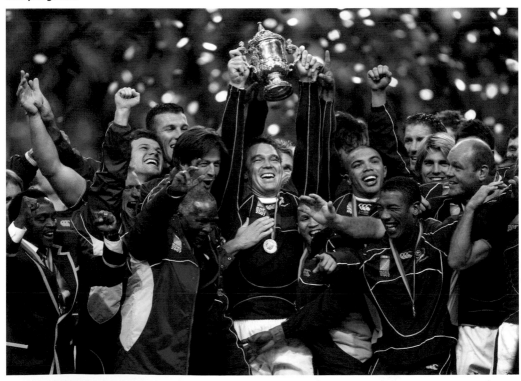

Having a word with the boys from France and New Zealand during the 2011 World Cup (right) and taking some shelter from the pelting rain and finding the Australians handy cover in Auckland during the same tournament.

The toughest but easiest decision of my career was when I sent off Sam Warburton and broke Welsh hearts in their semi-final against France in the 2011 World Cup, but I was on duty for the Welsh again when they played Australia in the Bronze Final.

It was my great honour to referee the All Blacks 16 times during my International career and each time, I was amazed and thrilled to be up close to the greatest team in the world and, of course, enjoy the Haka.

As a Leinster man, I also got to see just how special Munster were in the early days of the professional game. Here I award a try against them in the Pro 12 (above) and have a word with their captain Mick Galwey in the very early days.

I share a moment with my old friend and colleague, Nigel Owens from Wales and (bottom) IRFU president Pat Fitzgerald makes a presentation to me on my retirement from refereeing in 2014.

Ireland. We would normally land on a Tuesday, with the tournament taking place on Saturday and Sunday.

We'd train on the Wednesday, with the boys having given it a real lash when we landed. The guys were invariably destroyed by a double-dose of dehydration, taking in the heat and humidity as well.

I don't think I have ever seen anyone as ill as Paddy Johns after one such Hong Kong acclimatisation. He was as green as our jerseys. We had to get the metro to our first training session and he got sick in three or four bins. When we got to training he threw up again and in the end, just went for a walk.

I missed a Senior Cup tie in 1993 because of the Hong Kong trip but there was no question of staying at home, particularly as I was captain.

We had become quite adept at the condensed code by this stage and I was joined on the squad by Denis McBride, who was to become a regular alongside me. We were both very passionate about the format.

Others in this side included Brian Glennon, who broke my heart in the 1985 Leinster Senior Cup final with a brilliant try for De La Salle, Bill Mulcahy, whose father of the same name played for the Lions, Mick Galwey, Richard Wallace, Eric Elwood, Paddy Johns, Vinnie Cunningham and Jonathan Garth, who is now my brother-in-law, having married Lizzie's sister. We beat Italy and Hong Kong but were undone by Australia in extra time of the quarter-final.

Eric, Mick, Paddy, Richie and Denis were buzzing as we flew out on a Monday, two days after Ireland had walloped England 17-3 at Lansdowne Road. Gaillimh had a wide grin on his face despite the sore head that was the inevitable result of the celebrations, after he scored that famous try with Tony Underwood on his back and his sister running onto the pitch to give him a hug.

Gaillimh was one of the great characters of rugby. On the tour of Australia with Ireland in '94, he formed part of a trio with Keith Wood and Peter Clohessy that was dubbed the Limerick U13s. They were inseparable and got up to some serious high jinks. They knew how to have a laugh, that's for sure. They were good for the mood in a camp, especially when you were away on a trip like that. It was rarely boring with that lot around and you had to watch your back.

'Ernie' Elwood had arrived like a fireball and was the new sensation. He had made his Test debut by scoring 11 points in the win over Wales and followed up with another composed performance in kicking two penalties and two drop goals against England on only his second international appearance.

I got to know Eric pretty well and through an unusual set of circumstances, ended up being Best Man at his wedding in Barbados, with Lizzie being Tara's bridesmaid. When Eric moved to Dublin to work and play with Lansdowne, we lived close to each other in Sandyford.

We had a very similar ethos when it came to rugby. Like me, Eric left no stone unturned so we just gravitated towards one another. I knew what made him tick because it was the same thing that drove me. The desire to get better.

Lizzie and I had decided on a trip to Barbados in July to celebrate our wedding anniversary. We were out one night with Eric and Tara and when we mentioned that we had booked our vacation – more specifically, when we mentioned our destination – they just stopped, looked at each other and started laughing.

They had gotten engaged but hadn't told anyone as they were trying to decide whether to have the traditional Irish wedding, which would be a big affair given the size of their families and Eric's profile, or do something else. Eric is a very private, unassuming guy and he wasn't keen on making a fuss.

One of the options included the two of them jetting off to Barbados and getting married on their own. So when they heard we were heading there anyway, it was decided we'd travel together, with Lizzie and I filling in for the supporting roles.

We flew Aeroflot because it was the best part of a grand cheaper than BA but it wasn't a flight to remember. They were ruthless on the plane. A kid in front of us tried to take a second sweet and the air hostess grabbed it back off him. Lizzie's seat belt consisted of half a belt, with a strap on one side only. The seats didn't go back and you wouldn't go into the toilet a second time if you could get away it.

Once we landed, we had a great time though. Going with the tradition of the night before a wedding, Lizzie stayed with Tara at our villa and I moved in with Eric. That night, Eric and I had a drink in town and the next morning, after a swim and a workout in the gym, I bought him a round at the Royal

Westmoreland Golf Club as our wedding present. I'm not a golfer but you could see why it has such a reputation. It was stunning.

After that we got ready and arrived at the church. When the priest saw us, he came down with a puzzled look that immediately informed you that all was not right. Eric and Tara had forgotten to confirm the booking. Fair play to him though, he carried out the ceremony anyway. It was beautiful.

We went out to dinner that night and needless to say, swapped back to our villas from that point on.

▮▮▮▮

The quarter final appearance in Hong Kong was in March and it put is in fine heart going into the inaugural World Cup Sevens at Murrayfield the next month. Denis took over the captaincy, which I had no problem with as he was a natural leader anyway. I was the same and not having the armband made no difference to how I approached things.

Unlike many of the invitational events, even the high-profile ones, this was deadly serious. We did well on the first day to qualify from the pool into the main draw. Our very first game was against Samoa.

It was around 9am on a greasy surface and it was freezing cold. It suited us down to the ground. The Samoans, not so much. It was the perfect time to catch them as they as they loved the top of the ground and having won in Hong Kong, might have been looking beyond us. We were inches from conceding a try 20 seconds into the game but survived. Gradually we clicked into a rhythm and beat them 17-0.

We were full of belief now and carrying on the momentum from Hong Kong, beat France and Tonga too. There was a growing sense of belief in the camp and we prepared really diligently. It was great to be involved with a national team performing at the highest level.

People were beginning to sit up and take notice at home but unfortunately, the Aussies proved our stumbling block, just as they had done in Hong Kong.

The manner of the defeat at Murrayfield was even more galling though and drew parallels with the 15-a-side World Cup loss to the Wallabies in 1991. This time, a side including Michael Lynagh, David Campese and

Willie Ofahengaue waited until injury time to stick the knife in, having gotten the fright of their lives.

Richie got us off to a great start as he burned Campese around the outside for a try that Eric converted easily. Australia hit back with a brace from future Tonga winger, Semi Taupeaafe but Vinnie restored parity before Denis went over for a brilliant try. There's a photo of me planting a big kiss on his face after he touched down.

Crucially, Eric's conversion attempt hit the upright. It was cruel on him because he had been flawless over the three days. The significance of it was driven home when Willie O finally broke our cover and Lynagh added the extras to make it 21-19.

An Andrew Harriman-inspired England beat Australia in the final. Harriman was a try-scoring machine in Sevens. England had begun their involvement in this format with Mickey Skinner in the squad. He was a dirty player and brought the filth that served him so well at 15s to the Sevens game, where it had no role. It wasn't part of the game and it wasn't conducive to succeeding in it.

Unsurprisingly, England's management quickly learned that and jettisoned the abrasive flanker. Instead they brought in young men like Lawrence Dallaglio and Matt Dawson, who would win a World Cup with England 12 years later. Like that duo, Nick Beal and Tim Rodber played for the Lions. That was the quality you had at these Sevens competitions. They were just incredibly prestigious and great fun.

The line-up in Hong Kong for the 20th anniversary of that tournament in 1995 was stellar to the max. How about this for a cast of genuine world class protagonists?

George Gregan, Jason Little and Joe Roff (Australia), Richard Hill (England), Waisale Serevi (Fiji), Thomas Lièvremont and Denis Charvet (France), Eric Rush, Jonah Lomu and Christian Cullen (New Zealand).

What better environment to be in? I made my Test debut in front of a full house at Lansdowne Road in 1990 but every game in Hong Kong Stadium was packed to the rafters with 40,000 revellers demanding high-class fare. I didn't get to play in front of that type of crowd at any other time in my career.

Lomu was beginning to make an impact on the world stage, though the explosion would occur a few months later at the World Cup in South Africa. He only had a handful of caps at this stage and was still a teenager. He was an absolute beast when you stood up close to him, a mountain despite his youth. He finished up player of the tournament and we could see that he was going to be a phenomenon.

Eric Rush used all his experience to get his young team-mate extra motivated for New Zealand's crunch tie against Fiji. He used the oldest trick in the book.

'Aw man, you can't believe what Serevi is saying about you.'

'What's he saying?'

'He's telling people you're average and he'll eat you up.'

Lomu bought it hook, line and sinker. He was half demented going out onto the pitch. Fiji's defensive structure involved a line of six, with Serevi providing the cover. So when Lomu broke the gainline for the first time at the half-way line, he had no intention of seeking an unimpeded run towards the whitewash. Instead, he turned towards Serevi and ran right over the top of him on the way to scoring.

It makes you wonder if Rush pulled the same stroke the morning of the World Cup semi-final in Cape Town that July, the way he dealt with Mike Catt for the first of his four tries against England at the Newlands.

▐ ▌ ▌▐

As I mentioned, there was a pretty significant social element to these occasions. Just because I didn't drink alcohol didn't mean I couldn't enjoy that aspect of it however. I loved it, having the laugh with the lads. A lot of the time I was able to laugh AT them.

Frank O'Rourke was one of the rugby officials who was a very wealthy man in the rag trade. For one of the tournaments we had in Monaco, he took his power boat over. We were partying on the boat for most of the week.

Monaco was always interesting. In one of our first years there, we were unaware of a law dictating that you could not walk around with your top off. After one of our games, which had been played in 30 degree heat, we all stripped down to our shorts and headed around the pitch to the stand, where

Davy Hewitt's wife was sitting. We had to walk past Prince Albert while doing so and apparently it caused consternation, though we were completely oblivious to it.

One of the characters who made these weekends was Terry Kennedy. He was known as 'The Rat' and was a very funny individual. He damaged some ligaments in the first game of that weekend and as a result was ruled out for the rest of the tournament. That gave him carte blanche to indulge himself.

That night, there was a reception in the Hotel de Paris, which is on the square in Monaco. All the players were invited as guests of Prince Albert. Terry was on crutches at this stage but emboldened by his day of lubrication, approached Prince Albert.

You could see the bodyguards tensing up as he moved towards the Royal. They were trying to determine the threat to their ward. Were the crutches a cover? Were they, in fact, some form of weaponry? Was this an assassination attempt by a mad Irishman?

No, it was just Terry, drunk as a Lord.

While the bodyguards were assessing the situation, Terry had his arm around Prince Albert and was talking to him like an old friend in the clubhouse at Templeville.

'How are ya going Albert?' roared Terry, before embarking on a largely one-sided conversation with the Royal.

The bodyguards didn't know whether to shoot him or deck him or what? You don't speak to a member of royalty unless they address you. And you definitely don't touch them.

'Let me tell you about the time...'

Terry was a great man to spin a yarn. A really great guy, he could talk the hind legs off a donkey. So there he was, with an arm around the prince and sure what could poor Albert do only reply. It was hilarious.

David Beggy was always someone you wanted on tour with you. He was an incredible athlete despite liking a drink and a smoke. He could just keep on running all day and was a gifted footballer. His unpredictability suited the Sevens game and I pushed hard to get him involved. His love of a party suited that scene too.

He was a free spirit on and off the pitch. There wasn't a song he could not play on the guitar and he had a voice to match. Invariably, when things got going, he was at the centre of it. Every country had to do a party piece on the circuit and one year in Hong Kong, Jinksy did a version of *The Wild Rover* that brought the house down.

Jonathan Davies, Mark Ring and Ivan Tukalo were internationals who I would have played with at the Bermuda Classic. That was a 15-a-side invitational event. These were still common then. Brent Pope wrote about them fondly in his book. They have become another victim of professionalism.

Yes, they were an excuse to go on the lash but even though I didn't drink, we had a ball. One year, we all decided to rent mopeds but nobody would have a clue how to ride them. You'd know by the cuts and bruises as the lads staggered out on the pitch for training in the morning who had come off their moped twisted at 4am.

Training took place for the Bermuda Classic on Horseshoe Beach. You wouldn't find a more idyllic venue. It was training in the very loosest terms, killing an hour before the boys could go drinking again. We'd just throw the ball around a bit in a bid to put some small structure on things. Then go for a swim.

▐ ▮ ▐

I guess I enjoyed these trips even more because I only got to go on one proper Test tour. Even then, there was a pretty significant social aspect to it. The guys liked to blow off steam. In fairness, even the professional teams will do that but it is much more selective.

You had some great characters around the Irish squad at that time. Gary Halpin was a real messer who was living in London and was pally with Simon Geoghegan and Jim Staples. They were always playing practical jokes on one another.

He used to drive an old Citroen Diane and the two guys got a fish and hid it in lining of the car. As the days passed, the smell got worse. It drove him mad and he couldn't find it. God knows how long before the dastardly duo came clean.

When we were at receptions, we had a code that if you were stuck talking to somebody, you'd scratch your ear as a signal to the rest of the lads to rescue you. On one occasion, Gazza scratched one ear, then the other, while Frano and I just stood there looking at him with blank faces.

In the end he was ripping the two ears off himself as he struggled to extricate himself from a mind-numbing conversation. You could see the amusement in his eyes as he thought to himself, *good one lads* but that soon transform into anger and then desperation. You got your kicks whatever way you could.

Gazza is teaching in Wales now and we have had a few giggles since I became Public Enemy Number One in the Principality.

'I bet you don't tell the rugby folk you know me.'

'Dead right!'

He was the judge in the Kangaroo Courts in Australia, with Staples and Geoghegan acting as prosecutor and defence attorney respectively. It was carnage.

I got fined in Australia for failing in my assigned duties as aide-de-camp to the IRFU president, Mick Cuddy. Everyone got a job on tour, with the various responsibilities divvied out. Because I was a non-drinker and altogether too sensible, I was charged with looking after 'The Cud'.

'You're such a fucking organiser, make sure Mick is at every function in his correct attire.'

It wasn't as straightforward as you might think. Mick is a legend. He was chairman of selectors when Ireland won the Triple Crown in 1985 and is a very knowledgeable rugby man.

We got on great but being a diabetic, he was blind as a bat. So he might not always have the right clobber on. One morning he arrived at a team meeting with his runners on the wrong feet. I got nailed for $20. In fairness, Gazza didn't go do hard on me.

Mick's wife, Helen still thanks me to this day for getting him back in one piece. Mick endured a horrible tragedy many years ago when his first wife and children were killed in a car crash. He was very fortunate to meet Helen, who is a lovely lady.

I would still meet him when I was the fourth or fifth official at the Aviva. His eyesight is so poor now that Helen would have to tell him it was me.

'Mick, it's Alain, your favourite referee.'

According to Helen, he hates referees as a rule and I was the only one he would talk to. That must go back to our days Down Under, despite me failing to carry out my duties flawlessly and falling foul of the judicial system.

I am delighted to see that the IRFU has thrown its support behind the new, professional Sevens circuit, albeit very belatedly. Trying to qualify teams for the Olympics in Rio de Janeiro is the motivation but they have a lot of ground to make up.

There was no need to leave it so late. I am not sure why they were so suspicious of it. I know there was an issue of cost but it really does surprise me that they were so adamant in their opposition to joining the professional circuit, given that they have gotten most other things right in the past decade.

Denis and I tried to sell the Sevens concept to the IRFU when we were players. We believed passionately in it, as an entertaining form of rugby that excited supporters and filled stadiums around the planet. We invariably alternated the captaincy between us as players and combined again with him as coach and me the manager of a squad that won in Benidorm in 1998. We maintained those positions as we returned to Hong Kong the following March with a squad that included a young Shane Horgan and David Corkery.

We believed in it but the purists seemed to consider it an abomination, in much the same way as the stuffy cricket types view T20. But that shortened format has opened cricket up to a much wider audience. It will never be what counts the most within the game, but it is creating revenue for the sport, drawing in people that would not have been seen dead watching the game and developing players.

Sevens can do the same for rugby, especially with the scrum being such a problem in the 15-a-side game. It is pretty much a running game from start to finish. Again, it will never be of more value than the 15s game nor should it, but it has a role. It is happening now and it seemed bizarre that Ireland was the one Tier 1 country that wanted nothing to do with it.

It was frustrating that there was so much resistance at executive level.

Initially, it was probably because of the clashes with club games. I missed the odd game going to Hong Kong and Monaco, but I was invited to Dubai six or seven years on the trot and had to turn it down each time because it was in November, when there was just too much going on.

Yet it was always popular in Ireland. The crowds at the Belvedere Sevens at the beginning of every season were huge. It was the same in Kinsale. It was synonymous with having a good time.

What people need to understand now though is that just because we are a Tier 1 country doesn't mean we are going to go out there and dominate. Sevens is a completely different game. Portugal, Kenya and Papua New Guinea are just some of the countries doing really well now. The uninitiated will think that Ireland should just rock up and beat Kenya but the Africans would be favourites.

The IRFU didn't like when that happened a few times as Sevens evolved internationally and we showed up unprepared. They felt that losses to Tier 2 or Tier 3 countries reflected badly on their credibility, so they pulled teams out completely.

Now we're back and better late than never. Crucially, they have selected dedicated squads for both men and women. You need full-time contracted squads to compete on the IRB circuit and while that could be a drain on player resources, it is why they cast the net far and wide to pick up a wide range of athletes, not just rugby players. It actually emphasises how different Sevens is from the traditional format.

Having said that, the likes of New Zealand have shown how Sevens can be used developmentally. It's a great foundation for 15-a-side rugby, not just in improving attacking skills but in becoming accustomed to playing in front of large crowds.

Communication is so important. So is tackling, angles of running, spatial awareness, the timing of a pass and the ability to draw an extra defender. Ultimately, with ball-in-hand, it's about breaking the gainline and getting the offload away. This remains the most devastating skill in the 15-a-side game.

CHAPTER TEN

I met Lizzie McDonald at the Merrion Inn. It was a regular haunt for the guys I used to hang out with while Lizzie lived just around the corner in Sydney Parade. When I was working on the building site at the Merrion Centre, she would sometimes call around for a quick kiss and a cuddle rather than take the bus to UCD where she was studying French and German. Young love!

It became serious pretty quickly. We just clicked. Lizzie is just four months younger than me and is much more outgoing. She makes up for my ineptitude in the social stakes. In that way, we are very similar to my parents.

Lizzie has always been a stabilising force. She is very strong and has had to look after a lot of the homemaking while I have been away. And once I became a Test referee, I was away around 26 weekends of the year. If you had to go to the southern hemisphere, my absences were even lengthier.

Not much has changed now that I have started up my own business. More than once, I have been reminded by my kids that the reason I called time on refereeing was to be at home more often. It hasn't worked out that way.

That is why it is so important to pull my weight when I am around and I have no problem doing that. So I don't watch much rugby on television or anything like that. When I'm home, I am going to spend time with my family or look after the jobs that need to be done around the house.

Without Lizzie's support though, I would never have achieved what I did as a referee, nor could I put so much into developing the business. You need a stable support structure and she provides it.

Lizzie and I were going out with each other about seven years when we got married at Donnybrook Church on July 9, 1993. We were 26 but had known for a long time that it was going to happen. By then, I was working for Prudential Life, dealing in life insurance and pensions. There were great bonuses and between that and Lizzie's work we saved more than enough to treat ourselves to a fabulous honeymoon in The Maldives where we both did our Padi Cert diving qualification.

We had bought a house in Sandyford but when we got back to Ireland, it wasn't ready. So we spent the first week as a married couple in Ireland with Lizzie's mother, until the snag list was finally sorted out.

▮▮▮

We weren't in any hurry when it came to having kids either. It was always on the agenda but we planned to indulge ourselves first; to live life as a married couple before being tied down. We did a lot of travelling for the next five or six years before Mark was born.

When he came into the world in April 1999, we realised the error of our ways. It was like flicking a light switch.

'Why the hell didn't we do this sooner?'

This was what we wanted more than anything else. We finished up with four. Mark is 16 now and he was followed by three girls – Clodagh (14), Natasha (11) and Amy (7). I was there for all their births.

I wouldn't say I'm a disciplinarian but I am probably stronger on having a few rules around the place than Lizzie. But we're very lucky. They're great kids.

Mark played a bit of rugby for a while and was very skilful, switching between wing and scrum half. He had a lovely pass and we used to do a few drills out the back during the summer. Getting knocked about and being small as a late physical developer, lost its lustre and he gave it up. Now that he has grown up he has toyed with going back to it but kickboxing and the gym seem to have won out for now.

It was completely understandable. You see the kids playing now and they're huge. When you're playing against kids that size at that age, there's nothing enjoyable about it. I was never pushy with him or any of the kids about what they did so I had no problem with him giving it up.

Rugby is no longer a contact sport. It's a collision sport. More than once during the Toulouse-Wasps Heineken Cup final in 2004, my voice can be heard over the comms reacting to some of the ferocious hits.

'Jesus, that's gotta hurt.'

'How did he get up from that?'

But that was 11 years ago. Look at the likes of Victor Matfield or Bakkies Botha now in comparison to when they started out. They must be 20kgs bigger and I remember thinking they were the biggest men I had ever seen a decade ago.

It does concern me. The guys are getting bigger and stronger, the impacts of the collisions becoming more grievous. When I played, your second row was between 6'2" and 6'4" and might have come in at 100-110kgs. You've got guys playing in the centre now who are 6'4" and hitting 120kgs. That's ludicrous stuff. Someone is bound to get hurt when two men of that size crash into each other at full tilt.

I do think it's something the governing bodies could look at. Has it gotten to a stage where they should consider putting weight limits on players in certain positions? I don't know but it's worth investigating. Maybe they could put something like a 900kg limit on the pack. Something like 100-110kg for a player in the back division. It's just a thought.

They do it in New Zealand for junior rugby. Teams are determined by weight, not age. They would have a lot of Pacific Islanders who are naturally bigger than kids of the same age. So it's under 40kg, under 50kg, under 60kg, under 70kg. Not under 12, under 14, under 16 and so on. It's worth a discussion.

I'm looking at the guys getting smashed about now and we have all seen the damage done as a result of taking those knocks on an ongoing basis. Even if they are not missing games through big injuries, the cumulative effect of a decade of pounding has got to take a heavy toll.

Mark has decided at this time not to play rugby because he has taken up Sanshou, which is a Chinese form of kickboxing. There is no ground-fighting but it isn't for shrinking violets, with a variety of kicks, punches and throws. But he's fighting against people in his own weight category.

The excellent hand-eye coordination that made him a good rugby player has stood him in good stead and he became Irish junior kickboxing champion in his weight category in 2013. He is hoping the sport becomes an Olympic event in the future.

It was around 2004, when Mark was four or five, that we struck up a bargain where I would send him a signal before every game to let him know I was thinking of him. We decided that I would scratch my left ear just before kick-off. The cameras always go to the referee before the game gets under way and I would watch the big screen to await my cue. It is nothing anyone would have noticed but I did before every game, including the World Cup final.

Clodagh is our performer. She is a brilliant dancer and actor. Show her a move and she will pick it up straight away. To see her doing the Wii Dance is frightening. Mum swears it comes from her. It doesn't come from me anyway!

Natasha is a sports nut. She does Gaelic football, athletics, hockey, tennis, golf and basically anything she can lay her hands on. The point will come when she will have to prioritise but she hasn't gotten there yet. She's young and needs to enjoy it all now which she does. She loves it.

Amy has started gymnastics. I was watching her doing pull-ups a few months ago. At six! As I am with all of them, I was very proud. Beaming.

I only speak in French to Amy. It is a strange one because it is English with the older three. I did try to get Mark and Clodagh speaking French when they were younger. Natasha was only a baby at the time.

I thought it would be nice that they have something from their cultural background. And it might help them later in life too. I started with great intentions, got a BBC Muzzy French learning book that is ideal for kids, starting with the basics. I did it for a couple of weeks but lost momentum and then it got parked.

But when Amy was born, I just got this mad notion that I would always speak French to her. And from Day One, it is the only language I have spoken to her. If I am saying something she doesn't understand, I will repeat it in English. She doesn't speak to me in French so it probably would sound very strange to people outside the family.

It's great. All I'm trying to do is give her an ear for the language. She did wonder initially why I spoke French to her and nobody else in the house but it's second nature now.

They are all finding their own way. We don't push them and I suppose that's why they have all drifted to different areas. It means it's busy but we don't care if they're excellent or average or no good. I'm definitely no Earl Woods and you see that parent around all the time.

If they have the drive and ambition to be high achievers in sport or the dramatics or whatever area they choose, fine. But once they're happy, that's all I care about.

CHAPTER ELEVEN

Rugby was hurtling towards professionalism now and there were bound to be issues.

No-one was surprised when Frano got in trouble while on Ireland duty by doing a television interview wearing a t-shirt with a logo of a personal backer, rather than the official national team kit with Irish Permanent on the front. He was fined but while he has never revealed how much he got, you can be sure it was a big whack and well worth whatever disciplinary measure was meted out.

Discussions about contracts began with the IRFU towards the end of 2005. Other countries were well ahead of Ireland in this regard. The Union got it completely wrong at the beginning. They probably thought they had a lot more time to deal with it than was the case. They were slow to see the signs and deluded themselves into thinking the old ways wouldn't change. When it became clear that everything would be different, they weren't ready.

Myriads of Irish players accepted the big-money offers to go to England. This caused problems then with regard to them being released for the Test or provincial sides. It got to the stage where it probably would have been easier to have international training in London than in Dublin.

To be fair to them, the IRFU got their house in order subsequently, with their centralised contracts system now the envy of the northern hemisphere federations.

But back then, the blazers were so stuck in their ways and the press coverage often reflected that. The negative manner in which Leinster's first dipping of the toe in the waters of sponsorship in September 1992 was reported was a good example, although the design of the jersey might have had something to do with that too.

'Leinster branch has cast aside 120 years of tradition by changing the provincial jersey. The traditional blue jersey has been replaced by a new strip, a garish, striped concoction carrying the logo of the provincial sponsors ACC Bank. It would seem more appropriate for an Australia Rugby League team than a representative rugby union side. Nothing it seems is sacred anymore.'

The snobbery still drips off the page.

Most Ireland players signed their contracts on January 13, 1996 but that didn't stem the flow cross-channel. Paul Burke, David Corkery (Bristol), Eric Miller (Leicester), Paul and Richard Wallace, Paddy Johns, Eddie Halvey (Saracens), Keith Wood (Harlequins), Jonny Bell, Allen Clarke (Northampton), Victor Costello, Niall Woods and Gabriel Fulcher (London Irish) were just some of the Irish lured by the cash.

I accepted an offer myself to join a second division club with big ambitions. Moseley were financed by infamous Aston Villa owner, Doug Ellis, known as Deadly Doug because of his Continental penchant for sacking managers. You always knew when he was around because the Roller was in the car park.

Darragh O'Mahony, Henry Hurley and Martin Ridge were already there. As well as Trigger, 'Rock had also lost Wally and Woody. I knew it was over for me with Ireland so when the call came in November 1996, I decided to give it a go.

It was a good deal. I was 30 so a full-time professional contract didn't interest me. I continued working and only travelled over at weekends. What's more, I got paid whether I played or not. Otherwise I could not justify giving up so much time to it. It was the first time I ever received money to play rugby.

It was a crazy time for me because after I had agreed the arrangement with Moseley, I was approached by Cornmarket with a view to working for them as a mortgage broker. They offered me a fantastic package. I was very interested but with quite a bit of trepidation, had to explain that I would be flying out of Dublin every Thursday afternoon until Sunday evening. So I could only be in the office, three and a half days a week until April!

I was sure they would tell me to fuck off but thankfully, they understood and gave me the green light. Mobile phones had developed a bit by now and that meant you could be in contact with the office. I had one that was almost the size of a TV. It was monstrous but allowed me to pursue my five months of Birmingham weekends.

It was future Ulster coach, Mark Anscombe who was running on-field affairs and he contacted me directly. Mark took a lot of flak for his time with Ulster even though results were pretty good. I must say I enjoyed working with him. He had some good drills for improving the skills of players.

You could see why he didn't get on with everyone though. He is very direct but find me a New Zealander that isn't. If he thinks you fucked up, he'll tell you. He's not going to be cuddling you. It'll be a kick up the backside rather than an arm around the shoulder. If you knew what he was trying to do, you could wear it, but if people didn't, they didn't take to him.

While he was coach, I was playing all the time and we won 11 on the trot. It was a punishing enough schedule but I really enjoyed the rugby. It might have been the second tier of the English League but I reckon we would have beaten any team in the AIL at the time.

Then it seems that despite this brilliant run, his personality was sufficient reason to get rid of him. Deadly Doug, who was hardly the king of man-management himself, swung the axe once more.

Allan Lewis, who would become a member of Graham Henry's Wales set-up and is now in charges of the Wales Academy, was appointed as his replacement. Allan had a whole new idea as to what he wanted to do and because I wasn't around during the week, wasn't sure that I could contribute.

I was in one week, on the bench the next and getting paid regardless. But you want to play so it was a bit of a relief when it finished up in April and I no longer had to do that travelling, with the possibility of sitting on my arse – no matter how much preparation the international scene had given me for that particular experience.

I was still playing with Leinster while I was with Moseley and lined out in a couple of more Heineken Cup games. But just like Moseley, they were anxious to start tying people down to full-time professional contracts. Having begun a new job and with my 31st birthday approaching, it made absolutely no sense to throw away what I had built up in my professional career for the sake of one or two years as a full-time rugby player.

That accelerated my retirement from playing. When my contract with Moseley was up, that was going to be it for me and it should have been. But Kelvin Leahy, who I knew very well from playing with Leinster, contacted me and asked if I fancied coming down to Wanderers.

They offered a bit of pocket money and I did one more season with them in Division 2 of the AIL. It was enjoyable enough but my heart wasn't in it the same way it had been with 'Rock. I was past my prime.

I had always been motivated by getting the best out of myself on an individual level and then putting my shoulder to the wheel for the rest of the boys in my team. It meant something. But being paid to play is not something that's inflicted on you and of course it was welcome. So was the lifestyle and quality of preparation that went with it. Mind you, there were a lot of average players getting good money.

Good luck to them. I was moving on. I always presumed I would coach when I finished playing. I had already dabbled in it, starting with a women's team at Stradbrook.

The brilliant All Black and Samoa out half, Steve Bachop was with 'Rock at the time and his future wife, Sue was a former Black Fern i.e. she played with New Zealand women's rugby team. She was a stunning player, absolutely brilliant with ball in hand. Sadly, she died many years later after a long battle with cancer. She had continued her rugby involvement as a Black Ferns selector and assistant coach and broke new ground when appointed joint coach of Norths senior men's team in Wellington.

A few of the girls were talking with Sue about playing and it was thrown out there that some of them might like to give it a try. Nicola Doyle was the real driving force behind it and her interest got her husband involved subsequently.

Philip Doyle was playing mostly seconds and thirds rugby with 'Rock at the time. He went on to almost single-handedly make Ireland a world force in women's rugby, as head coach of the team that won the Grand Slam in 2013 and reached the World Cup semi-final after beating the Black Ferns for the first time the following year.

Back at Stradbrook, the girls asked Bash and I to do the training, which Nicola announced over the PA, would take place in the morning. About 14 girls showed up. Most of them had never even held a rugby ball and we didn't really know what to do with them.

So we started by showing them how to move the ball across the line, how to tackle and how to fall. It went from there. They were like sponges and couldn't get enough of it. Even though there was no league, we had about 40 girls at the next session. Eventually we got a team together and organised a couple of friendlies against other clubs with similar set-ups.

Bash works for the New Zealand academy now so the experience obviously stood to him.

I was actually asked to take charge of an Ireland women's team to play Scotland in Edinburgh in 1993 as a result of my input with the Rockettes. We held trials and training sessions in January, picked a squad and worked hard to get ready for the game.

Blackrock actually beat Terenure in Templeogue the day before to secure promotion to Division 1 of the AIL. We flew over with the girls that evening and though we lost 10-0, it was tremendous experience.

It is great to see where women's rugby is in the country now since that era and I am delighted to have been involved on the ground floor, before more qualified people took it on and got it to this point. It took up quite a bit of time but I enjoyed applying some of the things I had picked up from the many different coaches I had encountered through my career.

As I've said already, Eddie O'Sullivan was the best I had with his concept of thinking two and three phases ahead utterly revolutionary in that era. I had an awful lot of time too for Brian McLoughlin, who emphasised the link between forward and back play. Brian was great at identifying the strengths of the team and building around that.

At national level you had Ciaran Fitzgerald, Jimmy Davidson, Gerry Murphy and Murray Kidd. And at Leinster, Ciaran Callan, Jim Glennon and Paul Dean. There was nothing that really jumped out about them, but I don't mean that in a negative sense. In those days, most coaches were doing similar things.

I would not be critical of them though. Their commitment was total. Everything they did was to the best of their ability and because they wanted to have the team at its best. But it was an amateur era.

Jimmy D had his own approach, very individual. It was a little left-field as he was big into the mental side of things, visualisation. He was ahead of his time in that regard but players then would have considered it a bit hocus-pocus. I was young and happy to try anything.

Fitzy was a great motivator. He wore his heart on his sleeve. What he might have lacked technically, he more than made up for in positivity and pride. He was a very good forwards' coach too.

I often wondered how those guys would get on in the professional environment. It's such a completely different game, even the way you use the bench tactically. But really, it's unfair comparing coaches from the past with the current crop. They hadn't the science, the qualifications – and they were one selector out of a committee of four or five. Now, the head coach has total control.

Anyway, I tried to take the best bits from all of them in my time with the women's teams and also when I was manager of the Sevens. This was what I was going to do.

There were one or two approaches from junior clubs offering a start-up role on a player/coach capacity. It would have been perfect but by the time I finished up in May 1998 with Wanderers, I was already on another path.

One that would get me even closer to the action.

The best seat in the house.

PART
THREE

CHAPTER TWELVE

November 27, 2004. Ma'a Nonu is barrelling over for New Zealand's last try on the way to pounding Grand Slam champions France in Paris, 45-6. It is the end product of another perfect fusion of punishing brawn, grace and guile. The All Blacks are on fire and I am enthralled.

That might sound inappropriate given that I am the referee but this is a special night. Stade de France has crackled with electricity for hours before kick-off, in anticipation of the hosts' coronation as the best team in the world.

Les Bleus are coming off a comprehensive win over Australia, which on the back of their Six Nations dominance and New Zealand's average showing in the Tri Nations, has made them favourites to claim one of the most prized scalps in global sport.

Daniel Carter, Freddie Michalak, Tana Umaga, Thierry Dusautoir, Richie McCaw, Imanol Harinordoquy, Anton Oliver and Serge Betsen are all luminaries of this and any era. In the middle of them all is this little Dublin guy, concentrating hard and looking to remain in the shadows. A stage hand whose job it is to facilitate the stars while they put on a show.

And that is always the job. It isn't to command. It isn't to lay down the law. It isn't to be judge and jury. It isn't even to be a negotiator. It is to maintain an environment conducive to a good, clean game of rugby. The way I officiated, particularly at the breakdown, games could be really attacking and free-flowing.

If teams wanted that. There is nothing you can do as a referee if they don't.

You are in the background ideally. A facilitator. Not a dictator.

This is a surreal experience. My first Test appointment has come three years previously, almost to the day, but I have already done a World Cup quarter-final, something that carries a lot of meaning in the wake of my failure to make the grand stage as a player.

When the Kiwis are involved you can usually expect a spectacle and with the French supporters in a state of euphoria before a ball has been kicked, I just know that something extraordinary is about to unfold.

This is why I beckon the fourth and fifth officials to join me and my touch judges, Simon McDowell and Andy Turner on the pitch for the anthems. Four and five are always referees from the home federation and it is not protocol for them to cross the whitewash. They were hesitant but I insisted.

Being part of a wall of noise in the stand is not the same as standing in the middle of the bowl as it descends upon you from all sides. It is almost an assault on the senses, something that takes getting used to as a player and a referee. If you lose focus when your faculties need to be razor sharp, you cannot perform at optimum level.

I have done my preparations though. I have gone through my check list and am mentally solid. I have every intention of soaking these next few minutes up.

The people of Auckland must be able to hear *La Marseillaise*, such is the enthusiasm with which it is belted out. Once the French anthem is concluded, four and five head for the sideline, more than happy with their unexpected surprise.

But the best is yet to come so I call them back again.

The Haka is a cultural wonder and extraordinary to be around. It is pure theatre and the thrill of drinking in the emotion of the tribal war dance from six feet away never dissipated, even though I would referee the All Blacks 16 times in my 68 Test career.

They come back and at one stage, I look over at them. They're grinning from ear to ear. Having this front row pew is a rare privilege on an occasion like this.

The game itself is a master class. It starts at a frenetic pace and we have a minute and 49 seconds of continuous play. That doesn't sound like much but it is very rare to have that much at the start without a knock on, kick to touch or penalty. After all, you have 30 hyped up behemoths out on the pitch.

I don't realise it until awarding a penalty for a shoulder charge. The players are sucking hard. As Freddie Michalak prepares to take his kick I look at my watch.

Holy shit, that was unbelievable.

There is so much speed, so much brutality. Sweat and blood. Shouting and cursing. Flicks out of the back of the hand, scything runs and tackles that would cut a civilian in two. The ebb and flow on the pitch and its reflection around it from the supporters.

It's crash, bang, wallop. Beauty and beast. Force and subtlety.

'Ref! Ref! He's holding on!'

'Merde!'

'You fucking bastard.'

'Salaud.'

'That was high ref!'

Not much older than some of them, I cover every blade of grass on the pitch. When Nonu touches down in the 79th minute after a lightning exchange between backs and forwards from inside their own 22, I am waiting for him behind the try-line, ready to blow.

That brings a smile to my face when I see it because it says a lot for my fitness, which I always prided myself on. More importantly, it shows my game sense.

Being a scrum half honed my understanding of rugby. It developed my instincts for predicting where the ball was likely to go or what move is on? It isn't something I can explain but I just *know* what is on.

When I started refereeing, I was renowned for my running commentaries. Liam Toland mentioned it in a column he wrote in *The Irish Times* around the time of my retirement as I might remark on a good tackle or one he fell off on. Maybe a dropped ball.

'Bad hands 7.'

I'm sure he didn't always appreciate it but it was banter as much as anything.

It wasn't unusual for me to watch a game unfold and instinctively bark out the next move, as if I were watching on television or from the stands.

'Give it.'

'Straighten'

'Put it in behind.'

When something spectacular happened.

'Wow! Great try.'

Or.

'Fuck. What a hit.'

With increased technology and the referees being mic'd up, I had to curtail that habit. It was just the fan in me coming out; a human reaction. I could appreciate what was going on while still ensuring that the laws of the game were being adhered to and that teams attempting to produce positive rugby were allowed to do so.

Another area I learned to row back on was getting too close to the play. That was a natural result of coming so quickly from playing as a 9 for so long. Initially, I got in players' way a few times. Positional sense is a vital tool in the referee's armoury and once I learned to modify slightly from a player's perception to an on-pitch official's, it became one of my real strengths.

IIIII

This game produces 80 minutes of high quality and that is down to the players. You can only referee what's in front of you and just as a bad game is invariably the fault of the 30 lads on the pitch, the same applies to a good one.

The game is not about the referee. It's about the two teams and the official is there to assist them. These guys are giving me everything. When players cooperate, prepare to be entertained. Certainly, that was my goal as someone who loved freewheeling rugby.

I became known as a referee that was very hot on the breakdown because I loathed killing the ball. I wanted it out of there quickly. Over time, as that reputation became solidified, more and more of my games were open affairs because it was common knowledge that transgressions would be punished until a change in player behaviour was achieved.

There are no such issues here though. France have contributed quite handsomely to the early exchanges but New Zealand wear them down with the variety and breadth of their attack. Byron Kelleher is one lucky bastard to be the link between that pack, Dan Carter and a fantasy three-quarter line.

This is up there with one of my greatest memories on the pitch as a referee. It is challenged by the New Zealand clash with South Africa in Pretoria the previous year.

Obviously there's the World Cup final, which I would have remembered fondly if it had finished 3-0 and to be fair, it wasn't the most exciting game ever. My first ever Heineken Cup game between Saracens and Toulouse was a cracker. The first Heineken Cup final between Wasps and Toulouse was entertaining too, while the last one will stand out because it was my final game.

But in these two games, we probably got as close a glimpse to perfection as we are every likely to see on a rugby pitch. The All Blacks were awesome against high-powered opposition, with South Africa and France heavily tipped to prevail on home territory, against opposition that was perceived to be waning.

People think referees are predisposed to All Blacks. I had them 16 times and they won 14 of those games but that was just because they are the best. There is no conspiracy there.

I had France 16 times too and certainly in the early years, because of my background, there was a perception that I would be favourably disposed to them when making decisions. Pascal Papé certainly didn't think so! As it happens, France won exactly half of those Tests.

It might surprise people that I refereed England (20) and South Africa (17) more than the other two, given the misplaced belief in some sections of the rugby community that I was the go-to man for France in particular. I also refereed Wales on 16 occasions. That represents a fairly level playing field.

I could watch this game in Paris all day long though and make no apologies for that. I look at the action unfolding on the DVD and try to recapture my feelings and thoughts at that exact time.

It's easy.

I'm having a ball.

▮▮▮▮

Of course it hasn't all been positive. The Warburton sending off in the 2011 World Cup semi-final earned me my most negative coverage.

That wasn't difficult for me personally because the decision was the right one as Sam himself so graciously acknowledged, even if his coach, Warren Gatland couldn't. But the rules are there and clear.

As a referee, there were many more difficult days than that, when I could not control a game or generally felt that I had underperformed. My worst feeling was not having been able to change player behaviour, or when I got irritable with the players myself. In time, I developed triggers to avoid that situation that made me a much better communicator, because communication is an integral part of high-class refereeing.

One time I had to get an out-of-control Brian O'Driscoll to calm down as he thought I was favouring Munster against Leinster. Ironically, at the end of the same game, the Munster coach, Rob Penney accused me of being a cheat.

On another occasion, I nailed Leicester because of a beef I had with Richard Cockerill but I don't feel too bad about that. I didn't screw them outright in terms of making up transgressions, giving penalties that weren't there. I gave them nothing though and unlike my normal style, didn't miss any opportunity to blow the whistle. I'm not proud of it now, but he is an aggressive bloke who had crossed the line in terms of his treatment of referees and I reacted.

The good days far outshine the bad though. Many times over. The friends, the camaraderie, the Test games, the Heineken Cup finals, the World Cup final. The AIL games, the SCT clashes.

The privilege of being ringside, right in the middle of two heavyweights, immersed in the cauldron of some of the greatest sporting occasions the world has ever seen.

My God I was lucky.

Incredibly lucky.

CHAPTER THIRTEEN

I spent more than a decade haranguing referees, the archetypal chirpy scrum half, trying to run the game from the base of the scrum.

When my retirement as a player was announced at an annual conference held by the Leinster branch of the Association of Referees, there was a standing ovation. This was partly tongue-in-cheek because I was in attendance, now one of them, but there would not have been too many members who would have considered me an easy player to work with.

That relationship improved in the last couple of years, given that I possessed a greater understanding of the referee's job and was now a gamekeeper as well as poacher. I was able to put myself in the referee's shoes and as a result, give the man in charge less of a hard time than might have been the case in the previous decade.

I was the unlikeliest candidate to take up the whistle but a strange chain of events that owe completely to fortune altered the trajectory of my entire life, and I was on the path almost three years by the time I packed in playing.

It was towards the end of 1995. I was only 29, still playing for Leinster and having earned a Test cap that same year. Being at a loose end, I decided to call down to Stradbrook to watch the 'Rock 2nds play on the top pitch. There also happened to be a 3rd A game between 'Rock and Lansdowne on the back pitch and for some reason, the appointed referee failed to turn up for that. I often wonder who it was. I have a lot to thank him for.

It was a real *Sliding Doors* situation. You know the film, with Gwyneth Paltrow and John Hannah? It switches between two parallel universes, based on the different directions the Paltrow character's life would take depending on whether or not she caught a train.

So the ref was a no-show, I happened to pop into the clubhouse and the Lansdowne manager, Rory O'Connor spotted me.

'Rollers, you couldn't do us a favour and come down to referee the game for us? The ref hasn't arrived.'

I knew Rory well and it was a tremendous shock to us all when he was killed in a car crash two years later. He was a tremendous clubman, respected by everyone involved in rugby around Dublin. I suspected he might have lost his faculties though when he came out with that.

'I can't. I'm 'Rock.'

'You have no idea how difficult it is to get 15 boys out here. Please. We don't care. We just need to play.'

I always had a kit bag in the car and they were desperate, I agreed to try it. Rory found me a whistle and watch while I went back to my car to change.

I trooped down to the bottom pitch in a green pair of shorts over funky, multi-coloured cycling shorts, odd socks and a USA Sevens rugby jersey with the number three on the back. I wasn't thinking then that this was going to send my life onto a whole new trajectory.

Some of the guys were looking at me.

'What the fuck are you doing here?'

I was to become accustomed to that over the next few years.

Contrary to my expectation, I really enjoyed the game. Unlike playing, it came naturally. I got into it immediately, barking instructions at the players and we just got on with things. I probably wasn't doing a whole lot different from when I was playing as a scrum half, except that I wasn't actually touching the ball.

When the game finished, a number of the players approached me and said how much they enjoyed it. It was a more pleasant experience than I expected too.

In another quirk of happenstance, Ned Cummins had been assessing a referee from whatever game was on in the top pitch. He must have gotten bored of that because he decided to take a stroll down to our game and liked what he saw.

He asked if I would consider refereeing. I was taken aback and didn't really have a clue. My initial reaction was that it wouldn't be something I'd be interested in. I detested refs and they felt the same about me because I was in their ear all the time, much more of a dictator as a scrum half than ever was the case as a referee.

In those days, you would never know who was refereeing a match until the official walked into the dressing room.

'Oh fuck, not this dickhead.'

Then you were sitting next to him at a referees' seminar a couple of years later.

That this was the case can be attributed to Ned passing on a favourable report of my efforts to Owen Doyle, despite my lack of encouragement. Owen had been one of the top referees in Ireland for many years and had recently been appointed by the IRFU to be director of referees. It was a new position and Owen was an inspired appointment because he had a very clear vision of what he wanted.

He gave me a call. We agreed that I'd do a junior game every second Sunday. It was fun and I knew fairly quickly that this would be the next best thing to playing as it kept me in the thick of the action.

It just clicked. It was something I had a natural aptitude for. As a player I had to work feverishly hard for anything I achieved. I worked intensely hard as a referee too, because that's my nature, but the transition was much more seamless. It just came more easily.

I would have known most of the laws but throughout my career, I was never one for spouting off chapter of verse. I would know that Law 10 referred to foul play and Law 20 the scrum but I could not reel off all the subsections. I learned over time and thankfully the law book is such an easy read!

I think that had its advantages because it meant you didn't get caught up in the technical side of things. There are some things you have to know but experience brings that as well.

The biggest challenge for me was dealing with emotion. I used it a lot as a player but as a referee you have to be calm. It took a little time to get that right, as it did to make the necessary changes to my running angles.

My hard work as a player paid off as a referee too in the sense that because I had been reasonably successful, everybody knew who I was. When you walked into changing rooms, there tended to be an acceptance. They couldn't say I knew nothing about the game. They couldn't cast any aspersions about my fitness and ability to keep up with the play.

It became clear very quickly to players too what way I would referee. So much so that the guys used to see me and beg me to blow the whistle a bit. My former teammate, Victor Costello was one who hated when I reffed matches he was playing in. I have visions of him gasping for breath as I played another advantage, struggling to get the words out.

'Will you blow your fucking whistle?'

I allowed things to develop. I knew and understood what teams were trying to do, offensively and defensively. I wasn't going to blow as soon as I saw a transgression. I very quickly got this idea of materiality, of whether or not an offence had any relevance to what was occurring.

My progression was quick and it was another piece of good luck for me that I got into this at the same time as Owen started his job. He put proper structures in place and created a pathway for prospective referees to progress quickly if they were good enough.

Under the old regime, you did your time in the junior ranks and appointments had more to do with service and age rather than ability. It frustrated Owen to see good, young referees with real potential wallowing in the back pitches for five years before they could dream of getting a senior league. So he restructured the method of identifying promising referees, nurturing them and then promoting them in accordance with their proficiency.

I was one of the first beneficiaries of this new fast-tracking system which has since proved such a monumental success, with Ireland boxing far above its weight in terms of producing top tier referees when compared to rugby's other major countries. This is a credit to Owen and the IRFU.

If I had gone in under the old system, I would have had four or five years down in the junior ranks before I'd get a sniff of a senior club game. Under

Owen, I had refereed a Test match in that time frame.

Of course it didn't go down well with everyone. Established referees didn't like some flash young guy being pushed through that didn't have to put in the hard yards they had done, the years and years of slog, even if this process did not develop the necessary skills. You needed to gain experience but once you had proven yourself at a level, you needed to be tested once more, regardless of age or experience.

There was jealousy and Owen got it in the neck plenty of times. Nobody ever said anything to me but they said plenty to him. I suppose I was his guinea pig but he was investing a lot of faith in me. He was a mentor at the start and remained my go-to guy right to the end.

What was very important was that there was a consistency there for me. With different assessors, it can happen that you are told to do completely contrasting things from one week to the next. When you're getting conflicting messages, you need a coach, somebody to bounce it off who knows you and understands the job.

Owen knew me as a player, he had reffed me. He grew to know me as a person and learned what made me tick. He would distil what I had been told and be very direct in his assessment.

'I was told to do this.'

'Fuck that, that's rubbish. That's not what we want to do. This is what we should work on.'

I realised very quickly that this was the man to listen to.

I was also lucky in that Ireland did possess a lot of international referees who were willing to share their knowledge, people like Denis Templeton, Brian Stirling and Stephen Hilditch. So while I might have an assessor at a game, someone like Denis, Brian or Stephen would travel as well to do a coaching report. That was invaluable. I am delighted to be able to pass on some of that expertise by coaching elite and pre-elite referees now myself.

I had to postpone refereeing full time until finishing as a player. The plan was to get going when my time with Moseley was up but I opted to accept the Wanderers offer, which delayed it another year.

In my first year refereeing full time, I got an AIL Division 3 game between Suttonians and Ards. There was pandemonium. You have no idea the abuse that Owen got as a result of putting me in for that. Older referees were spitting feathers. And the blazers weren't happy either.

I remember it vividly because it was one of only two games that survived the snow that weekend. When I went out to do my warm-up, I could see that there were an awful lot of alickadoos around. As the game began there were more there. Referees, administrators, old buzzards clinging to the old ways.

They were there to watch the new kid fall on his arse. Make no mistake about that. I remember laughing to myself.

Bring it on.

It just made me more determined. I refereed the game very well. I flashed a couple of yellow cards when I could possibly have managed the situations but for somebody in their first season, the movement, the communication, lack of controversial decisions – it proved the merit of my appointment.

That was a bit turning point within the establishment because the reaction after that was positive. I won over a lot of them that day. A few others were more intransigent and the jungle drums continued to beat. It didn't matter how well I had done, how good I might be. I shouldn't have gotten that game over someone who was refereeing longer. That's how they felt and how they always would feel. Owen never buckled under that sort of pressure though and I prospered as a result.

I was on my way.

CHAPTER FOURTEEN

Players, coaches and supporters were taking to my style of refereeing. Having played at a high level earned me an initial cache of respect which wouldn't have saved me had I not been up to the job but gave me a bit of credibility starting off. Nobody could say I hadn't done it on the pitch, that I didn't understand the game.

At the beginning of the 1998/99 season, Jim Glennon and Ciaran Callan brought me to the UK to officiate at what was supposed to be a gentle session between Leinster and Rotherham. They planned to practice some scrums and lineouts before having a 20-minute game.

It was carnage. There was a massive flare-up and nobody was surprised that Trevor Brennan was in the middle of it.

The teams got through about an hour of scrums and lineouts without incident but it didn't take long for the free-for-all to break out. From the kick-off, Trevor nearly took a guy's head off. Right then I hadn't a good feeling about it. It descended very quickly from there.

There were fights, teeth knocked out and stitches inserted. It was like being in A&E. It was beyond brutal. It was a practice session but I had to call it off, it was such a bloodbath.

I didn't see what happened initially to start the fighting, as Leinster scored a try and I was following the play. Apparently, Trevor retaliated to a late tackle with a kick. As is the norm in these situations, four or five players joined in so I told the respective coaches that I would call it off if there was any escalation of hostilities.

Rotherham's restart from the try didn't go 10 metres and as the players were coming back for the scrum, a Rotherham player bumped into a Leinster player. Who knows if it was accidental or mischievously intentional with the hackles raised? It was sufficient for the whole thing to flare up once more, the heavies wading in with concussive blows, unburdened by the presence of television cameras or media.

I immediately called a halt to the entire proceedings, although I'm not sure Jim was best pleased. But I had better things to be doing in my free time and it was out of control. I know for sure Jim wasn't pleased with Trevor because he dropped him from the squad subsequently.

Trevor is a lovely fella that I have a lot of time for. We always got on very well. Whenever I am in Toulouse, I call into his pub De Danú to say hello. He'll throw his arms around me and offer me a bite to eat on the house, knowing I don't drink. We'll chat about old times.

He was a hard man on the pitch but the opposition always knew that it was easy enough to get under his skin. His disciplinary record wouldn't have been great for a long time but it improved significantly in the latter half of his career and like I said, you couldn't meet a nicer man.

He comes from a tough background and had it harder growing up than most people he encountered on a rugby pitch. He had to help his father run a milk float when he was young and the death of his younger brother naturally left its mark.

I was a senior player when he came into the Leinster set-up and spoke to him quit a lot. As a result, we tended to sit next to each other when we travelled. Being thrown under the spotlight in a professional environment took some time for him to adjust to but he did it well in the end.

I was delighted that the move to Toulouse worked so well for him. He reinvented himself in a fashion, while remaining true to himself. They appreciated what he brought to the table in France and he built a wonderful life there. He is amongst a select group of Irishmen to win two Heineken

Cups. I was referee for the final he lost in 2004 thanks to Rob Howley's remarkable late try but I don't think he holds it against me.

IIIII

That type of outbreak was a rarity thankfully. It soon became apparent that I was about giving teams the platform to produce quick, entertaining rugby.

One example was an astonishing AIL game in which Ballymena emerged from Dooradoyle with a 44-38 victory. The teams produced 10 tries between them, which was an indication of their ambition. For good measure, the kickers were in stunning form as well, with only one miss out of 15 off the tee. It was a day we all enjoyed, perhaps the Garryowen folk a little less so.

That was the type of match that boosted my reputation and was being noted positively. It wasn't just about me knowing the laws and applying them properly; it was the type of games I was overseeing. And when there was a consistency in the nature of them, everyone, including Owen took note.

I was selected as a Level 1 referee for the first time at the beginning of the 2000/2001 season alongside Donal Courtney, Alan Lewis, David McHugh, Bertie Smith, David Tyndall and Murray Whyte.

My first interprovincial assignment involved Munster and Ulster at Thomond Park on September 29. It was a momentous occasion but I came back down to earth with a shuddering bump when Dad died three days later.

I remember absolutely nothing about the game but it had been an emotional rollercoaster of a time as Dad's health had been failing gradually and we knew things weren't good. Still, it will always play havoc with you when your Dad is dying.

The appointments for the Heineken Cup had been announced by this stage and I was scheduled to reach another milestone by getting my first European game, in the Heineken Cup, involving Toulouse and Saracens at the Stade Municipal.

The tie was only a couple of days after Dad's funeral but there was never any question of me not taking it up. He wouldn't have wanted me to miss it and I'm glad I didn't.

It was a memorable occasion, with the stadium packed to its 30,000 capacity. The commentator for the host broadcaster was none other than Pierre Salviac, who had been part of the French TV crew that came to Ireland to interview me when I was named to make my Test debut against Argentina 10 years previously.

Pierre was completely taken aback when he saw me walk out onto the pitch.

'What are you doing here?'

Of course he had seen the name of the referee but did not realise it was the same individual. Apparently he spent the first five minutes of the match talking about me in his commentary and how he had interviewed me and my French father.

The reaction when I walked into the dressing rooms for the first time to issue my instructions to the players was similar. Again, I would have played against a number of the Toulouse boys in particular, only a few years earlier.

'What the fuck are you doing here?'

Franck Tournaire was bollock naked and he just stood there looking at me. They were completely taken aback that a referee could speak to them in French. They warmed to me straight away.

Darragh O'Mahony, who I used to stay with when I was over at Moseley, was playing with Sarries by now and he told me afterwards that he promised his teammates they would get a fair crack of the whip because neither the occasion nor the home crowd would faze me.

I wore a black armband in memory of Dad, and Darragh asked me how everything was? I could feel the emotion welling up and fought to keep a lid on things. It was the same during a stoppage in the game when Christian Labit asked me what the armband was for and I had to explain. That was a struggle because I couldn't help thinking how much it would have meant for him to see me doing my first European game in his homeland.

It was an amazing game. Saracens won 32-22 and Darragh got one of the tries. Thomas Castaignède buried the knife in the heart of his compatriots with 22 points from the boot, including four penalties, two drop goals and two conversions.

I got talking to Thomas after that game and we have remained friendly since. We just seemed to click and he was very kind when asking about Dad.

We have caught up many times over the years.

I was on a high coming off the pitch because what was the biggest match of my career had gone so well when I was approached by a member of the French production crew to do an interview. I was brought up some steps and duly explained how it transpired that this Irish son of a Frenchman was refereeing at such a level.

When it was over, I thanked them and returned to the changing room.

Then I broke down.

Needing to be mentally prepared going into the game, I hadn't allowed myself go into that other area. It was only when the whole thing stopped and I had that one second to reflect that I lost it. The other officials were in there too but they knew what was going on. They gave me my space and I got myself together again.

The other exceptionally difficult game was the first Six Nations Test I did between Scotland and France the following March. The November prior to that, I was given the Wales-Romania game in Cardiff as my first Test but Scotland-France was tougher because of France's involvement. I was overcome with emotion when *La Marseillaise* was played. It was still just a bit raw that there would be so much he wouldn't see.

As I got older, I built up the experience to handle those emotions better. For the World Cup final, when the anthems were being played, I definitely had a thought for Dad but not to the extent where I was in trouble on an emotional level. It was just a moment of reflection.

I wanted him to be proud and I know he was.

▪️▪️▪️▪️

The season ended with the AIL final between Cork Con and Dungannon at Lansdowne Road in May, with the Ulster men winning their first and what remains to date, their only title. Indeed they were the first club from the northern province to claim ultimate honours.

David Humphreys guided the victors astutely, finishing with 26 points and earning the man of the match gong, but his rival for the Irish jersey, Ronan O'Gara was unavailable for Con due to being on Lions duty. He was undoubtedly a huge loss to the Temple Hill crew but it is doubtful if he would have made up the 46-12 deficit.

The game was memorable for another reason too as it was the first in Ireland outside of a Six Nations tie to have the video replay system in place. The IRFU were responding to the controversy surrounding the failure to award a try to John O'Neill in Munster's gut-wrenching one-point Heineken Cup semi-final defeat to Stade Francais at the Stadium Nord the previous month. There were no television match officials officiating in Heineken Cup games at that time.

The IRFU didn't want any such controversy surrounding the domestic scene's marquee game and so installed four remote control cameras with zoom lenses and a 180 degree sweep to supplement the RTÉ cameras.

David Tyndall was in the booth. Known as Fr Ted, because he was a reverend, David was a regular AIL referee and was the accomplished type of official you needed in the booth with the technology being used for the first time. We worked together in a lot of games over the years and got on very well. He was a great character.

Fortunately, the game passed off without incident. It was nice to be part of a day like that, especially when a club was experiencing that kind of success for the first time. Of course I would have preferred to have done it with ball-in-hand in a 'Rock jersey.

That was in the past though. Now I was one of the premier referees in world rugby, having been very recently appointed to the international panel by the IRB. Still only 34, I was the poster boy for the IRFU programme as overseen by Owen.

I was his guinea pig but could not have been mentored in a better way. The experiment was working. With each fast-tracking up a level, I flourished. There was a touch of sink-or-swim about it at time but if you proved yourself in one sphere, it made sense to test yourself at the next level.

The ultimate examinations lay in wait.

CHAPTER
FIFTEEN

How rare is it for a player with a full Test cap to referee at the same level?

Very.

When I was selected to officiate as Wales played host to Romania at the Millennium Stadium on September 19, 2001, I was bridging a 29-year gap back to New Zealander Frank McMullen, the last man to join the ranks in 1973, when England stunned the All Blacks at Eden Park.

It had been way back in 1953 when Ham Lambert took charge of his final international as a referee. Ham (short for Hamilton, as in Noel Hamilton Lambert) had been the last Irishman to do it but he had one over on me in that he played cricket for Ireland as well.

Pretty remarkable as his feats were, they fell short of the amazing New Zealander, Eric Tindill. Eric was a senior international player and referee but astonishingly, repeated that achievement in cricket, when he followed a career as Test player for the Black Caps by umpiring at the highest grade.

I wasn't in that league but what I had done was unusual and I remain very proud of that. I don't know why there haven't been more ex-players from any level coming through to referee, not to mind internationals. The fact that it hadn't happened in Ireland for almost half a century told its own tale.

Having played at a high level has to stand to you, particularly if you were in one of the decision-making positions at half-back. Former players didn't always make the transition well though.

There was one guy who played provincial level rugby in Ireland and was an excellent player but was a pretty dreadful referee. It was amazing to see someone who had played at that level that could be so detached from the feel of the game.

The way he spoke to players, his actions, his body language - he just didn't have any empathy with the game and the players. He had no sensitivity or depth of understanding. It was no surprise that he didn't progress and gave up eventually. It's only when you give someone a whistle that you know for sure what you have or don't have.

Nowadays however, you have the likes of John Lacey, who played Heineken Cup with Munster and is now a top flight official bound for the eighth World Cup in England and Wales alongside fellow IRFU product, George Clancy.

New Zealander, Glen Jackson is a former Waikato Chiefs and Saracens out half who is making the same journey and was fast-tracked in a similar fashion to me.

At a domestic level, ex-Munster, Connacht, Leicester and Ireland A scrum half, Frank Murphy is moving up the levels quickly too. Gary Conway and Andrew Brace are a couple of others going the right way within the IRFU programme.

Another Ireland international scrum half, Ciaran Scally gave it a go when a knee injury forced his premature retirement. Sadly, the injury was so severe that he could not continue refereeing either. He couldn't even do a figure of eight. It was a pity as he was very keen.

Most satisfying is the increasing number of females getting a chance to prove their ability. Helen O'Reilly became the first woman to be picked on the IRFU's national panel at the end of 2014 after establishing herself as one of the top female officials on the planet after the Women's World Cup earlier in the year.

She has done well in Division 2 of the AIL and earned promotion to the A panel as a result, which makes her eligible to referee Division 1 games and to be an assistant referee in the Pro12.

Former Ireland captain and Grand Slam winner, Joy Neville has been promoted to the interprovincial appointments level after showing well in Munster, where the likes of Pamela Browne and Wendy Fitzpatrick are also flying the flag.

It is brilliant to see and I hope it continues. With Owen still in charge it will. If you're good enough, you'll make the grade.

▮ ▮ ▮ ▮

I still remember the warm glow of satisfaction that accompanied the notification that I would be getting a full international. It came via a phone call from Owen and was a nice moment for both of us when he told me about Wales-Romania at the Millennium Stadium on November 19. There were nerves on the day, without question, but the pervading feeling was one of excitement that such an opportunity had been presented to me.

It had taken me an entire career to accumulate three caps as a player but after just two years as a full-time referee, I was in the Test arena. It was a bit of a whirlwind.

The flight to Cardiff was one of the bumpiest I can ever remember being on. Fr Ted was one of my TJs and he must have blessed himself about six million times with his rosary beads. We were all fairly green staggering onto welcome *terra firma*.

The game was easy as Wales hammered Romania 81-9. One-sided affairs invariably present few problems to a referee because of the reduction of intensity. Play is more open which means there aren't too many set pieces. You're just keeping things moving.

When I played against Argentina as a 24-year-old, I hoped that it would be the start of a lengthy run. I never took anything for granted but that experience would have acted as a reminder not to get ahead of myself, even if things were happening more easily for me as a referee than ever was the case in my playing days.

Thankfully, this wasn't to be a false dawn and I went on to referee all the best teams in all the major fixtures at all the premier stadiums. By the time I took charge of my last Test at the Millennium Stadium - almost 12 and a half years after my first at the same venue - I had travelled the globe and stewarded 68 internationals.

Unlike the professional referees, I did that while holding down a full-time job and having a young family. I did my best to ensure that there would be as little upheaval as possible both at home and in the office.

With work, particularly as the advances in technology made communication so easy, that never really created a problem. By the mid-noughties, I had developed a big team at Cornmarket which helped. But I was always able to contact clients and carry out business.

If I was in the southern hemisphere I would work when I woke up in the morning, dealing with all my emails until about 11am. The middle of the day was free because it was night at home. I would have an early dinner then and go from about 7pm to midnight, as that was morning back home and it was live work in real time.

I had to take all these days out of my holidays which meant I rarely got away with the family. We did try and squeeze in a couple of holidays between Christmas and the New Year, when everything was closed, but even at that I still had to get back for Cornmarket's annual sales conference on January 4.

Every other trip, the half-days on the Friday, the half-days on the Monday morning, the 10 days in the southern hemisphere, it all came out of holidays.

I was on a part-time contract with the IRFU but the retainer increased when you made the IRB panel. As you went up the food chain, you had to travel more and the retainer and match fees reflected that. Because all my tax-free allowances were used with Cornmarket though, I was losing 53% of the whole refereeing income on tax. But I never did it for the money.

The professional referees were expected to do a certain amount of work outside of the games themselves, with club teams within their federation's auspices. They were at the beck and call of their employers. Apart from the odd workshop and seminar that I had to attend, my only commitment to the IRFU and IRB was to do the actual games.

I never considered becoming a professional referee for the same reason that I wasn't going to go that route as a player. The IRFU could not pay me what I was getting in the financial sector.

I don't think refereeing has to be a fully professional job in the northern hemisphere. It does in the southern hemisphere as there is much more travel involved. Some of the boys might be away 170 days a year between Super Rugby, Six Nations and the Rugby Championship. You couldn't hold down a job with that sort of absenteeism. So all those guys are professional and if they're told to go to Australia for three weeks, they just pack up and go.

Still, I was away a lot and when you're not at home, there is obviously a knock-on effect. You cannot help with the homework, attend the kids matches, put the plaster on the grazed knee. Lizzie took all that on board and made my refereeing career possible. Even with that, I was away from home 26 weekends in 2012. It was a huge factor in prompting me to retire.

I did my best to manage the situation. In 2011, I was appointed to do the first game of the Tri Nations series, with South Africa travelling to Wellington to take on New Zealand at Westpac Stadium. Normally, you would arrive around 10 days in advance to get the body clock in order when travelling between the hemispheres and it tended to take a few days to recover after returning too.

I handled jet lag pretty well but I didn't want to be away that long in July, especially as I was going to be back down in New Zealand for two months from August. We didn't advertise it, because it might not have been perceived as the best preparation but Paddy O'Brien gave me his blessing to make it a truncated trip.

I left Dublin on Wednesday and landed in New Zealand on the Thursday afternoon, going straight to bed on arrival at my hotel. I had to stay up all night and watch the British Open while I did some work. It was the year Darren Clarke finally garnered his first golfing major so there was plenty Irish interest.

I maintained that sort of a schedule, keeping Irish time by sleeping all day. The match was on Saturday and with a flight at midnight, I left for the airport straight from the stadium. I was back at home in time to see Clarke get his hands on the Claret Jug. That was extreme but I didn't want to be away any longer than needed to be the case.

▐ ▌ ▌ ▐

Getting my first Six Nations game on March 23, 2002 was another breakthrough. It meant more than my Test debut because I had never played in the Six Nations, or the Five Nations as it was until Italy joined in 2000. There was more of a sentimental significance too because of Dad.

While I don't recall where I was when Owen rang me to tell me about my first Test appointment, I recall everything about the call for this one. I was at one of Cornmarket's monthly seminars. To be specific, I was in the toilet.

'Rollers. The appointments are out for the Six Nations.'

'Tell me I've got one.'

I hadn't slept the night before thinking about the possibility.

'Please, please, tell me, I got one.'

Owen can be a real bastard at times. He keeps you hanging there. Given the way Paddy O'Brien dragged it out in Paris for the World Cup final, it was probably good training. Owen was actually more of a bastard though because he didn't just drag it out. He said I hadn't got it.

'I don't think you're gonna be happy.'

'Fuck. I didn't get one.'

A pause.

'Ah no, you did.'

'You bastard!'

'Scotland-France. Murrayfield.'

'You bastard! Fucking brilliant.'

I jumped up and down in the toilet. I was absolutely over the moon and then had to head out to the seminar as if nothing had happened, because the official announcements hadn't been made yet.

Owen did that to me a few times in subsequent years. He got some sort of sick kick out of it. I should have been ready for it but he always caught me.

The last time, with the Heineken Cup final that I finished my career with, he did the exact same thing.

'Rollers? They've just come back. We've got details about who's doing the match. I'm really sorry.'

'Ah fuck. I was hoping for the best. Who did they give it to?'

'You jammy bastard.'

'Bastard! Absolutely brilliant!'

I always felt when I was refereeing internationally that I was representing my country. That meant a lot to me. I didn't forget why I was there and how I had gotten there.

But this was nothing like the build-up to receiving my first cap as a player. And it did not beat playing at any level, never mind for your country. But it was close. And it has to be better than coaching because you are right there in the middle of it. You just can't touch the ball.

▮▮▮▮

This was the real big breakthrough in terms of being an international referee. It was Scotland against France in Murrayfield with points at stake. You weren't being examined in this type of environment. You had made it.

There might also be a perception that I was predisposed to France because of my background and that they had an unfair advantage because I could speak to them in their native tongue. Of course that was nonsense. Until that point, it was all the other teams that had the advantage because frustration at not understanding what was going on tended to be what sparked Gallic combustion.

When I did speak in French, I always repeated the message or instruction in English so that everyone understood. The same applied from English to French. It was certainly an advantage for me in terms of being able to referee and France appreciated having someone that could communicate with them. It removed a vital tool for opponents against *Les Bleus*.

Not everyone was impressed with my bilingual skills. Former England and Lions hooker, Brian Moore is just as pugnacious in the commentary booth as he was on the pitch. He once said that it didn't matter to him that I could speak French fluently, as it just meant that I could get it wrong in two languages! Great line.

I had a lovely build-up to the game as I refereed my first Leinster Senior Schools' Cup final between St Mary's and Belvedere the Sunday before. Given my background in the SCT and losing a final, it was great to play a part. St Mary's came out on top on a freezing cold day, complete with snow and hailstones.

I got an amazing letter from the parents of the Belvedere players subsequently, thanking me for the way I reffed the game and how I dealt with the boys. Even though they lost. I was totally taken aback that they went to that trouble. It was an incredible gesture.

In Edinburgh six days later, the spoils belonged to France and Bernard Laporte's squad went on to bag a Grand Slam.

█▊█

I only refereed Leinster twice because I was a former player. Both games were against Munster and were torrid affairs.

The first occasion was in April 2002 at Musgrave Park and I had to speak to both captains in a bid to get them to address player behaviour. It was getting out of control. The spilling rain transformed the ball into a bar of soap and any opportunity to take a shot, cheap or otherwise, was taken. It finished 6-6, which tells you all you need to know.

I managed to keep all the players on the field I think even though they were trying hard to force my hand at times. I know I had to talk to Mick Galwey, who was Munster captain, and tell him this couldn't continue.

'Help me out here.'

'I'll have a word and sort them out.'

Gaillimh had been involved in a few skirmishes himself, not least with his former teammate Brian O'Meara, who was now in the Leinster colours. But he got the lads to cop on and we didn't have too many issues after that.

The second time was probably more eventful and it arrived 12 years later, my final season as a referee. It always matters when it's Munster and Leinster but by now, the clubs were superpowers, multiple winners of the Heineken Cup and the domestic battle was being played out on the international stage.

There is a possibility that Munster were carrying some gripe against me into the game. Certainly they were unhappy with my handling of the Pro12 defeat to Ulster in Ravenhill on January 3. Nobody likes when you send Paul O'Connell to the bin!

Alan Quinlan cut loose on RTÉ afterwards.

'The better team won tonight but there were three shocking decisions in my opinion by Alain Rolland.'

He thought I got it wrong when penalising Peter O'Mahony and then Paulie for getting their hands on the ball, illegally to my mind after calling that a ruck had been formed, or that I didn't award a penalty after Munster were held up mauling over the Ulster line.

As was often the case with Quinny when he was playing, he was calmer once the red mist disappeared. So he doled out some sugar in his newspaper column later that week, declaring his respect for me because I explained my decisions to a player.

He was adamant I had had a poor night though and could take the criticism. Whatever about the first part, he was right about the second.

In the same column, Quinny wrote that he knew from his playing days that he could not push me too far. I'm not sure he always displayed that knowledge on the pitch though!

We got on well. He was a serious operator as a player. You always had to watch him. He was one of those guys you'd have a word with beforehand.

'You need this whistle today Quinny? Or will I referee this one?'

It was a joke delivered with a smile but you were sending the message too. He'd give you the mischievous grin and then go and rub everybody up the wrong way in his own inimitable style. He was yappy, forever trying to help you with his suggestions, while having a word with the opposition too. He was also liable to do anything. But he is a good guy who made the very best of himself.

▌▐ ▐ ▐▌

So maybe Rob Penney was carrying a grievance. Mind you, when the prospect of me doing their Pro12 game in March 2014 came, both the New Zealander and his skipper (O'Connell) said I was the best man for the job.

Pascal Gaüzère was the original appointment but he got injured during the week and at short notice the options for replacements were thin on the ground. Once Owen contacted me, I was more than happy to do it if the teams gave the green light.

It was always going to be an issue for supporters. Munster fans would be convinced that I would screw them at every turn, while their Leinster counterparts would reason that I was being stricter on them to overcompensate for the fact that I was a former player.

Anyway, both Penney and Matt O'Connor agreed. I was delighted because this is one of the most intense rivalries in rugby. That makes it very tough because of the derby nature of it, the history and the fact that it is always so physical. It just has a different dynamic to all the other interpros.

Nigel Owens will tell you that it is one of the most difficult games to referee. But he loves it and I would have given anything to referee them in front of a full house at the Aviva.

The irony is that a game that ended with the losing head coach calling me a cheat began with the best player to ever wear the green jersey absolutely losing the plot with me because he thought I was giving Munster everything!

Brian O'Driscoll may have shared Blackrock as an *alma mater* but that cut no ice in the Aviva. I gave Munster four scrum penalties in the first half, which Ian Keatley kicked to put them into a 12-3 lead. I think the visitors had given away two or three penalties for slowing the ball down and suddenly Brian came from 30 yards away screaming.

'They're fucking killing the ball.'

I was taken aback to be honest. I didn't expect that from him and to be fair, it was nowhere near normal behaviour from what I can gather. It wasn't normal for any rugby player though. He was gone crazy. It was 'fuck this', 'fuck that'.

It was extraordinary. Clearly, there were a lot of factors. This was his last season and we were now at the business end of the campaign where significant issues were being decided. Also, it was Munster. He wasn't alone in being psyched but he was out of control as nearly every sentence delivered to me had a 'fuck' or something spicier in it. It just goes to show that even the best can be overwhelmed.

Brian was sailing perilously close to the wind, screaming that I was giving Leinster nothing in the most disrespectful of language. If this continued, I would have no option but to send him packing with little more than 20 minutes elapsed.

Jamie Heaslip was the Leinster captain and I called him over.

'I don't know what's going on but you need to calm him down.'

Jamie knew it. He could see the way Brian had lost it, contesting decisions, demanding decisions, with aggressive language and posture. Thankfully, he got through to him. Brian modified his behaviour. It was to his and Leinster's benefit as he scored the only try of the game in a comeback win.

He came up to me afterwards and apologised but in truth, it was apparent that he was still a bit pissed off with me. Once he acknowledged that he had gone too far, it was fine by me and that was the end of it.

We would retire at the end of the same season though his career was by far the more celebrated and rightly so. He was an incredible player and a brilliant leader for Ireland, Leinster and the Lions.

It was a privilege to be fourth official when Brian played his last home Test in the Aviva against Italy. I still have the card that Mick O'Driscoll gave me to mark his substitution. He signed it for me afterwards.

'This will be the biggest cheer you ever get for coming on,' I told Fergus McFadden before communicating the message to Nigel Owens and sure enough it was!

ı▮■▮ı

Penney was a whole different ball game. I wasn't aware of any of the issues he might have until Owen sent on his coaching report and when I saw that I was taken aback. Scratch that. I was angry.

Had I read newspapers, I would have had an inkling. He didn't refer to me but was clearly agitated when claiming that post-game reports were not being passed onto referees.

'Some of them probably get lost in the ether.'

That was bullshit. Owen always sent them on to the Irish referees anyway. Penney also implied that any referee with a job could not perform at the level required and given that I had just officiated the game in which his side had been beaten, there could be no doubt he was talking about me.

'You'd love to think that (the reports are) all being passed on to the referees and being discussed deeply, because we do put the effort in. But I do query whether there's been the in-depth support or education for the referees when they're busy men themselves.

'Some of them aren't professional or full-time but at the end of the day their decisions cost money and livelihoods so it's a position that needs to be treated with a great deal of respect.'

He got to address me directly in his report to Owen, in which he surgically got stuck into me. There were a number of issues, including a claim that I spoke with Leinster scrum coach, Greg Feek at half time. I don't know where he got that idea; it never happened. I didn't speak to Greg or any other team official.

Anyway, it was all part of the picture Penney was trying to paint.

'Very disappointing performance across the board and I'm sorry to say, prior to this game we outlined our reservations about Alain's appointment but were given assurances that he would not be compromised by his Leinster relationship. Unfortunately we feel our trust was misplaced. We have highlighted several actions by Alain that we feel compromised his impartiality. Please respond in some detail to our report as if we are not correct in our assessment, we need to get the learnings very quickly.'

Needless to say, Owen's response was swift.

'There's quite a bit in your report but we'll revert later in the week. I'm sure you will not be surprised that I wish to comment on your final paragraph. It's really not acceptable to question Alain's impartiality. It was a difficult task for him in a match which is always challenging and the idea that any mistakes which were made were due to bias is not credible and is an unworthy challenge to his integrity.'

Owen forwarded the report to me, offering a brief summation of the drivel within it. He directed me to that final paragraph. It was the only part of the report I read.

I emailed Owen the following.

'Hi Owen, I will not be doing any work on this report as a result of his comments as they are completely out of order. I did not have any conversation with Greg or anyone else for that matter at half time.'

The insinuation in the report was that as a former Leinster player, I was making decisions in their favour. Brian O'Driscoll certainly didn't think so! But Penney was saying I was biased, so to my mind, he was calling me a cheat.

He could have easily said I had a shit game and left it at that. Instead, he went over the top on me, questioning my integrity. It's the only time it happened but once is enough. I would never be swayed by former loyalties.

Accusing a referee of cheating is the worst thing you could ever say about him. That he would purposely go out to screw a team, to do them out of the game, to make up decisions against them. That was wrong.

You always had an opportunity to respond to any issues brought up in the report but this was so over the top, I told Owen that there was no way I was even going to acknowledge it. Fuck him.

I ▮ ▮ I

I must make a confession though. There was one occasion in my entire career when I went out on the pitch with the intention of nailing a team. By that I mean that I was going to blow the whistle against them every opportunity they gave me.

In other words, I was going to be a 'Gotcha' ref.

To explain, a 'Gotcha' referee is one who will pull for every transgression with glee, whether it has any material effect on the game or not. These officials are easy to spot because they like to be the centre of attention. They are Little Hitler types, drunk on the power the whistle gives them and keen to abuse it.

You will know them too by the quality of the games they are in charge of. They are generally poor because teams have no chance of building up momentum. You don't get to go through the phases with these guys because the law book has been swallowed and is being regurgitated with monotonous regularity. Tries aren't that common in such games.

Judging the materiality of an offence is critical. What part of the pitch are you in, what effect the offence has had and so on. The best referees are the ones who get these calls right more often than not.

Anyway, on January 15, 2011 in round five of the Heineken Cup, I turned 'Gotcha' on Leicester and penalised them every chance I could get. And I went into the game with every intention of doing so.

Tigers head coach, Richard Cockerill was never the most likeable individual as a player and nothing changed when he went into coaching. He is just confrontational all the time and has no problem picking rows.

The 'nobody likes us, we don't care' mentality is central to the Leicester ethos and allied to a savage workrate and total buy-in surrounding the club culture, has brought them phenomenal success. But off the pitch, a lot of the guys that people might have formed bad opinions about were dead on.

Martin Johnson is one example. You would think he'd strangled a baby kitten on live television the way people in Ireland still go on about him after he refused to switch sides before the Grand Slam decider in 2003. It was brilliant leadership though. He could not back down and his teammates, as so often was the case, followed his lead.

Johnson was a dominant figure, with a reputation as a surly and intimidating individual on the pitch. He is a huge man but he was very respectful and a good communicator. You could speak to him, knowing that if you needed to get a message to players, he could be relied upon to do so, unlike Steve Borthwick or Pascal Papé.

Martin was one of the great captains I dealt with, along with John Smit, Fabien Pelous, Thierry Dusautoir and Richie McCaw. Lawrence Dallaglio was another although he and his England colleague might not have possessed the same humility as McCaw.

Johnson and Dallaglio were very similar. They were brutally single-minded and tunnel-visioned but they knew how to work with a referee.

I recall them going head-to-head when Wasps played Leicester. These two guys were the best of friends playing for England but they were passionate about their clubs and detested one another when in opposition.

You knew beforehand there was going to be skin and hair flying but having those two guys around was an immense source of comfort to me. They were like a safety net because if it was teetering on getting out of control, those two could get their players to pull back from the edge if I asked them to. They would recognise you had a problem and deal with it.

There were others, and Borthwick was a prime example, who gave you nothing. You were on your own with those guys. But Johnson and Dallaglio were good captains, good guys. It's ironic that I could not work with Steve when he was a captain and we hardly ever saw eye to eye, because in my current role as a consultant with World Rugby I have a very good working relationship with him as he is the forwards coach for Japan.

My point about Johnson here is that I had no issue with Leicester or the type of player they had, particularly in the pack. I admired them and what they stood for. It was just that Cockerill is not a guy you could like, even if he was a guy you wanted with you in the trenches.

He has described himself as belligerent and that is an accurate description. It is just his manner and he is the same way with everyone. It was no surprise when Martin Castrogiovanni had such a massive cut at him last year, not least because Castro has always been fairly combustible too.

Anyway, that never affected how I refereed Cockerill or Leicester before this game or subsequently. If you were nailing every guy you didn't like it would be a Gotcha gourmet.

No, the fact is that he got under my skin because of completely over-the-top comments he made about Donal Courtney, the former Irish referee who was the ERC match officials performance manager, in particular, while he also stuck the knife into another Irish official, Peter Fitzgibbon.

Fitzy was in charge of the Tigers' home tie against Perpignan in the fourth round of their Heineken Cup pool in December, which ended in a draw. Beforehand, Cockerill held up the game for five minutes, claiming that he had not been aware of a change in the start time, even though it was widely publicised and of course Leicester would have received official notification. He was a real ass about that.

Afterwards, he criticised Fitzy's handling of the game although bizarrely, he absolved him when accusing Perpignan of killing the ball all day. For that charge, he turned his sights on Donal claiming that Donal had told him beforehand that there would be "zero tolerance" at the breakdown and that Fitzy hadn't exercised that zero tolerance.

I never responded to criticism of myself but this really pissed me off. I carried that anger into the following round when I was appointed to do their trip to Parc y Scarlets and I pretty much gave them nothing.

When we called into the dressing room for the pre-match instructions, I asked him what time he wanted to start the match at? He looked at me funny but said nothing. He knew what I was getting at.

Some people might view this as semantics but I wasn't cheating because

I was observing the laws of the game. Nobody would have known what my thought process was. I never gave a penalty that wasn't a penalty. I was taking the opportunities Leicester gave me and they tended to give you plenty.

Normally, I would have given them the benefit of the doubt for many of these transgressions or let them go if they were having no material effect. I played advantage where I could because I liked a flowing, entertaining game. Here, I was punishing every indiscretion, no matter how petty or how little effect it might have. I was being a Gotcha ref.

There were many times where I could have managed a situation, had a quiet word, as the situation didn't really have any materiality but I said, *Fuck you, I'm going by the letter of the law today.* So I wasn't doing anything wrong but I wasn't giving them any room for manoeuvre.

Just give me a reason to punish you? was my thought process the whole time.

I never refereed unfairly to influence a result and Leicester won the game. I was disappointed in myself afterwards though. It was unprofessional behaviour and shouldn't have happened. It never did again.

▮▮▮▮

That wasn't me at my finest, but I would not cheat. I would not penalise teams for no reason. I would not ignore blatant transgressions that that had a material effect on a game. I don't believe that any referee operating at that level would. To claim that a referee would is to go at the very heart of what he does and who he is. It places a huge cloud over the entire game.

So when Penney implied that of me it was the only time I was really angered by anything said about me.

He said that I was seen having a conversation with Leinster's scrum coach, Greg Feek and was influenced by him after making so many decisions at the set piece in Munster's favour in the first half. That was not the case.

But really, it was the implication that I would be biased that pissed me off. I'm not sure he would have gone that route if he had been sticking around. But it hadn't gone well for him in Munster since he had arrived from New Zealand and they had lost to the old enemy. Now that he was fucking off to

Japan at the end of the season, he felt the shackles were off and he could say what he wanted. It was wrong.

Being accused of purposely attempting to systematically make biased decisions for or against a team because of loyalties to another, of trumping up charges and seeing penalties that didn't exist. That's vile. Yes, I went out once to give a team nothing, or to penalise them whenever they broke a law which I'm not proud of, but all the decisions I made were there.

Of course mistakes are made, just as they are by players and coaches. I have made plenty of mistakes. What you hope is that your mistakes don't affect the end result. Even legitimately penalising Leicester every time I could didn't cost them the game, as they beat Scarlets.

Penney insinuated that I blew for penalties that didn't exist and ignored those that obviously did. He implied that I either passed on some information to Greg Feek or hatched a plan of some sort to improve the scrum situation for Leinster, after Munster had gotten those early penalties at the set piece.

He could fuck right off to Japan.

CHAPTER SIXTEEN

The big games kept on coming and making the cut for the 2003 World Cup was phenomenal. Of course I felt I deserved it given my trajectory and performances, but it was still a significant achievement given my youth and the fact that I was refereeing at international level less than two years when the tournament kicked off.

Being given a Tri Nations game on July 19, when South Africa welcomed New Zealand to Pretoria's Loftus Versfeld Stadium, was the last big test before the World Cup to see what level I could operate at. I was well aware of that and there were plenty of butterflies before that. But the competitor always relishes these kinds of challenges.

I had been in Durban 11 months previously as touch judge for Dave McHugh in one of the most infamous Test matches of recent times. The All Blacks provided the opposition then too but after the game, everyone was talking about a big, fat nutter called Pieter Van Zyl, who attacked Macker, leaving him with a dislocated shoulder.

Macker always blames me because I called a scrum for a knock-on he hadn't spotted, and it was during this stoppage in play that Van Zyl took it upon himself to register his dissatisfaction with the referee's performance in the most inappropriate fashion.

It was surreal. I was on the far side of the ground and he was already on the pitch when I saw him out of the corner of my eye.

Where is this guy going?

He wore some sort of green camouflage gear with the Springbok jersey and dark trousers, and just seemed to blend into the surroundings. Nobody noticed him until it was too late. Suddenly, he's having a go at Macker, dragging him to the ground.

Woah. Fuck.

I started to move forward and fortunately Richie McCaw and AJ Venter were very quick to react, ensuring the situation didn't become even worse. I think McCaw landed a bit of a haymaker on him. Someone did anyway because when Van Zyl emerged from the ruck of players, he was sporting a bloody nose.

I sat up with Dave most of the night because he was in a bad way. He was getting sick and I was afraid he might choke. Then the following day, we were in the courthouse.

Van Zyl was absolutely crazy and completely unrepentant. He said afterwards that rugby was about fans like him. What a nut job. The most disappointing aspect of it all was that a South African radio station carried out a poll and close to 50% of those that contributed agreed with the lunatic's actions.

I was staying in the same hotel as the All Blacks. It was amazing the attention they were getting in this rugby-mad nation. They were rock stars. There were people around them all the time but they were so generous with their time and always polite. A smile, a word, pose for a photo and sign an autograph. Really grounded.

One time, I was by the pool getting something to eat and one of the players – I think it was Aaron Mauger – was strumming a guitar. It was great to see them in that sort of environment, so relaxed.

There was a bit of focus on me beforehand because Australia coach, Eddie Jones criticised Steve Walsh and his officials after South Africa had beaten the Wallabies in Cape Town seven days previously. I was calm about it though. Looking forward to it. It proved another thrilling experience.

Sometimes people downplay the role of the national anthem at these events but quite apart from the pride people feel about it, there are some places where it just explodes and creates a torrent of emotion and enthusiasm. It adds to the atmosphere.

My top three anthems for home teams are *Bread Of Heaven*, *La Marseillaise* and the South African hybrid of *Nkosi Sikelel' iAfrika* and *Die Stem van Suid-Afrika*. *Bread Of Heaven* is amazing when the roof in the Millennium Stadium is closed. If Katherine Jenkins is singing it, that's a bonus. *La Marseillaise* has that typical French flair and flourish.

Fuck me though, the South African supporters are passionate. The All Black being in town obviously stirs the blood, and the 'Boks were fresh from beating Australia but you knew it meant something to the people.

The anthem comprises five of the country's most common languages and as a result, embraces the entire nation. It starts slowly and builds up to a rocking, throbbing, ear-splitting crescendo created by the majority of a 53,000 capacity crowd.

The first four sections are sung in Xhosa, Zulu, Sesotho and Afrikaans. The conclusion is in English and the whole thing seems to get louder by 50 billion decibels.

Sounds the call to come together
And united we shall stand
Let us live and strive for freedom
In South Africa our land.

It was electric listening to that in person for the first time. The depth of feeling was clear from the start but when it flipped to English for the climax, it was like that Tango ad, where your man comes out of nowhere and slaps you across the face. I looked across at my TJs. Chris White was just about holding it together but Eric Darriere was in floods of tears. It had that sort of effect.

Next up was The Haka. This was my first time refereeing New Zealand so even the prospect of being up close for an event that transcends rugby was exciting. With Carlos Spencer leading, it didn't disappoint.

'Ka Mate, Ka Mate, Ka'Ora, Ka'Ora.'
Spine-tingling.
After those 10 minutes, I am pinching myself. I can't believe I'm here.

I have always been able to enjoy the pre-match build-up and then get myself in the right head space for the game itself and the same applies even in these circumstances. The zeal of the supporters continued as proceedings commence and when the Springboks went ahead through a Louis Koen penalty, it skyrocketed even further as the place erupted. The hairs were standing on the back of my neck.

It was 26 degrees but while the temperature isn't a problem, being at altitude was a little bit of an issue. I had been in Windhoek the week before for Namibia v Samoa and only got to Pretoria two days before the kick-off. As a result, I noticed that I was catching my breath a little even in my warm-up. My mouth was bone dry. It took me 10 or 15 minutes to adjust but once I got my second wind it is fine.

Incidentally, I met Craig Joubert for the first time in Windhoek as he was my touch judge for the game there. We got on exceptionally well from the start.

The fact we were both young guys flying through the system probably had something to do with that. Mind you, I was a couple of steps ahead of him on the ladder at that juncture because he was still only 25.

Craig would go on to join me in the select group of World Cup final referees in 2011 and while I was disappointed not to get the nod for a second time, it was tremendous for Craig and I gave it everything as his assistant.

Watching the DVD of this game again makes me cry as I look at the brilliant Joost Van Der Westhuizen, who is now battling a form of MND. It was his last game on South African soil.

He was an incredibly gifted 9. I encountered him first-hand on the Sevens circuit and he loved the freedom the shortened format gave him to express himself. He was so skilful but standing at over six foot had the power to take the game on himself. He was a nightmare for opposition back rows.

When I went into the changing room beforehand, we had a little exchange. It was just a bit of small talk between members of the scrum halves union but I treasure it.

A guy at the other end of the age spectrum playing that day was Jerry Collins. He went on to have a brilliant career too. A typical Samoan, he was so physical with and without the ball but had all the skills too. When you were tackled by Jerry Collins, you stayed tackled for a while. The only guy I saw with bigger biceps than Jerry was Pierre Spies.

Jerry was killed with his wife in a car crash in France at the beginning of June 2015, while his four-month old baby daughter survived, reportedly because Jerry wrapped himself around her. The tragedy shook the rugby community to its core. Jerry was only 34, Alana a year older.

▐ ▌ ▌ ▐

It was very difficult to communicate with the players due to the constant din. There was a knock-on in the first play.

Oh shit.

The last thing you want is a fucking scrum straight off the bat with two sets of forwards wired to the moon. You want to run them around a bit initially to smooth some of the edges off them. At that time, we didn't have the same problems with the scrums that are so endemic now and thankfully it passed off without incident.

The first penalty of the match was against Richie McCaw for offside. So was the second but I got it wrong. He was so fast that he made the tackle and was up on his feet to play the ball before the ruck had formed. The third penalty was against him too.

I pinged him for my first three penalties but I still say that he is without a shadow of a doubt, one of the best players I ever refereed. People are always complaining that officials let him get away with murder but that wrong decision I made is a testament to his extraordinary skills, strength and quickness.

The All Blacks scored the first try after a bit of magic from Carlos Spencer but Koen kicked a drop goal from just inside the opposition half and the place went berserk once more.

What is he at? I thought, as he shaped to kick, but the way that ball flew at altitude he would have slotted it from his own 10m line.

The expectation beforehand was that the Springboks would keep it tight and try to outmuscle the All Blacks. They probably should have. Instead, they played expansively and Stefan Terblanche, who later played for Ulster,

knocked on with a try apparently certain.

The opening 20 minutes flew by at breakneck speed. And no-one was quicker that Dougie Howlett.

At one stage in the first half, he collected a kick close to his 22. I was standing about six or seven metres in front of him but he was 10 metres ahead of me before I had barely a chance to turn my body. It was mind-boggling acceleration from a man who is now a Munster legend.

Howlett put New Zealand ahead after a little switch play in midfield that ended with a lovely pass out the back door when tackled from Aaron Mauger. The execution of the skills at that speed was incredible.

At one stage in the second half, I played an advantage on the All Black 22 for a Springbok knock on. After a few phases of play, they found touch on half-way but I called back the play for a scrum. Owen pointed out afterwards that it was the wrong call and I would agree now. The advantage was over. It worked out well though as they broke upfield and ended with a try. Not that the South Africans might have looked upon it in that light.

They broke so quickly that there was one moment of huge doubt when Rokocoko was tap-tackled just after receiving possession. Watching from behind, I could see him losing the ball and then somehow having it again and racing over for the try.

Hold on. What happened there?

When the ball had flipped up, it rebounded off the retreating Springbok hooker, Danie Coetzee back into Rokocoko's arms. It looks wrong but there's no offside line because it's open play. I'm running with my arms up signalling play on. What I'm thinking is, *I hope to fuck I have this one right.* Thankfully, I did.

New Zealand cut loose in the second half. Howlett ended with two tries, as did Joe Rokocoko, while Mauger and Kees Meeuws also touched down. It was a record win (52-16) for the All Blacks over South Africa and the most tries (seven) they had ever gotten against them.

That was one of the most complete games of rugby I've ever seen, up there with what they produced in Paris the following year. The problem for them was that they couldn't get it right for a long time when it came to performing at a World Cup.

Like every World Cup there has been, they went to Australia as prohibitively short-priced favourites. Not for the first time, they endured disappointment but my tournament could not have gone much better.

❚❚❚❚

That was the pinnacle so far. To me, New Zealand v South Africa is the biggest game in world rugby, bigger than the Bledisloe Cup. Rugby isn't the national sport in Australia. It very definitely is in both South Africa and New Zealand. The whole country is behind them. That is why I was given this game.

Can he hack it?

I did and was selected among 16 referees for the World Cup. I would say I was pencilled for a quarter-final after Pretoria, as long as I avoided a train wreck. Macker joined me in Australia but there was no joy for Alan Lewis, the former cricket international who went on to have such an excellent career as a rugby referee.

If I had known that the venue for my first World Cup assignment was a former graveyard, I might have been a bit unnerved, but Brisbane's Suncorp Stadium didn't bury me or France, as they trounced Fiji 61-18.

The Pacific Islanders may have taken a heavy beating but that game will always be remembered as the day the great Caucau announced himself to the world.

Rupeni Caucaunibuca is one of the game's mavericks. His laidback nature means that he wasn't always in peak physical condition and you would love to have seen him fit for 10 years. I'm not sure there was anyone else with his natural flamboyance, even though Fiji breeds that class of player. Of course if you changed his natural characteristics, you might have lost that flair that entertained so many as well.

He scored a try against France that remains one of my favourite of all time. Fiji got possession deep in their half and as usual, were looking to run it. Caucau received a pass half-way between his 22 and the 10 metre line with a wall of French defenders in front of him.

He seemed to glide at full tilt around Aurélien Rougerie, making the tall winger look like a garden gnome in the process. Rougerie was trying to ease him towards the touchline and there wasn't a whole lot of space but with an almost imperceptible change of direction and a very perceptible but fluid acceleration, he was gone. It was like he floated.

That's if you can float while crossing the ground with the pace of a cheetah. He sped past Harinordoquy on the outside before dipping inside once more past the despairing tackle of Nicolas Brusque. It was a clear run to the posts from there but what he did in a matter of seconds took your breath away.

Not literally, I hasten to add, as I am proud to say that I was only about five strides behind Rupeni when he dotted down. That was pretty good going given his speed and athleticism, even if he did ease off the gas a bit having left the opposition in his wake. I don't think it got try of the tournament but it must have been right up there.

I had to send him to the bin later on, along with Olivier Magne, after they had gotten involved off the ball. He was suspended for two games afterwards but in his first game back, scored two glorious tries against Scotland. I consider it a real honour to have been on the pitch when this great talent became an international star.

Next up was Georgia-Samoa and that was fairly straightforward. Samoa won and the game produced the lowest number of penalties in the tournament.

If people want proof that you can only referee what the players give you, it is my penalty stats for that tournament. Because I followed the game producing the lowest number of penalties, with the encounter that accumulated the most when Canada and Tonga went toe-to-toe.

People might characterise referees as fussy or *laissez-faire*. While there are whistle-happy people out there, it really does depend entirely on the players. You go from giving out seven penalties in one game to 27 in another, it can't be about you.

Canada v Tonga was one of the dirtiest games I ever did, with scraps breaking out everywhere. It was chaotic. I had to dish out a couple of yellow cards to try to cool things down but the whole game was a shit-fight.

Reviewing the game afterwards, you did question whether you could have done anything different and there wasn't a huge amount. The Canadians were angered by an injury to their skipper Al Charron late on in what was his last of 76 internationals but he got injured in a legitimate tackle.

Obviously my bosses were happy enough as I got the England-Wales quarter-final back at the Suncorp. This was a definite seal of approval because there was a potential for this to be a fiery game, given the traditional rivalry and the prize of a semi-final on offer.

A shock was on the cards for a long while. Wales outscored England three tries to one and were leading 10-3 at half time. Early after the resumption, Jason Robinson went on one of his magical runs, beating five players with that phenomenal gas and killer side-step. He drew a sixth and sent Will Greenwood over in the corner.

That sent England on their way and Jonny Wilkinson kicked 23 points to put Wales away. The out half was the hero as Clive Woodward's men went on to win the World Cup by virtue of that nerveless drop goal against Australia.

I was an ultra-confident operator by this stage, even though I had only refereed eight Tests before the World Cup and was now up to a grand total of 12. The Test in Pretoria had given me a tremendous boost. I knew it had gone well and former Australia prop, Chris 'Buddha' Handy mentioned the possibility of me going on to do the World Cup final towards the end of that game.

I would have had no problem doing a semi-final or final at that juncture but of course they were never going to give the big one to a rookie, less than two years after he had done his first Test, even if they felt themselves I was capable of it.

They had been hugely supportive but had I gotten the final and it had gone horribly wrong, they would have been heavily criticised for not going with a safe pair of hands.

I was pretty much told, 'Look you've had a fantastic tournament' and it was clear from subsequent appointments that I was now one of the IRB's go-to referees. Even before I left Australia towards the end of November, the referees' manager, Steve Griffiths told me I would get France-England in the Six Nations on March 27. This was the biggest game in northern hemisphere rugby at the time and the fact that they were making that call four months in advance was significant.

I had moved to the highest level.

CHAPTER SEVENTEEN

By now, a definitive professional rugby season had been firmly established. The World Cup and Heineken Cup had been inaugurated in the course of my playing career and from humble beginnings, grew to dominate the game. The latter is now the most coveted prize in club rugby but of course the World Cup is the ultimate.

So the term 'World Cup cycle' came into being, referring to each four-year period leading up to the global event.

That doesn't detract from the Six Nations and The Rugby Championship, the major club tournaments or the Lions tours. But in the same way that Cheltenham looms over the entire jumps racing season, planning for the World Cup in terms of player development and peaking at the right time is the ultimate aim of the national federations.

So it was with me. Once I had made the decision that my rugby future lay in refereeing, I approached it every bit as seriously as playing.

Like any manager, Owen was pivotal to this process. As one World Cup ended and a new cycle began, we would sit down and discuss where we were and the areas we could improve on. Then we set targets. If you don't have a target to work towards, you won't be motivated to improve. That applies in every walk of life and referees are no different. The good ones will have goals and work towards them.

For Australia, I wanted to make the panel. That was ambitious but I made it. Having done so, there was only one possible aim thereafter; to be refereeing the World Cup final in Paris in four years' time.

As one of the top tier officials, you had to want that. There were probably eight or 10 of us striving for it but I was in a very strong position and I knew it. Everything from that point until Paddy O'Brien made his announcement was geared towards realising that dream.

By around 2005, I was firmly established in the top echelon of referees and our plan was to widen the gap between me and the rest. If we saw that someone was improving, we made a very clinical commitment to finding even more of an edge. We would never accept that the current standard was good enough.

And it was 'we'. Referee and mentor. We were always looking for another percentage or two.

Take my communication for example. When I started, I was so focussed on the task at hand that I sometimes gave the impression that I wasn't approachable. Owen would get feedback of that nature from teams and you couldn't ignore it because that is part of the package. Communication is probably THE most important tool in a referee's armoury. Without it, you cannot work with teams.

So I made a conscious effort to improve that, starting off with the pre-match chat in the changing rooms beforehand. You're not there to be the clown doing party tricks but you can't be all business either. There has to be a happy medium. As someone who wouldn't be gregarious by nature, that was difficult but I got better at the small talk as time elapsed.

I trained as hard as ever but I trained smarter, with much more expertise having come into the game.

For the last decade or so of my refereeing career, I worked with a strength and conditioning coach named Karl Gilligan and he was invaluable in ensuring that I was in peak shape. Allied to things like giving up chocolate, sugar and generally having a real handle on my diet, knowledge meant I was in better nick at 40 than 25. The only thing missing might have been half a yard of pace and some hair but I was still pretty rapid across the turf.

I brought a whole new benchmark to training, eating right. The other referees looked at me having my porridge for breakfast, with five or six egg whites. I'd have my protein shakes during the day and train really hard. I felt it was important to look in physically good shape too. Players noted that.

I learned about mental preparation too and that developed over time. In fact I was improving in this aspect right up to when I hung up the whistle. It isn't fair on players to come at these things half-assed, particularly now that this is their livelihoods. You owe it to them to be ready and able.

One tool I used was to ask myself the question *Do I need it?* to prevent me blowing too quickly. Sometimes you might be too quick off the draw and the ball was there. So that phrase buys you a second.

The important thing is to come to the right conclusion. Mental clarity is imperative in achieving that.

Sometimes, life can get in the way though. I never found work an issue but there was one game where my focus was off after a bad week of preparation, although I didn't think that was the case at the time. Mentally, I was off and it showed.

It was Italy-Scotland in the Stadio Olimpico in March 2012 and Mum found out in the week before that she had breast cancer. I didn't tell anybody and just did the game. It was a bit like the England-New Zealand game when I was a bit tetchy and even the commentators noticed it.

What I think now is that at my very core, I didn't care. I didn't think it would affect me like that in terms of doing the game properly but it clearly did and the two teams deserved better than what I gave them, even if they weren't on fire themselves. But I was having far too many conversations that were too long and too cranky. I made too many decisions.

I did consider pulling out but Mum would have killed me had I done so. It was a tough one but in hindsight, I should have because I just wasn't there.

'What the fuck were you at?' was Owen's immediate response.

So I told him while failing to prevent the tears falling. It was a very worrying time. My mother is such a rock and seemed indestructible to us. She has held us all together through our lives, through the restaurant going to the wall, Dad's illness and his death. She is a beacon of positivity and endurance.

I broke down the first two or three times I told people about her having cancer. I found it really difficult to get it out. She means the world to us.

Mum is fine now, thankfully. She turned 70 last November and it was a real celebration, though she didn't want any big deal made of it. But she is a big deal so she had no choice.

▐ ▌ ■ ▌ ▐

A lot of what we do is pictures, so we need to tell ourselves things as well as players. If we are at a breakdown and it's just the tackle but it's not a maul, players are allowed to do an awful lot more once it becomes a ruck.

So you are sometimes saying to yourself, *don't get tackled, now it's a ruck* to ensure that you are refereeing the right facet of play. That helped me a fair bit.

As I got into it, I found myself saying these phrases less because they were happening automatically. I practised them, just as I did my passing and box-kicking when I was playing. If I felt there was a particular game where I needed to work harder at something or was going through a stage where I was getting to the breakdown a split-second later than I should maybe, I found it a handy tool. You don't want to miss the first infringement.

Visualisation became a really important part of my pre-match mental preparation. For example, you might know from previous games that the scrum or the breakdown was going to be challenging. Without predetermining anything, you needed to have a plan in place as regards what you were going to do and say. You must have a process worked out.

In the week leading up to the game, I would spend 15 minutes in a quiet place to think about that. Stepping that up though, I would do the same when running so that my heartrate was up and thus be replicating a match situation when I'm under pressure, tiring and sucking hard for air.

When you get close to the goal line, you've got to be attentive. Don't get caught out of position. How do I make sure I don't get caught of position? I don't want to be going closer than three metres to the breakdown. If I do go in to find the ball, make sure to get back out to the 10-12 channel.

These are things you are thinking about at home or doing a bench press. But to really make sure you can rely on these thought processes in a game situation, you have to think about them when your heartrate is racing beyond

180 towards 190.

I do a running drill where I start my first two minutes on 10km per hour. Then I increase it every minute from 12km per hour to 15 and back down to 12. I repeat that from 12-16kmph and back down, 12-18kmph and back down and finally in the last set, I bring it up to 20kmph.

When I'm on 20kmph, I am working really hard. This is when I bring in my visualisation.

Positioning. Don't get too close.

When you are able to do it under that physical and mental duress, you'll be okay. You are just rehearsing and reinforcing. It makes a big difference. Referees that appear to have all the time in the world and seem to have everything under control have processes. They have prepared for all eventualities.

Positioning was also something I worked on. You need to be in the place that allowed you to move to the next stage without any delay and without getting in the way. That isn't as easy as it sounds. Sometimes I was a bit lazy in this regard because I was very quick. So I might be a bit late leaving one stage to get to the next. I'd walk then sprint.

'Rollers, you need to run, then walk. Not the other way around,' was Owen's message.

You don't want to risk missing the first infringement so I would prime my touchies to give me a kick in the arse if they saw me walking.

'Fucking run Rollers.'

In the early days, I would get too close to the players, thinking as a scrum half rather than a referee. In one game between Leicester and Stade Francais I got stuck at the bottom of a ruck because I had been anticipating the play to go one way, and at the last second, the player cut back straight into me and I hit the deck.

I was pinned and couldn't get the whistle to my mouth to stop play. The players stopped of their own volition, picked me up, dusted me down and had a good laugh at my expense. I had to do better and I did.

Owen is razor sharp when it comes to this type of stuff. I was probably a nightmare for him initially because I could justify every decision I made. Ironically, given that I was a referee so long, Lizzie reckons I have little respect for authority. I'd have a row with a Garda if I thought I was right. To be fair,

I certainly had little time for referees until I became one.

It took me a little while to realise that you don't have to justify every call you make. Sometimes you're wrong.

'I'm not fucking wrong! Look under Law 10… I'm entitled to call that.'

Eventually I developed the notion of materiality. Was there need for that sanction? Look how quickly the ball was gone. I was too quick on the trigger. It sunk in that Owen was just giving me constructive feedback to make me better. If I took it on board, I'd be a better referee.

It is just like coaching a player. When you see something you have passed on coming off in a game, it's a great feeling. I am getting that with some of the work I am doing with referees now. There is tremendous satisfaction in seeing them take the information on board and improving as a result.

I had a checklist that I went through before every game. It contained a number of these phrases or reminders, covering the aspects of the game I needed to focus on, be it in terms of the game itself or me and my triggers. I added to them routinely over the years.

I would do it just before the comms went on. Find a small private compartment for a minute and go through the bullet points to reaffirm them in my mind.

Be the facilitator and don't get frustrated

The three Cs – conscious, courteous, calm

Specific and factual when talking

Quality decision

Arrive at the breakdown facing the goal line

No closer than 3m to the gainline

Run then walk

Don't get left behind, anticipate

Stick to my parameters on foul play

Watch for coming in from the side

Binding at scrums

Obstructions at lineout

Kick-offs

Fully bound at the maul

There are more. The three Cs were important for me because I could get snappy and lose my composure quickly. The temperature would rise in a heartbeat.

I'm actual proof that you can change your behaviour. Every action is your responsibility but you need to acknowledge your weaknesses and then have a process to address it. It's the same with players and 'That's the way I am' is not an excuse. You can control it.

The process is first to identify the problem. So with me, the identification is that my tolerance levels are reducing. As soon as that happens, you realise you need to defuse it and I had my triggers. Repeating the three Cs was my initial approach.

There were some occasions after I had been tetchy in the first half where I came in, blew off some steam with the lads and then read my list once more. You have to get your focus back. That's your job.

‖ ∎ ‖

There were some significant ticks along the way towards the World Cup. Being appointed to my first Heineken Cup final in 2004 was a wonderful landmark. To have my Irish colleagues Donal Courtney and Dave McHugh as TJs and Alan Lewis as TMO made it a tremendous success for Owen.

It was fantastic to be part of this competition as it expanded and became the most relevant club competition in world rugby. I was extremely fortunate to get to referee three finals, finishing my career with the 2014 decider. Had Leinster and Munster not been so successful, I would probably have gotten more and it was nine years before I got selected for my second.

That didn't bother me. I am an Irish rugby man first and foremost and if I couldn't get a final because Irish teams were involved, I was delighted with that.

That might sound like bollocks but it's genuine.

Until John Lacey came along, I was the only man to both play and referee in the Heineken Cup. John played in the 1997-98 campaign and scored four tries for Munster. He is doing an excellent job with the whistle now.

My first Heineken Cup decider between Stade Toulouse and Wasps at Twickenham was only my 12th appointment in the tournament and my first in the knockout stages. It was an amazing game remembered for its dramatic conclusion. I walked off the Twickenham pitch afterwards thinking, *How the hell did Wasps win that?*

Toulouse had an unbelievable offloading game. Their first try just before half time by Yann Delaigue came at the end of a passage of play that included so many passes out of the tackle. Many of them were executed under extreme duress, one-handed or over the top. They should have had another two tries really.

Having said that, the Londoners led for most of the game despite Toulouse dominating possession and territory. Yet Wasps, with Lawrence Dallaglio at his most defiant, defended in a manner that became their calling card under Warren Gatland. Shaun Edwards' influence was there for all to see, just as it was when Wales made a record 250 tackles in their 23-16 Six Nations victory over Ireland in Cardiff last March.

Some of the hits were savage. Wasps always brought that physical intensity, with Joe Worsley and Paul Volley supporting Dallaglio brilliantly as backrow enforcers. Toulouse had big men in the pack too, like Trevor Brennan, Fabien Pelous and Finau Maka.

It wasn't until four minutes remaining that Jean-Baptiste Ellisalde brought Toulouse level at 20-20 and you would have banked on Guy Noves' outfit driving on from there, even if they might need extra time.

What unfolded next did so almost in slow motion. Clément Poitrenaud was the Toulouse fullback in the perfect position to deal with the situation but he waited and waited, expecting the ball to either bounce into touch or continue its momentum to the in-goal area.

Agonisingly for the Frenchman, Howley's kick was judged to absolute perfection and held up. At the last second Poitrenaud reached for the ball as the veteran Welshman bore down on him. For a split-second, he even had it in his hands.

Howley was upon him now though, his eyes wide like a lion pouncing on prey. He dived forward, with nothing to lose and managed to slap through Poitrenaud's hands, freeing it from his opponent's grasp and grounding it in one motion.

I know all this now having seen the footage many times since but in that moment, I did not have a clue whether it was a score or not. Nobody did. Not even the players involved. You could see the despair in Poitrenaud's eyes. He feared the worst and was hoping for the best. Howley didn't celebrate. He was unsure.

There was real suspense as I went upstairs to Lewy. A score and Wasps had grabbed a spectacular victory. Be assured that I was as excited as anyone by the drama of it. You love being involved in a spectacle like that.

'Try, yes or no?'

'You may award the try.'

Holy Shit! I thought and raised my arm. The place went ballistic.

The unbelievable France-New Zealand Test in Paris came along at the end of the year and the big games kept on coming. Six Nations, Tri Nations, Heineken Cup.

The Six Nations was hugely exciting in 2007 and in circumstances that were similar to this year's denouement, three teams could win the title on the final day. This time Ireland lost out to France on a score difference of four points, after conceding a converted try in the last play of the game.

I had Wales-England in the Millennium Stadium and by the time we kicked off, Ireland and France had both won. England needed to win by 57 points to claim the overall honours and that was never going to happen.

Nevertheless, with the hosts having lost every game, England were hot favourites but Wales love giving their old rivals a bloody nose.

Those twin motivations propelled them to a stunning performance, particularly in the opening quarter of an hour when they flew into a 15-0 lead thanks to tries from James Hook and Chris Horsman.

England brought it back to 18-15 by the interval with tries from Harry Ellis and a typically brilliant effort by Jason Robinson. They drew level in the second half but Hook kicked two penalties either side of a drop goal to send most of the 74,500 fans home in ecstasy.

I had South Africa-New Zealand in the Tri Nations next and then France-England in a World Cup warm-up. It was all boiling up nicely for the big one.

CHAPTER
EIGHTEEN

My experiences as a player with Ireland taught me never to take anything for granted but it would be a lie to say that the sense of anticipation about the naming of the referees' list for the World Cup was the same as four years earlier. It couldn't be because I knew I would be there. The type of fixtures I was getting told me that.

With Ireland, I never played two games in succession. As a referee it was week-in, week-out, top games. You knew you were rated. That fuels your confidence and performances improve more as a result as long as you don't get cocky.

So when the tournament came around, I fixated on getting the final.

It was a strange dynamic within the group of referees at a major tournament like this, completely different to the norm. Generally, you get a game, do the game and move on. At the start of the Heineken Cup you'd like to get the final but the final is seven months after the competition commences. There are no finals in the Six Nations or Rugby Championship.

At the World Cup, you are there as a group staying together and working together for two months. That is a completely different environment. There are 12 referees there, all chasing the Holy Grail. Yet we have to combine as a team during the course of the competition.

Some guys really struggle with that. It was very obvious at times and you still see it on occasion, when something happens and you wonder why the TJ didn't provide the information to the man in the middle.

I flipped it around, reasoning that being helpful generally around the place or to whoever was refereeing while you were a touch judge, would enhance how the selectors saw you.

Of course it crosses your mind that by making a guy look good you are strengthening his case to get one of the knockout games and especially the final, at the same time undermining your own opportunity. But that's the World Cup environment for referees. Working together while retaining personal ambition.

That's not to say you grieved if a rival made a fuck up. You weren't thinking it was great but I would doubt if you could be human and for it not to cross your mind that a bad mistake represented docked marks and could only boost your own case.

While I cherished the notion of getting the final and felt I had a very strong argument for getting it, I had seen in 2003 what it looked like when a ref arrived to do the final. There were one or two guys that almost went through the motions in the pool matches because they expected to get the final but they stuffed up as a result and put themselves out of contention.

I was a man on a mission and being in the top two or three would mean nothing if I didn't perform in each of my games at the tournament. Having told us how they were going to make the appointments, it was clear that I needed to get a quarter-final so that became the shorter-term focus.

Lewy and I were the Irish referees selected, with Simon McDowell amongst a panel of touch judges. Lewy and I were chalk and cheese as individuals. I'm quiet and he is a complete social animal.

We really drove each other in an era when we were two of the top refs in Europe. I considered it a blow when he was selected ahead of me to do the Heineken Cup final just before the World Cup, in which Wasps beat Leicester in Twickenham.

I was gutted because I thought I should have gotten it but gave my all as Lewy's touch judge. I wasn't resentful at all, just disappointed. On the day, he was the man and we had to work as a team despite the rivalry that had pushed us to improve all the time.

In fairness to Owen, he knew us both well and the decision must have been difficult for him. I think maybe my standard might have dropped to a seven out of 10 in one or two games and Owen felt with the World Cup around the corner, I didn't need a high profile game to go wrong on me. He made the judgement that I could do with being out of the spotlight for a little while. I would have to say he was right.

▐ █ █ ▐

Wales-Canada passed without incident but I had to send off Namibia's No 8 Jacques Nieuwenhuis during their 87-10 loss to France for a dangerous tackle on Sebastien Chabal. Nieuwenhuis had scored a try against Ireland in the first round and is now a referee himself in South Africa.

I had no option but to pull out the red card having warned him twice for high tackles already. When he levelled Chabal I just reached into my pocket immediately. He had to go. France ran riot and finished with 13 tries. Vincent Clerc nabbed three and Jean-Baptiste Ellisalde notched up 27 points.

England-Tonga was my last group game and when the quarter-final appointments were announced, I had England once more in the quarter-final against Australia. Lewy got South Africa-Fiji, making it the first time two Irishmen were refereeing at that stage of a World Cup. It was another massive testament to Owen's work.

Before the game the Aussies were doing plenty of chirping about England gamesmanship. They either didn't get the irony of that or didn't care.

Australia head coach, John Connolly focussed on the throwing of England hooker Mark Regan into lineouts, claiming that the player he had formerly coached at Bath had a tendency to literally step over the line. He made a submission to Paddy O'Brien about it, saying that England picking him was a statement of intent.

Clearly, coaches that do this are trying to plant a seed in a referee's head. Sometimes, they might have a word with you in the pre-match chat.

It never worked with me. I would deflect any comments made directly, letting them know in no uncertain terms that the previous game was irrelevant to this one. I adjudicated on what was happening in front of me.

So I took no notice of Connolly's comments. It was a big game for them and it was huge for me too. I knew I had to nail this one. Get out without any controversy, not be a factor in the game. I managed to do that.

Mind you, the first set of scrums was really difficult and challenging. There were four resets before I gave a penalty against Andrew Sheridan, a decision he wasn't happy about. It just required a significant amount of refereeing and concentration. There was a brief exchange of opinions between the front rows after the second collapse.

This was a real examination and it was absolutely imperative that I kept my composure. I had to be patient but firm and felt I managed the situation well. All the work done with Owen bore fruit there and the front rows got their act together as the game wore on.

Having been a scrum half and spent so much time at scrummaging practice to work on timings with the hooker, I grew to understand the scrum better than most backs. I would never claim to know everything about what goes on in the inner sanctum of that particular demonic workplace but am clear on feet positions, angles, bindings and so on.

Ronan O'Gara wrote in the *Irish Examiner* not so long ago that the time had come for a former front-row player to be in the booth with the TMO. He said he hadn't a notion what was going on in there and that he thought referees were guessing.

Some are, because they haven't the foggiest. You can see when that is happening. Some guys know they have to give a penalty but don't know who transgressed and just pick one side.

The difficulty for referees now is that teams are being coached to win penalties at the set piece. As someone who is involved in training young referees now, it is impossible to give them all the information they need because of how teams are approaching it.

If players and coaches bought into the scrum being a straight-up contest, you wouldn't have half the messing that we've seen the last few years. When a scrum is collapsing all the time, it's not because of the way I tell them to crouch, bind and set. I don't make them take the wrong angle. So it's player attitude and coaching.

I would observe a number of things before the ball goes in. How's the bind for the loose head? Is his head and shoulders above his hips? Is he tight on his hooker or is he sticking his arse out and working his way in? How's the tight head binding? Where are his feet?

So if the ball goes in and doesn't come out, I must decide from what I observed before the put-in what the reason for that is. It's not always the team not putting in that is responsible. Sometimes the team with the ball will try to push up out of a scrum to give the impression they are dominant and the defending pack is transgressing.

You have to have all that in your mind before the ball goes in and then in a split-second, make a decision as to why the scrum wasn't completed.

Scrums have become a massive issue but should not be neutered. They are not just a means of restarting a game and should never be. There is an opportunity to contest for the ball. But what is happening now is that more teams are viewing it as a chance to win a penalty, especially if it's within kicking distance, rather than a means of getting quick ball to get something going.

There are more ex-players becoming referees now though not so many former front-rowers. However, even if you did have a hooker take up the whistle, I'm not sure it would make a difference. A lot of the time guys pick themselves up after a collapsed scrum with no notion as to who was responsible because technically, there are so many ways of doing it. That's the kind of minefield it is.

▎▐▎

We got on top of it though and the result was in doubt right to the end. With less than three minutes remaining, England were leading 12-10 thanks to four Wilkinson penalties when I had to penalise Joe Worsley for coming in on the side. There is a part of you in that situation that doesn't want to give it because of the enormity of the situation and the attention it draws on you, but I had to. It was a clear transgression.

I can still see the look on Joe's face. He trudged back towards the goal line with his hands on his head, clearly distraught. It reminds me of Paddy Wallace after conceding the late penalty in Ireland's Grand Slam decider against Wales two years later. On a human level, I felt terrible for him and while it wasn't that I wanted Stirling to miss, I was pleased for Joe that his stupid penalty wasn't so costly. Of course by dragging his kick a couple of feet wide, the pain was Mortlock's.

From a selfish point of view, the miss guaranteed that I wouldn't be linked to the main story the next day and that was always the aim. Mind you, the transgression was so clearcut it is Worsley who would have been criticised. The margins can be very fine at times.

When you have a game as tight as that in the last 10 or 15 minutes, you are not looking for marginal decisions. They have to be obvious. Your mindset is completely different to a one-sided affair when you're coasting, letting a bit more go. You're judging things on the materiality and when one team is 20 or 30 points clear, there is a lot more room for manoeuvre.

With a margin of one or two points, you are incredibly focussed. The Heineken Cup semi-final I did between Leicester and Cardiff at the Millennium Stadium in 2009 was another example.

There was so little between the sides that they ended up being separated by a sudden death penalty shootout. In the last 10 minutes of normal time and even more so in injury time, you could see that it had affected the players themselves. There were collisions but the players were almost tip-toeing around because they were afraid to give anything away. They were being super-compliant.

In that situation, you want the teams to decide it. In an ideal world, one outfit orchestrates a try and they are deserving winners. You don't want to be the one who decides it so if there is a penalty, it has to be absolutely definite that the player came in from the side or that the loose head dropping was definitely the cause for the collapsed scrum. There can be no doubt because you don't want to be the difference between winning and losing.

Everybody makes mistakes and you go out knowing there are bound to be one or two. It is human nature. In those last 10 minutes though, there is intense scrutiny on every decision and non-decision. You need courage to want to be in this situation and not hide from it.

CHAPTER NINETEEN

The days immediately following Paddy O'Brien's announcement about my selection to referee the World Cup final were hectic. After a few minutes crying on Joël Dumé's shoulder, I composed myself and rang Owen. I couldn't talk. Then I rang Lizzie and I couldn't talk. The emotions were rendering me, not just incoherent, but mute.

The media demands were a little overwhelming in the next few days, particularly for someone not accustomed to it. It was an area I advised Craig on when he got the 2011 final. Get them all out of the way as quickly as possible and then cut yourself off from Wednesday afternoon. You need to start focussing on the game then.

I had an advantage in that regard though as in 2011 the announcement wasn't made until after the semi-finals. Four years earlier it was after the quarter-finals and I would not have a semi-final to prepare for either. So I could be a bit more relaxed about it.

The goodwill from Ireland was tremendous. I took calls from *Morning Ireland* and many other shows, while the recently-elected Taoiseach, Bertie Ahern sent me a letter. The Irish team had travelled with very high hopes after a couple of good years under my old coach Eddie O'Sullivan but for some reason, it never clicked for them in France. Me getting the final was no consolation but generally I think people took a small bit of satisfaction from that and certainly, I would have felt that I was representing my country.

I got it on the double though because in France, it was treated almost as if one of their own had been appointed. So I told my story and Dad's story many times over those few days.

▮▮▮▮

Because I wasn't involved in the semi-finals, I could go back home to see the family and do some work. I had commuted at regular intervals anyway. That made it very different from 2011 in New Zealand when I spent 57 days away from home.

Romain Poite and I were the only two referees that didn't have any of our family out at some stage of that trip. I enquired about it alright but it would have cost 10 grand and as Lizzie said, if we were going to spend that sort of money, it would be on a holiday destination of our actual choosing rather than one of necessity, where I wouldn't be around half of the time. I found that very tough to be away from them all so long but she was right adamant she didn't want to go.

She would not have had the best memories of travelling to the southern hemisphere for the World Cup anyway. In 2003, she came down to Australia for the knockout stages, when we would only have games at the weekends.

We were based in Coogee, which sounds idyllic, but Lizzie was seven months pregnant with Natasha and had a four-year-old (Mark) and two-year-old (Clodagh) in tow. What's more, Clodagh caught the fucking chicken pox when we were there!

That caused a bit of grief for the other referees because as soon as our team doctor heard about it, he wanted to give a vaccination they have in Australia for chicken pox to anyone who hadn't had the condition before. I remember Walshy ringing his mother to find out if he had had it. The answer was no so it was a jab in the ass for him.

There were no such difficulties with France and I returned to Ireland as the World Cup final referee, catching up on some work and dealing with the builders working on an the extension of our newly purchased home in Foxrock.

The place was a bit of a mess and we had to improvise on a lot of things. I remember Lizzie handing me dishes through the window for me to dry. I would then have to go around the back and tiptoe gingerly across the new tiles to find somewhere to put them away.

There was no fear of getting any notions of myself that's for sure. It was a brilliant few days though and nice to get completely away from the bubble of the World Cup, where the tournament was all everybody talked about. That normality and balance was vital in the lead up to the biggest day of my refereeing career.

∎∎∎

Lizzie and Mark came back over with me. Mum and her partner Richard, who has been a brilliant companion for her since Dad died, made the trip as well. We went out for a bite to eat with the rest of the officials the night before the game and everyone was in great form.

Mark was only seven, not really aware of the scale of the event taking place but still knowing there was a big match coming up. On the day, I went for a walk with him along the Champs Elysees and we had a lovely time. We both have a soft spot for crepes so we stopped at a stall to pick up some.

We bumped into George Hook along the way.

'Howya Rollers. All set? You've been doing a great job.'

He is as gregarious away from television and radio as he is on it. I know he isn't everybody's cup of tea but he's a great character.

We returned to the hotel and went to sleep at around 2.30pm until 5pm. I would do that on a day when there's any late kick-off. I wouldn't last otherwise. It wasn't because I was a non-drinker that I was in bed before midnight as a player, earning the Cinders nickname. It was because I love my kip.

It was an indication of how comfortable I was feeling though. There were no real nerves. Anticipation, most definitely, but not so much that I couldn't sleep. It's probably why I was able to combine work with top flight refereeing for so long. I could catch up on the shut-eye on planes and in airports no problem.

I felt fresh when I got up, showered, shaved and put on my Number Ones. Then it was onto the team meeting with the other officials from 5.30pm to 6.15pm. Joël Jutge and Paul Honiss were my touchies, with Lewy and Walshy four and five. Stuart Dickinson was TMO.

It was probably difficult for Lewy, as it was for the other guys. But being from the same Union accentuated it. If the shoe had been on the other foot I would have been fucking gutted. I'd have been delighted for him but hugely envious. That's human nature so I would have no problem him feeling like that.

All you asked was that once the call was made, they gave their best to ensure the game went smoothly and no-one noticed us, if at all possible. That's what I would do every time, without question.

I took them out for lunch and went through all the procedures, just like I would for every other game. We discussed touch, touch in goal, foul play and so on, every conceivable aspect so that we had all the bases covered.

For example, when play is going on I am looking at the ball. The leading TJ is looking at the ball. The trailing TJ stays back and keeps an eye on the bodies, even if there is a kick or a long pass. That is imperative because so much can happen when guys are getting up from a ruck or a scrum. And there are still two of us watching the action.

That was the type of thing we went through and when that was done, we were ready to be collected at 7pm to take us to the stadium. It was a three-car cavalcade. I travelled with Joël, Paul and Stuart. Lizzie, Mark, Mum and Richard were in another car and Mark loved the idea that we had two outriders leading the way. He felt very important! Poor Lizzie was planking it for me and I would say she barely watched the game. Mum was the same.

We were there in 20 minutes. It was time.

| ■ ■ |

The game itself won't go down in the annals as one of the great finals. Big games can be like that at times, when there is so much at stake. Nobody wants to make a mistake so even the semblance of a risk is avoided.

Overall the tournament had been pretty dour. It was largely a kicking tournament and after it was over, there was a loud clamour for change. The World Cup is the game's shop window and for those two months, it wasn't all that attractive. The IRB changed a number of laws subsequently in a bid to address that and they were largely successful.

As usual, I enjoyed the razzmatazz and the build-up. I told myself to take it all in because I might never be there again. I had worked hard for this very moment and sacrificed a lot. So had my family. It would be a shame if I couldn't appreciate it. It was a massive responsibility but it was a privilege too.

One of the real standout moments was when I blew the whistle and Jonny Wilkinson kicked off. It was as if the whistle had a direct link to every camera on the planet. A gazillion lights went off and for a nanosecond you were aware of it, almost in a different place. Then you were into it and the game was off. Down to business.

England got there relying on Jonny but it was similar with South Africa and Percy Montgomery. Neither side was expansive but the Springboks in particular were very good up front. They had pummelled England 36-0 in the pool stages but Brian Ashton's men turned it around pretty impressively to get to the final.

The Springboks had too much power in the end though and won 15-6. It was in keeping with the tournament in general that it was decided on penalties.

There was one try opportunity and it was a major talking point afterwards. It came to England, very early in the second half and had they scored, it might well have changed the course of the game.

It came from a brilliant sniping break by Matthew Tait and when the ball was recycled, Mark Cueto dived for the corner, with Danie Roussow making the tackle. In real time, it was just impossible to determine whether or not the winger had gone into touch before dotting down. So I had to refer it to Stuart in the booth.

He took a long time to come to a decision, looking at every conceivable angle. He wanted to be sure and of course, he needed to be, but it took an age.

There was nothing I could do about it. When I saw the replay first I said to Joël 'Jesus he looks in touch.' So I made the decision that if Stuart went that way, I would go back for a penalty because Schalk Burger had slowed the ball down illegally.

In hindsight, I should have binned Berger too because he slowed it down enough to merit that. I don't know why I didn't but it's not the reason England lost. It would have been the right decision though.

There was a lot of doubt immediately afterwards whether we had made the right decision on the try. The discussion continued in the changing room.

We had our meal and the guys had a few beers in when somebody went online and saw the photograph that proved definitively that Stuart had made the right call. There were inches in it but Cueto's leg was clearly touching the line before he got the ball down. I was so relieved for Stuart because he was the one getting it in the neck, with many insisting he had gotten it wrong.

It was only then that Paddy O'Brien allowed himself a drink!

There was a nice moment at the final whistle when South Africa captain, John Smith shook my hand and gave me a big hug. It was just an off-the-cuff, emotional reaction by him at reaching the pinnacle of a rugby player's life as captain of a World Cup winning team. I just happened to be the closest person to him.

John refers to that a lot now when he gives speeches, joking that he feels sorry for me that I had to be subjected to it.

I worked with some great captains but John was top of the list. He was South Africa's 50th captain and they picked a good one for such a landmark appointment. He is an out-and-out gentleman and I always had a very good rapport with him.

As a consultant with World Rugby I spend a bit of time with the captains of the teams I'm working with now, explaining how there's a certain way to approach a referee. It's about the timing and tone of your query. What you say and how you say it. That is very powerful in terms of getting the ref's attention. Not that he is likely to change a decision but if things aren't going your way he's more likely to help you sort it out.

John was brilliant at this. He knew what buttons to press at the right time. All the top guys did. It's important not to make the referee feel like he is the enemy. Ultimately, everyone wants to achieve the same thing so you're better off working together to do that.

There was a bit of controversy in the GAA world about an article written during the summer claiming that the Kerry footballers made a special attempt to get the referee onside. They considered the claim an affront. I don't understand why. It is just a sensible thing to do. It might not get you anything but a working relationship is vital.

The article was written initially in the context of the All Blacks apparently making a clear decision ahead of the 2011 World Cup to engage the referee positively. Having previously deemed the official as someone they couldn't control, they now felt that they could have some impact.

It isn't anything furtive. It's just about getting on the referee's good side. They would credit a call made against them when it was an obvious one. They would be mannerly. Have a chat during a break in the play and perhaps attempt to plant a seed. Richie McCaw was always good in this regard anyway.

There is nothing underhand or sly about this. Good captains have this art and the relationship between the referee and captains is integral to the production of an entertaining game of rugby. It just makes sense though that if you piss off a referee, it's going to be tough to get a 50-50 call. John understood that and we had a tremendous working relationship. I was happy for him at the end and left him to his celebrations.

I had gotten accreditation for the family to go to the post-match reception but got a big surprise when I ran into Mum as I walked in from the tunnel to the changing room after the game. Standing right there, with a big smile and the hint of a tear.

'How he hell did you get here?'

She had just blagged her way in. Even the thought of it makes me smile now. That's Mum. Gift of the gab and a flutter of the eyelashes.

She wanted to be there for me when I came in. We were both thinking the same thing, how great it would have been for Dad to see me in this setting, refereeing the biggest game in rugby, in Paris. He wasn't unfortunately, but we were.

CHAPTER TWENTY

Getting back to normality wasn't a big problem because I had been commuting over and back to my job as General Manager of Cornmarket's mortgage division. There was a tremendous reaction from people but particularly from the rugby family. I was blown away by the sense of goodwill, the kind words and the presentations.

We jumped straight into the Heineken Cup and my first game was back in Paris, at the Stade Jean-Bouin, where Stade Francais played host to Harlequins. Fabien Galthié was the Stade coach and we always got on well, bound by our ties in the brotherhood of scrum halves and a shared philosophy in how the game should be played. He had a restaurant too that served duck like no place else I had ever tasted!

I went into the Stade dressing room to do my customary pre-game boots' check and chat with the front rows but before I could start Fabien stood up on a bench and said a few words.

'On behalf of the whole team and club, we have to say it's an absolute honour to have you here.'

Fuck sake! I'm thinking, *I'm about to referee these guys.*

He wasn't blowing smoke up my arse though or trying to get me onside ahead of the game. It was genuine. I found it very humbling and didn't know what to say. It was a bit embarrassing.

'Thanks very much for your kind words Fabien but it's back to business now,' was just about the gist of my reaction.

Stade won comfortably enough and afterwards, their wing-forward, Remy Martin came into the ref's changing room.

'Alain, I just want to say thank you. It was amazing being reffed by you. We just love when you ref our games.'

The reception in France was always good because of my background but it rocketed to another level after the World Cup. They considered me a French success story. So I posed for photographs and signed autographs.

After the game we went to an amazing function at Roland Garros, where tennis' French Open is held.

When that was over, I arranged to meet up with the two motorbike police who escorted our mini-cavalcade to the Stade de France from our hotel for the World Cup final – Patricia and Louis. Patricia came to our hotel to meet us and we met up with Louis at a place where a lot of their colleagues hung out.

As we walked in the door they let out a huge roar to greet us. So we joined them, had something to eat and they had a few beers. As occurred through the entire weekend, they would not let us pay for anything. It was the cheapest Paris weekend you could ever imagine. David Wilkinson and Alan Rogan were my touch judges and their eyes were on sticks. I had to explain that it wasn't like this all the time!

Before that, I had done a club game down in Cork Con. Kenny Murphy came up to me.

'Jaysus Rollers, bit of a drop from the World Cup final to coming down here. What did you say and to whom?'

'I never forget my roots, Kenny.'

It was banter but my approach to doing an AIL game was the same as the World Cup final. They were expecting one of the top referees in the world. That was the standard so if you couldn't be arsed, you were letting them and yourself down.

I was still committed to ensuring that I could facilitate the two teams being able to play. That was really important because the last thing I wanted was to suddenly think it was about me. The moment you think it's about you,

you're dead. You will be found out because your decision-making will suffer.

So I had no difficulty motivating myself. I had raised the bar and even if a dip in level might be better than anything they were accustomed to, it would not be what they were entitled to from me.

As is often the case, I needed some experience to gain this understanding. I did a warm-up game in Belfast once before a Test and I made a few mistakes. Afterwards, Stephen Hilditch had a quiet word with me.

'You owe it to those teams to be refereeing as well as you can because they don't often have the opportunity to get top referees at their games. They are entitled to that. You have to give them what they are expecting and should never, ever take doing the job correctly for granted.'

That struck a chord with me. Every time I went back to a club or schools' game after that, I gave it my best shot.

There is another positive to doing these games too in that you are not mic'd up and there are no cameras. That means you can have more banter with the players and in a less sanitised fashion, which invariably makes them very enjoyable indeed.

It also makes it easier to change behaviour. I recall doing Young Munster against St Mary's once and there was some messing going on at one side of the scrum. I cut to the chase.

'You do that again you'll be off so fucking fast your head will spin.'

That short, sharp shock tends to be effective in such a testosterone-fuelled world but unfortunately you can't do that when every word you say is being blasted around the world.

▮ ▮ ▮ ▮

Refereeing a World Cup final is the ultimate taste of success. There are two responses to that. Your hunger is satisfied or you want to sample the delights once more. My appetite was far from sated. So when I met up with Owen to look at the next four years and what I wanted to achieve, being referee of the next World Cup final was top of the list.

Not everybody would have ranked me as top referee in the world. It might have been number two or number three. But I had been selected to do the final so to my mind, there must be some perceived gap in my favour. I had to work to maintain that gap at least, if not widen it. Set the standard that everyone else needed to strive to get to and when they did, have already moved on to another level.

Staying at the top is always harder than getting there because everyone wants to knock you off your perch. The real challenge started now but I was motivated to do whatever it took. It was all about keeping a bit of daylight between me and the rest.

It was really important that I avoided a train crash and I managed that throughout my career. Everyone makes mistakes but there was no game where I refereed so badly that a team lost directly because of my officiating. Plenty of coaches and players might disagree of course.

There were games when I didn't perform at optimum level. There were occasions when I failed to change player behaviour and reacted poorly to that. These were the kinds of areas I needed to focus on to get better.

I had a very bad day at the office for the England-New Zealand Test at Twickenham in November 2008. It wasn't that I got a lot of decisions wrong but England didn't come to play and clearly had a plan to disrupt New Zealand by any means.

They wouldn't be the first team in history to attempt that but there are methods of dissuading teams in terms of sanctions but I could not get England to change. That failure made me irritable and that irritability was there for all to see. The unwillingness of their captain, Steve Borthwick to help me in any way poured fuel on the fire.

Ironically, one of England's greatest captains, Martin Johnson had just taken over from his former teammate, Andy Robinson as head coach. Borthwick was the complete opposite of Johnno and Lawrence Dallaglio, not to mind John Smit and Richie McCaw. He couldn't give a shit what I was saying or doing. He definitely wasn't going back to his players and laying down the law to them.

This wasn't the first time I had issues with Steve. In the 2006 Heineken Cup semi-final, he was skipper of a Bath team taking on Biarritz in San Sebastien. The roles were pretty similar. The French side was blessed with the talent to punish teams by playing an expansive game. Bath wanted it to be a dogfight.

Borthwick was captain and at half time I told him he needed to talk to his players. If he did, it wasn't to tell them they needed to get their act together because the penalty county was 7-1 in Biarritz's favour in the second half.

Maybe he didn't like me. He certainly didn't give the impression he wanted to work with me and that was always going to cause problems. Yet I had England quite a bit before the All Black game. In fact in the 11 months before it, I refereed England five times and there was no inkling of a problem.

We had one this time though and it obviously came down to England aiming for maximum negativity.

My first mistake was that I never saw it coming and I should have. It had been a tough autumn for England and they had been booed off Twickenham when shipping five tries in a heavy defeat to South Africa.

This was a Grand Slam match for New Zealand, having already beaten Scotland, Ireland and Wales. England were under huge pressure and with Johnson in charge, the supporters expected a show of defiance. They provided a little bit themselves when offering up a deafening rendition of *Swing Low Sweet Chariot* during The Haka. But the team wasn't good and they were always going to be embarking on a damage limitation exercise.

I was feeling good, with the Wales-South Africa Test two weeks previously having gone well but the first two New Zealand lineouts took a long time to get going, while the first scrum had to be reset and was very unstable. But I was far too quick to act. I probably got caught up in the occasion a little bit and became too excited.

I spoke to Borthwick for the first time after around 20 minutes. England had conceded eight penalties after half an hour and both Lee Mears and James Haskell had been sent to the bin. Most teams try not to give away more than eight in a match. At one stage, Danny Care dived straight over the ruck and I should've carded him too but I was trying to manage the situation. It was a fucking stupid penalty.

I talked to both captains then. As Richie McCaw moved towards me and Steve, the England captain waved his New Zealand counterpart away dismissively as if to say 'Fuck off, this has nothing to do with you.' I had to explain that I wanted McCaw in on the conversation too. There was a lot of tension and a massive undercurrent all the way through.

Two minutes into the second half I binned Toby Flood for a high tackle. A lot of people would have said it was a bit harsh. It was a penalty kick but not necessarily a yellow card. I could have left him on but with my mindset and so many infringements, the card was out of my pocket before the guy had hit the ground. It was the reaction of a completely annoyed referee.

It was obvious that I wasn't getting the message across as the penalty count totted up. My body language wasn't good as I started to get frustrated with my inability to influence the actions of the English pack in particular. I was not helping with my tone and my reactions to the players. In all, I dished out four yellow cards to English players.

'Are you trying to kill yourselves here or what?' I said in exasperation at one point. Luckily for them, Dan Carter had a rare off day, proving that he was in fact human by missing five of 11 kicks at goal. It still finished 32-6.

That was a poor performance by me in terms of managing the game. When I was doing my review, I was mortified. I made a solemn promise to myself.

Jesus, I don't want to see that person ever again.

Borthwick was surly but I responded in kind as they continued the use of unlawful tactics to prevent the All Blacks from spinning the ball got to me completely. Or more to the point, my inability to put a stop to those tactics. I just didn't handle it well.

So I was not blameless for how it went down. I lost the plot and got really pissed off. Here we had New Zealand coming to Twickenham. Two of the best sides in the world in front of a full house but one of those sides had no interest in playing.

I got ratty, and dismissive. I use a five minute clip from that game at business conferences now to highlight how bad communication looks, from a verbal and body language point of view. It does not make for pretty viewing.

Even when England had quick ball, they didn't let it out. Care was marshalling forwards around while it sat there in front of them at the base, five metres out from the All Black line. That contributed to my state of mind. Even watching the tape now it drives me mad. If we were under the current 'use it' rule it would never have been allowed stay there that long.

I do feel though if Lawrence Dallaglio had been captain, I could have said

'Lawrence, you've had three penalties now, do you want to have a word with them?' and he would have addressed the situation. Steve just did not seem to have any interest in doing that.

I don't think I had ever encountered that level of wilful negativity before, where one team was trying to play and the other did not want to play. Neither had I been confronted by such a blatant unwillingness to cooperate. I didn't react well to that. I was just thinking that this shouldn't be happening. The harder I tried, the more frustrated I got and the worse I became in dealing with the English players and Borthwick. They just got under my skin.

Even watching the tape now an hour into the game and my notes mirror the ire I felt in real time.

'Yet another stupid fucking penalty by England. Easter for diving over.'

I told him he should be gone to the bin. I was trying to keep players on the pitch but had lost control. I eventually had to bin Tom Rees five minutes from time for slowing the ball down at the breakdown. It was head-wrecking.

I learned to establish triggers to employ when I recognised that the blood was beginning to boil and that I needed to calm myself down. I used buzz words to help defuse myself, so I don't get caught up in the emotion of things as I did that particular day.

It was Owen who gave me the triggers. The main one was the term 'soft hands'. If he said it to me once in my career, he said it a thousand times. Rugby people will recognise it as relating to sympathetic handling or disposal of the ball, so it really resonated when Owen applied it in terms of the mind.

I had always had the tendency to get a little tetchy and we recognised it as a problem, particularly after this game. So this was my 'count to 10' tool.

Soft hands.

Of course it meant that I had to recognise what was happening during a game to address it. In time I did and was able to deploy my trigger to refocus and resume control. It would go too far to call it a watershed moment, given where I was in my career at that point, but there are some games you take a lot from and this was a massive learning experience.

▮▮▮

There was one other fallout with England during their Six Nations match against France at Stade de France in 2010. I was TJ for Bryce Lawrence and I ended up telling Mike Ford to fuck off. Mike was the England defence coach, having filled that position with Ireland before that and of course he is now head coach at Bath. Soft hands didn't get utilised in this situation but then I wasn't the referee and he was being a giant pain in the ass.

Entering into the last quarter of the match England were chasing the French lead and the ball was kicked directly into touch by an English player who was just outside the 22. The player contested the decision, claiming he was inside his 22 but he wasn't.

As we made our way off the pitch, Ford approached me in a very aggressive manner, arguing that his player had been inside the 22. I told him he wasn't. I don't mind someone disagreeing but Ford's manner and body language was disrespectful and threatening. He also made some negative remarks about Bryce so I told him to fuck off.

Bryce and Simon McDowell were only a few feet away and Simon looked at me in absolute horror. He hadn't heard the context of the conversation, just me telling a member of the England team's backroom staff what to do with himself. We had a bit of a laugh about it in the changing room afterwards when I explained.

That wasn't the end of it though, as about five minutes later, England's director of elite rugby, Rob Andrew arrived in. Ford had obviously been mouthing off.

'Did you tell one my coaches to fuck off?'

'I did.'

'I'm reporting you to Paddy O'Brien.'

'Be my guest.'

I think it was during this match that he had been seen on TV constantly approaching Paddy during the match giving out about countless decisions. It was bizarre and not something that happened very often in the middle of games. It certainly wouldn't be considered acceptable behaviour.

So I spoke to Paddy anyway and explained the situation. I never heard another thing about it.

One man I never had any problem with was England forwards coach,

Graham Rowntree. Even when I was persona non grata, he would talk to me. He was a very upfront and honest guy, extremely well respected and knowledgeable. I would talk to him about the machinations of scrummaging and he was a fount of knowledge. 'Wiggsy' is a straight guy and a pleasure to work with.

‖ ∎ ‖

Good referees in any sport have a sequence of actions they intend to take to effect change in player behaviour if needed.

You start by managing the situation. Sometimes things happen where you move straight into card mode, because of the seriousness. Sam Warburton's dump tackle in the 2011 World Cup semi-final is an example of that.

But if you're talking about non-compliance at the scrum or the breakdown, which is where 75% of penalties come from, you go into management mode first. That means speaking to the players. Take opposing props after a few collapsed scrums as an example.

'Listen guys, this is not what we agreed beforehand. You need to be working harder on your feet positioning. You need to work harder on where you're putting your binds. Between the two of you, you're making the scrum very unstable and we've only got on issue on your side where it's coming down. So we need to sort it out. Do you understand me? Fine.'

The scrum goes down again so the situation escalates from management to sanction mode. In some instances, management works and you don't need to escalate. If it doesn't, you move on to sanctions. These are penalties to start with. If they don't change player behaviour, you bring it to the next level.

'I have spoken to you and made it quite clear. You told me you'd do something and you haven't. I've penalised you both. We're now at the point where if you don't sort it out, I will get both of you off to the bin and we'll get somebody else in to do it.'

That will sort it out eight or nine times out of 10 but on the rare occasion it doesn't, you have to follow through. That is where a lot of referees let themselves down. They issue the warning but then don't produce the card. That damages their credibility and as a result they tend to lose control because players don't believe they are going to be punished.

A lot of team sports are like that but rugby in particular. It's a game of huge physicality and as a player, you are pushing it as far as you can. You go right up to the line. Some edge over it, willing to risk a penalty to test the referee and see what the boundaries might be. If they get away with things, they keep going.

So you have to see it through. I have binned two props and restarted with a scrum. When the two new guys come in you explain to them that because of the difficulties that the scrum has experienced until now, the next sanction is a red card. That might seem harsh on fellas who have had nothing to do with the original problems but the ball is in their court. If they want to stay on the pitch they comply. The threat of a red usually sorts them out.

|▮▮|

My problem with that England-New Zealand game is that for all the penalties and yellow cards I gave, I didn't change player behaviour. That was the failure. If you go to that point where you are trying to manage, and then you're giving out sanctions, and there's no change in player behaviour, there's something wrong.

In my view, the issue was with my lack of management, on the basis of how I communicated with Borthwick. That was why I didn't have any buy-in from him when it came to attempting to change his teammates' conduct. I was too snappy with him and I'm sure he was thinking, *What a prick*.

Walking off the pitch, I knew it wasn't good. Having to dish out four cards was an indicator because I don't like to flourish them. So I was disappointed. There could have been a couple of more too that I could have justified technically but I turned a blind eye to them. It just got to the stage where I felt it would have to be something really big. As it was, England played most of the game with 14 players and were well beaten.

But I would have been turning a blind eye to something more important if I had hidden behind the laws. It was the fact that the players were continuing to commit offences that was the issue. I didn't alter the way the game was going and reacted dreadfully to that. I had to take the lesson on board and I did.

❘❘■❘❘

It is a source of pride now that one of the things I was credited for as a referee apart from my understanding of the game, was how I communicated with the players. There has always been a respect from the players that while they didn't always agree with my decisions, they knew what was going on. That is why there would have been very few games in which there was friction with the players.

It is top of the list of requirements for referees to succeed in my opinion. If players don't understand what you're trying to achieve, disaster will ensue, as I found out to my cost in Twickenham.

It starts in the changing room beforehand, how you talk to the teams. It is imperative that you get the balance right between being definite and dictatorial. Also, that you don't back yourself into a corner. Once you commit yourself to something, you have to carry it through.

There were a number of Heineken Cup games where there was a real undercurrent, where it might have gone wrong but having learned from the Twickenham experience, I was able to change player behaviour.

Anytime you referee England in a Six Nations game, there is an undercurrent because there is a real rivalry. When you have France against Wales, you know the two teams don't hate each other and they're going to go out and play. England are the team that everyone loves to hate. They just carry that mantle. Teams could be losing to everybody and they go to another level against England.

That hunger brings needle with it. Scotland, Wales, France and even Italy, who wouldn't have any huge history with England and aren't always competitive, all bring a bite that Scotland-France or Wales-Italy would never possess. You need to work hard in these games to make sure they don't boil over.

So you prepare on the basis that they're going to be in each other's faces from the very start. There's an awful lot of sledging going on. The patronising tap on the head to a player that has just given away a penalty in a bid to spark a reaction.

You get that a lot in Test matches involving England and Heineken Cup ties in which English clubs are playing. Delon Armitage did it in the 2013 Heineken Cup final when he pointed a finger at the last Clermont defender, Brock James before crossing the line for a try. It was showboating, rubbing an opponent's face in it.

I had a word with him about it and told him to cut it out. I could actually have restarted play with a penalty to Clermont under the laws for unsportsmanlike behaviour.

People generally put the enmity with English teams down to history but it's more than that. Most of them tend to play in an aggressive fashion. They try to intimidate, to bully, to dominate. That is fine of course but there are occasions when it can be perceived as being disrespectful by opponents and that ratchets up the tension.

Sometimes you can sense if the magnitude of the occasion or the atmosphere has gotten to players; that they are too wound up. When this happens, you need to have a word with the captains very early on to defuse the situation.

It is about understanding the game too. I didn't play Six Nations but watched a lot of it from very close to the action. I had some Test experience. I played in the Heineken Cup, in serious interprovincials and big club games when the club scene was massive in Ireland. I played in the bear pit that is Limerick.

That is a considerable advantage when it comes to understanding what is in a player's head leaving the changing room and then managing unfolding situations.

When I see a guy doing something, I can usually understand it, because the chances are I've done it myself. Particularly in the area of sledging. I could be quite a mouthpiece as a player. So sometimes you can think to yourself, *I know why you did what you did* and if it doesn't have materiality with regard to what happens next, you can just have a word.

You are supposed to come down hard on sledging. It doesn't happen very often but when it did, I tried not to make deal of it. You place it in context. You don't make an issue of it, you just have a quiet word.

'Don't do that again.'

'What did I do?' They always play injured and innocent.

'You know what you did. Don't be doing it again. Don't tap the guy on the head, rubbing it in. If you do, I'll have no hesitation in flipping the penalty over.'

And it won't happen again.

You generally go by player reaction as well. If something is done and the player doesn't react, it gives you an opportunity to nip it in the bud. But if a guy takes exception to something said or done and tries to take the other guy's head off, you have to deal with it differently.

The insults aren't usually that bad. I never went for comments about a guy's wife or mother and directed my attempt at mind games in other directions. If my direct opponent wasn't playing well, I'd tell him in no uncertain terms.

'Jesus, what are you at with your passing. You're giving him no chance. Don't you ever practice?'

I would never have stepped over the line with regards personal stuff but you'd hear it. Rubbing it in over a conceded score or penalty is always more likely to spark a reaction though.

CHAPTER
TWENTY-ONE

The sudden death penalty shootout that decided the 2009 Heineken Cup semi-final at the Millennium Stadium was one of the most extraordinary situations I have ever been involved in. It ended in devastation for Cardiff and in particular Martyn Williams, when the Wales flanker missed his kick, giving Jordan Crane the opportunity to send Leicester through.

It was an unfortunate ending to a thrilling encounter, which concluded with the Tigers prevailing 7-6 on penalties, after extra time had finished with the teams deadlocked on 26-26. Only one other major match had been decided in this fashion before, a French Championship final in 1984 between Beziers and Agen.

Despite the uniqueness of the situation in terms of the competition, there was no confusion about what would come at the end of extra time. We had been briefed as to what all the potential eventualities might be.

That was my first ever extra time game. Remarkably, my second came seven days later and again, it too went all the way. It was an AIL final between Shannon and Clontarf at Thomond Park. The teams could not be separated on 19-19 at the end of normal time.

On this occasion, the method for deciding the tie if they remained level at the end of extra time would be different. The winner would be the team that scored the first try.

That meant Clontarf needed to score in extra time and they very nearly did but Max Rantz McDonald couldn't quite hold the ball as he stretched out in a one-handed attempt to dot down. He was denied by inches.

Just like the Millennium Stadium, there was no score in extra time at Thomond Park and Clontarf endured further AIL final heartbreak. It was Shannon's ninth league title, this one thanks to a new-look outfit with an average age of 25.

Everyone would prefer a replay I think but in the absence of that, the first-try method of finding a winner was slightly better than the penalty shootout. The ERC changed the rules for the European competitions after what happened in the Millennium Stadium, to a situation where you just had three nominated kickers. I think that is fairer than bringing it down to flankers and props kicking at goal.

Just over 12 months later, I had Cardiff once more in the Amlin Challenge Cup final against Toulon at the Stade Velodrome in Marseille. Having presided over their heartbreak, I would have had to have been made of stone not to be pleased for them when they took the silverware by virtue of a 28-21 win over a team that would go on to dominate club rugby in the northern hemisphere.

That wasn't in my thinking while I refereed the game naturally and had no effect on my decision-making. It was just a human reaction, having seen their torment at first hand. I was particularly pleased for Williams, who missed the crucial kick in the shootout. He had given so much to club, country and rugby in general, it seemed cruel that he would have suffered in such a manner but that's sport at times. Now, he had something significant to celebrate.

▌ ▐ ▌ ▐

It was an amazing honour when I became the first Irishman since John T McGee in 1896 to referee a British & Irish Lions tour game in South Africa in 2009. The endurance of this great bastion of the amateur game in the professional era has been questioned in recent years, as the tourists failed to win a series between 1997 and 2013.

It is massive though and you only have to ask the players what they think of it to get a feel for what it means. It's the pinnacle for them. You don't ever see a player turning down an invitation to play, put it like that. Earning a good living from the game has not diluted the significance of that red jersey. The Lions are an institution.

I got to do the game with the Emerging Springboks at Cape Town's Newlands Stadium. The whole trip was an amazing experience. I spent the previous week in Durban because I knew the weather would be miserable in Cape Town. It always is so I left it as late as possible to fly in.

The Lions were staying in the same hotel as me in Durban. It was a lovely spot, right on the beach and it was nice to get a few days of sun in. The Lions supporters were brilliant and the atmosphere was incredible. They had the big 50 foot jersey with them on the beach, having had all the boys sign it.

Zane Kirchner and Wian du Preez, who were future Leinster and Munster players, lined out for the Emerging Springboks against a Lions team that included six starting Irish players and one more as a replacement. It wasn't a classic by any means, but the heavy rain had a lot to do with that. It finished 13-13 with a try in the corner and touchline conversion denying the tourists' midweek team a 100% record.

Paul O'Connell was the squad captain but Ronan O'Gara led the team that night and he was his usual self! I can understand why because while the captaincy was a massive honour, there was huge pressure with it I'm sure. He is an intensely focussed individual on the pitch anyway and would have been desperate to make an impression.

There was absolutely no chit-chat whatsoever at the coin toss. I thought there might be some small bit, given that there were two Irishmen. He wasn't having any of it however and I can see why. He is deadly serious about the game, as I was and by that juncture, would have been deep in focus. It is an approach that worked for him and made him one of the most successful players Ireland has ever produced.

▮▮▮▮

The traditionalist in you will always feel sad when an old ground is torn down, particularly when so many memories are interwoven with it. That is certainly how I felt about Lansdowne Road.

I played there a few times, most memorably when making my international debut. Prior to that, I lost a Leinster Schools' Senior Cup final with Blackrock and later on refereed a final there, as well as an AIL decider.

I brought Mark there for the Heineken Cup semi-final in which Munster thumped Leinster in 2006, the day after I had done Biarritz-Bath. As a Leinster man, that hurt but it was an incredible occasion.

It was pretty decrepit as an international ground however and needed to be redeveloped. Aviva Stadium was the result and after begging Owen, I got to referee the first game ever played on it, on July 31, 2010.

It was a combined provinces game involving academy players so there was no significance to it other than it being the first game. I'm not big on sentimentality but I just wanted to be part of the occasion when the first ball of any kind was kicked in the new stadium.

Paddy Jackson, Iain Henderson, Craig Gilroy, Luke Marshall and Martin Moore were amongst the youngsters to play and Gilroy scored the first points with a try. There have been many bigger games since but there will only ever be one first. It was nice to be there for it.

CHAPTER
TWENTY-TWO

The 'I Hate Alain Rolland' Facebook page is liked by 8,973 people. That will probably skyrocket on the back of being mentioned here. The last comment was posted on January 23.

'You're still a cunt!!! I aint forgot yet.'

The page was established in 2011 as a result of me sending off Wales captain Sam Warburton early in the 2011 World Cup semi-final against France in Auckland. It was described by the Welsh commentator as 'one of the most controversial decisions in the history of the World Cup.'

Wales lost the game though you couldn't say they did so as a result of being numerically disadvantaged, given the amount of opportunities they spurned. Had they been more clinical, they would have won and perhaps the criticism aimed in my direction over the subsequent years would not have been so vitriolic.

There was nothing too menacing really. I never had to get a panic alarm installed in my house, unlike the English soccer referee, David Elleray. Neither did I get death threats of a really serious nature, unlike Wayne Barnes after the 2007 World Cup quarter-final in which France beat New Zealand.

Most of what you saw on the internet was funny. There is a photo of me out there with a white beard and turban superimposed on it to make me look like Osama Bin Laden.

That is not to say that I didn't empathise with the players and supporters. I understood people were reacting emotionally, particularly in a country like Wales where rugby is not just the number one sport but a key element of their identity. Losing that game hurt.

There were threats but nothing you would take seriously. It was mostly social media stuff, where people tend to make wild comments from the other side of a screen and a keyboard. One comment under the profile pic on the 'I Hate Alain Rolland' page says that as a mortgage broker in Dublin, I should be easy to find.

One man wrote to me for about three years to tell me how useless I was, although he never signed it. He could not comprehend how I was still refereeing major games such was the level of ineptitude I had apparently displayed. I read the first couple and they were quite amusing but it got to a point that I would recognise the handwriting and just chuck the envelope in the bin.

Initially he sent me one every month or two. Then it slowed down to a trickle and finally, his anxiety seemed to have relented.

That was, until my retirement. The IRFU sent me an email saying that another letter had arrived. Curious, I opened it up. The message was simple.

'About bloody time.'

|| ■ ||

'Don't fuck up.'

So Lizzie would say to me every time I went out the door to do a game. It was a joke, part of the routine as I left for another airport.

While her delivery was laced in humour, this was actually the main target going out on the pitch. You wanted to facilitate a good, entertaining game but most of all you did not want to make the type of mistake that would affect the result of a game.

While there are many that demur, when it came to sending off Sam Warburton in the 2011 World Cup semi-final against France, I didn't fuck up. It was the right decision, as Sam acknowledged afterwards. There was no doubt in my mind at the time and none has entered since. Not a scintilla. It was a dangerous tip tackle on Vincent Clerc and the laws say that's a red card.

Despite it being correct in the eyes of the law and in the eyes of Sam himself, that did not stop many people subjecting me to fierce criticism. I never minded that from supporters because supporters by their nature are led by the heart. Their reactions are emotive.

You would have thought that some of the pundits, be they former players or coaches would have known better though. They should have.

Their problem though was that they were considering factors that I could not consider. The enormity of the game, how early it was and so on. Factors that have no place in the decision-making process of a referee.

People say I ruined the game but Wales had numerous chances to win, right up to the very end, when an actual wrong decision by me awarded a penalty that could have put them through to the final.

Now that would have been the greatest irony of all.

▐ ■ ■ ▐

Everything had been going according to plan. The four pool games went smoothly, with the marquee clash between New Zealand and France at Eden Park the standout in terms of being a heavyweight affair. It didn't really look it at the time mind you as Marc Lièvremont selected scrum half, Morgan Parra at 10. Richie McCaw and Dan Carter flourished and the All Blacks won 31-17. You wouldn't have suspected that this would be the pairing in the final.

While I didn't get a quarter-final this time, that was not a cause for concern because unlike 2007, it was decided to give the semi-finals to the top two officials and then select the referee for the final when those games were played.

That meant it was down to me and Craig Joubert, the young South African who had been my touch judge for the Namibia-Samoa Test in Windhoek eight years previously. He is an outstanding official but I was happy that I had done everything right and was in a good position to join Craig's fellow South African, André Watson as the only man to referee two finals.

Some decisions you make are difficult and some are easy. This was easy because there was an action that had a very clear and defined consequence. It was a dangerous tackle. There might have been no malicious intent involved

– I am certain there wasn't – but that is not a consideration. Neither is the magnitude of the game or the fact that only 17 minutes and change had elapsed.

The picture was very clear. As soon as Warburton made the tackle, I thought, *Oh shit*. I knew what I needed to do and it wasn't something I would enjoy. But it was unavoidable.

Warburton brought Clerc's legs over shoulder height. That constitutes a card of some nature. What colour depends on the landing. The law states clearly that it is the tackler's responsibility to take his man down with care. If he can bring his opponent down on his backside, he will get away with a yellow. Neck or shoulder and it's a straight red, no discussions.

Clerc landed heavily on his neck and shoulders so it was a straightforward decision to make. Sometimes you think when you've seen something, *Is it a red? Am I sure?* That internal conversation did not occur here. I was certain and I was right.

My record is there in black and white. I did not produce many cards and flashed very few reds in my career. There were only two in Test rugby and by my calculations, just nine in total. That's out of roughly 500 games. I wasn't trigger happy. I wasn't a Gotcha ref and I didn't want to be the story. After it happened, I was well aware of the significance. I knew that it would be a talking point. I would have loved to avoid that scenario but you must make the right call.

I have no doubt that there are referees who might have thought 'Hang on, this is big, this is a World Cup semi-final and only a few minutes gone' and taken the easy option with a yellow. You need balls to make a decision like that.

Lawrence Dallaglio argued that I needed to show common sense and not spoil a World Cup semi-final. But if that is a consideration for a referee, where do you draw the line? If someone knocks a guy out after five minutes, do you let that go because of the circumstances? Like fuck you do.

Most of the criticism afterwards centred on external factors, not the offence. You are a professional referee and nothing else matters apart from the laws of rugby.

That it was a World Cup semi-final was irrelevant. So too that we were still in the first quarter. Sam didn't mean it and it was a big guy tackling a small guy? Immaterial. It wasn't a spear tackle, he didn't drive his man neck first into the ground? No bearing on the issue at all.

You have to strip out the emotional side and deal with the facts, which is a message I deliver at a lot of the conferences I do now.

The only way to ensure that the crowd or the noise or any of the other outside elements don't influence you is to plan for the eventuality. If you are just reacting to the action, wondering, *How am I going to deal with this?* you might not always make the correct judgement.

As always, we had a match official meeting beforehand and one of the things discussed was the tip tackle. We were shown a number of clips and developed a process.

If the feet went past the horizontal mark, the referee had only to decide what colour card to show, rather than award a penalty and then consider whether additional action was required. As mentioned already, the colour of the card depended on the landing. It was very specific and very clear.

We had similar discussions about the breakdown and the scrummage. All the clips relating to these areas of focus were sent to the coaches. It was communicated to them very clearly what we would be looking out for and what was expected of the players.

When it came to looking at the action itself, once I saw the feet coming up I thought, *Oh fuck, there's a card coming here*. And I concentrated immediately on the landing. When Clerc came down on his neck area, it was black and white. Shoulder or above is red. No debate.

Once the decision was made and Sam was gone, it was back to the game. Whether it was right or wrong – and I had no doubts on that score – I wasn't going to dwell on it. The ship has sailed. It's like a sent email. You can't get it back so don't torture yourself. There was an hour still to play.

You can tell when a referee is dwelling on an earlier decision, wondering if he fucked up? If that is your frame of mind, mistakes will follow. You have to be strong mentally. During the game is not the time to analyse it because there are hundreds more decisions to make and you'll make a mess of things if you aren't concentrating.

So I did my job and did it well enough, though I might have gotten a couple of penalty decisions wrong. That happens and I would hold my hand up to them. The Warburton red wasn't one of them though.

| ▮ ■ ▮ |

The eagle-eyed reader will wonder how the materiality that I have referred to pretty regularly within these pages fits in here. It doesn't. Materiality doesn't apply to foul or dangerous play. There is no room for interpretation in those areas.

That is not the case for many of rugby's laws. Most technical areas are open to interpretation and two referees with the same book of laws might well apply them differently. My interpretations revolved around having an open game. That applied to the scrum and breakdown areas, which statistically are responsible for the vast majority of penalties. It also applied to the advantage rule.

A rugby referee could probably blow the whistle every time there is contact and find a law to justify doing so. The key is knowing when and when not to blow it. Somebody could do something wrong but if it had no impact on what happened next I don't have to blow the whistle. There may have been a technical breach of regulations but if the transgressor's team did not gain an advantage as a result, I will let the play go.

The really good referees understand this. The others are the Gotcha refs, who can't wait to blow the whistle. They don't see themselves as facilitators in the background. They want to be centre stage, whereas it's the players that should be in the limelight.

If I saw a flanker attempting to slow down the ball illegally but failing to do so, I will let it go because the team in possession have still managed to get the ball out quickly. But I will always have a word. It is important to let the guy know that he was spotted and that he is treading a dangerous line.

Rugby allows referees to give direction more than other sports. If you're warning a 7 to get his hands off the ball and he responds accordingly, that suits everyone and you don't have to stop the play. You want to give teams licence to play while making them understand that if they cross the line, you'll nail them.

One situation you might have to think about is a penalty in front of the posts five minutes from time that could decide a game. The materiality there is huge and so you'd be inclined to award it rather than wave play on. Of course if you are going with a penalty advantage, the ball is literally in the attacking team's court if they want to have a kick at goal.

That is very different from what people tried to argue about the Warburton case though, in terms of how early it was in the game. If you left that action go it would have been open season. The tip tackle would have been lawful for the rest of the game.

I would have failed had I allowed that situation to occur. It was clearcut.

▮▮▮

People went apeshit. Lizzie was very concerned and it was tough for her being on the other side of the world while she watched the British pundits in particular tear strips off me. She wondered what the consequences might be for me in terms of refereeing in general or if there would be some lunatic out there looking to shoot me?

She rang to check out my state of mind but I was fine.

Stuart Barnes described the red card as 'diabolical'. Francois Pienaar said I killed the game. Mark Cueto, Ben Foden, Rory Lawson, Doddie Weir and Mike Tindall were all critical. Interestingly enough, Pienaar changed his mind the following day.

Wales defence coach, Shaun Edwards insisted that intent should have been taken into account but the law doesn't allow for that.

The IRB referees' manager, Paddy O'Brien said that the decision was 'absolutely correct in law and in keeping with the clear instructions that match officials have received in recent years regarding dangerous tackling.'

The independent judicial officer also said that I took appropriate action and administered a three-match suspension to Warburton. The Wales captain escaped a lengthier ban due to his 'outstanding character, disciplinary record and remorse.'

That was a very appropriate description of Sam. I knew all about the type of individual he was from refereeing him before that anyway but his response to what must have been a very difficult time for him personally just accentuated the impression.

When I issued the red card, he put his hands to his head, turned and walked off. There was not a hint of dissent, though in other sports you can imagine the bile that might have spewed forth. I think it's fair to say that at first, he felt he had done nothing wrong and to accept the decision without question in those circumstances spoke volumes for the man. It was a tremendous example for any kid watching.

So were his comments after seeing the footage. He acknowledged that he had committed a sending off offence.

'The IRB said if you lift up a player and drop him it's a red card and that's exactly what I did. I can't complain. There was no point in appealing against it and I didn't have a leg to stand on really.'

It is no wonder he is a leader of men. It didn't make any difference to me personally that he did this. But it was huge for the game of rugby in my opinion and because I love the game, I was glad he made that public statement.

While there was plenty of negative reaction, I received many emails and messages from medical people and parents of young rugby players thanking me for making the correct decision. People wanted to be able to know that they could send their children to play a game where dangerous play was unacceptable.

I received one letter from a quadriplegic who did not suffer his injuries from rugby but could identify with the potential dangers. He emphasised that player safety was paramount and anything that might put a player in a wheelchair, even accidentally, needed to be weeded out as much as possible.

It was an extraordinary reaction in that sense and very humbling. I didn't need it to justify my decision because the laws did that. But it brought into focus the importance of the game and when Sam reacted as he did, he served the game of rugby. He will always have my utmost respect.

▮▮▮▮

Warren Gatland didn't care what his captain was saying. The facts meant nothing to him. He conveniently ignored what Sam acknowledged, that the referees had communicated with the teams beforehand that this was exactly how we would address such a tackle. He needed to lash out and apportion blame and Warburton saying it was the right decision would not get in the way of that.

The New Zealander opined that a yellow card would have been the correct sanction – which isn't the case in law – before focussing on me making an immediate decision without consulting my two touchies or looking at the big screen.

'I just thought that decision ruined the semi-final; we had our chance taken away.'

Clearly Gatland was fuming so much after the sending off that he paid absolutely no attention to what happened in the rest of the game. You would think from his comments that France pulverised a disillusioned Wales as a result of their numerical advantage.

The game finished 9-8. James Hook missed two penalties. Stephen Jones struck the upright from a fairly straightforward conversion attempt after Mike Phillips' try. Leigh Halfpenny was just short with a penalty attempt from distance with five minutes remaining.

So it was absolute bullshit to say their chance had been taken way. More clinical execution would have won them the game and gotten them to the World Cup final.

He was still going on about it at the start of the Six Nations. How about this for a contradictory statement?

'I just think he got it wrong. This is my personal opinion – and I understand that under the letter of the law he was right – for me, it was the intention.'

By his thinking, the first 20 minutes should be refereed differently to the remaining 60. The laws are to be ignored if necessary. Obviously, a referee can't do that.

There might be a suspicion that Warren was never my greatest fan, even before this. We played against each other in the AIL when he was with Galwegians but I don't recall there being any issue arising out of those games.

Certainly he criticised me on a number of occasions in his capacity as an *Irish Times* columnist, even before 2011. Four years previously, he had a go for my performance in the World Cup final.

To be specific, he said I had a good game before picking at a slew of mistakes. He argued that I should have binned Schalk Burger for slowing down the ball. He was right on that one, as I admitted earlier. There was more though.

'If the English hadn't suffered the rough edge of the officiating with regard to the decisions it would have meant a six-point game going into the final 15 minutes and that certainly would have changed the complexion of the match.'

Later on, he said South Africa got more of the 50-50 calls. I would hate to have seen what it would have taken for him to think I had a bad game.

In 2010, after a Six Nations game in which England beat Wales 30-17 at Twickenham, the visiting head coach complained that I should have gone to the TMO when judging that Tom James had knocked the ball over the dead-ball line when trying to gather possession with the score only 20-17 to England. Yet again, footage showed clearly that I made the correct decision.

Yet anytime we met, he was always very civil. Of course he wasn't going to do anything to piss me off because he knew I would have his team for other games.

There was a funny postscript to the whole thing when Warburton opted to stay around for the IRB dinner that would take place after the World Cup final. He was taking a flight from Auckland to Brisbane and as luck would have it, was on the same plane as France.

He was one of the last getting on the flight and as he tells it, noticed a few of the French players sniggering. They were aware of what was about to happen.

There was only one seat left unoccupied. When Warburton looked down, he could scarcely believe his eyes.

His companion for the journey?

Vincent Clerc.

▮▮▮▮

Many speculate that I was overlooked for the 2011 final because of the massive attention surrounding the Warburton sending off and I think it had to have some bearing on it. It wasn't the main reason though.

My mind is always drawn to an incorrect penalty I gave for offside that gave Halfpenny that late opportunity to snatch the semi-final for Wales. I have mentioned before about how certain you need to be in the last 10 minutes of a tight game like this. You cannot make an error.

I actually had a bad feeling about it as soon as I blew the whistle. As

Halfpenny was lining his kick up I was saying it to myself.

Fuck. I might have gotten that one wrong. If this goes over, I could be in trouble here.

It was right on target but dropped marginally short. That was a relief but it didn't erase the mistake and if there were one or two others during the game, they might have added up to go against me in the head-to-head with Craig.

When you looked at it clinically, there was less heat out of Craig's semi-final than mine. Had I gotten the nod, the red card would continue to be a talking point. But in my heart of hearts, I feel that had I gotten that late penalty decision right, I would have had a better chance.

There are always conspiracy theories of course and in France, they like to posit that with Paddy O'Brien being a New Zealander, he would have preferred an official that would not be able to communicate with the French players in their own language. While they would always have been more comfortable with me refereeing because I could explain decisions clearly to them, you cannot give any credence to such a line of thought.

I was gutted to miss out although there is no doubt that having done it already did alleviate the pain somewhat. Still, I wanted it again so it was excruciating. When Paddy told us, I couldn't lift my head up off the floor. I felt everyone was looking at me.

I also felt that some of the guys would have been relieved that I didn't get it. While we were a team with good camaraderie, be in no doubt as to the extent of the rivalry. It would have killed one or two of the guys had I gotten a second one.

I got over it pretty quickly. I was going to be Craig's assistant so I dedicated myself completely to helping him. And I was genuinely delighted that it was him, if not me. He was only a couple of days short of turning 34, so it was a great birthday present. He was young but unlike me in 2003, had significantly more experience at international level.

'Welcome to the club' were my first words to him.

I gave him as much advice as I could from my own experiences and in the game itself, I tried my arse off for him.

❙❚❙❚❙

It is customary for the IRB to give you a break from a team or country after you have had some difficulty or controversy with them. It just saves everyone involved a lot of hassle and allows things to die down a bit.

After the issues with England in 2008, it was 15 months before I got them in a Test again. Then, Paddy O'Brien rang to give me the heads-up before the appointments were announced publicly. I was delighted to get back into it. I knew why they did what they did but never felt that I needed protecting.

Having had that experience, I wanted to get back into Wales sooner rather than later. Whatever you were going to get from supporters was coming, no matter how long they kept you away from them. Wales is the nearest country to New Zealand in the northern hemisphere in terms of their rugby fanaticism. They weren't going to forget.

The slagging is still going on. I never have to show my passport at passport control. No matter who is there, they know their rugby and recognise me. They just giggle, give me a bit of faux abuse and wave me through.

I wasn't kept away from Wales as long as England. There was some talk that I would not have them for the rest of the season. That was ridiculous. Owen was being very cautious but I told him we couldn't avoid the issue and at some point they would have to throw me back in. The situation had a danger of escalating the longer they left it.

It was an eight-month gap when I refereed the national side against the Baa Baas but I had been back to Wales for a few club games by then which served to break the ice.

The first game was a Heineken Cup tie in Parc y Scarlets in January, with Northampton making the trip to play Llanelli. I was very relaxed about it. Lizzie gave me the usual 'Don't fuck up' line as I left but this time, she added a rider.

'Watch your back.'

Beforehand, Llanelli coach, Nigel Davies said that I couldn't be blamed for following the laws of the game. That might have helped in lowering the temperature a little and was certainly appreciated.

Not that I was in any way concerned. I went out early enough to do my warm-up. There weren't many in at that stage but I did hear one man to say to his son 'That's the fella that sent off Sam.' He said it loud enough for me to hear it and intended me to do so.

Quick as a flash though, a woman beside him retorted.

'Don't worry ref, we still love you here.'

I just smiled and carried on. You were going to have the banter but it was nice to have someone defend me.

The announcement of my name produced a chorus of boos that could be heard in London and so did my face appearing on the big screen. I just smiled. You have to take these things on the chin.

I noticed that there seemed to be a lot of police around. There were four in the tunnel alone, more outside the changing area. Bob Yemen was the Wales referee manager, known universally as Domo (director of match officials) and I queried the increase in numbers with him afterwards.

'Hey Domo, what's the story with all the cops?'

'They're for you. We just weren't sure how things would go. All it needed was one lunatic.'

I laughed, thinking it was a bit OTT. I hadn't considered the possibility of someone trying to exact retribution. But I guess when you think of Pieter Van Zyl and Dave McHugh, it wasn't inconceivable.

But it all passed without incident and over the years, the booing got quieter. They were to be finished with me pretty soon.

CHAPTER
TWENTY-THREE

I returned from New Zealand confident that I was still operating at the very top of my game. I had produced another good four years of refereeing and there was no reason why I could not continue through the next cycle to Twickenham in 2015.

While my performances weren't dropping, there was a group of hungry, young guys who were improving all the time. Craig was almost 34 when he did the World Cup final. I was 45 when I assisted him and while I had no concerns about being able to do the job to the highest capacity at 49, I had little interest in doing so if getting the final wasn't a realistic possibility.

There was no problem with my fitness and conditioning. I was as disciplined as ever. Having said that, the last six or seven months before going down to New Zealand, I had probably started eating food I wouldn't normally. So when I returned I made the decision to go off carbs until Christmas.

After 10 days I had lost an inch around my waist and my weight was down to 80kg, having been at 84kg in 2007. I was probably too bulky then because I was chewing the gym around that time. As I got older, I felt that carrying that muscle around the pitch was harder so I backed off. Combined with the diet, I actually dropped down to 76kg but when I saw myself on TV, felt that I had lost too much weight and got myself back it up to 80kg, which I felt was just about right.

Coming towards the end of the 2012-2013 season, I began to consider my future. Having been forced to retire himself from a knee injury that ended his playing career, Joël Jutge had taken over from Paddy in a role now defined as high performance match officials' manager. We get on well and had an honest chat.

'What are your thoughts on the World Cup?'

'Right now, I'm going.'

That was fine but then he threw the curve ball.

'Alain, you've refereed at three World Cups, you've refereed everything there is to referee. Do you really need to do another World Cup.

'What do you mean?'

'Well what have you to prove? What is there?'

Owen had a phrase he used to repeat a lot.

'Get out with them wanting more.'

That had always been to the forefront of my mind and Joël knew it. I wanted to retire at the top of my game, with people praising me rather than saying I should have hung up the whistle two years earlier. I wanted to go of my own volition rather than be pushed.

At this stage I was refereeing as well as anyone. I could go to 2015. But were they going to give the final to a 49 year old? It would be a gamble in much the same way as giving me the final in 2003 might have been. They didn't need to take that risk.

Did I want to go away for another two months, even if it was the UK and I could commute every few days? Did I want to do that in the knowledge that the final was more than likely not available to me?

Joël definitely got me thinking.

Around the same time I took some gardening leave from Cornmarket to take up another role as a director of sales for a new online hotel reservations website, greatstay.com. I didn't stay long there but I was certain that I would not return to my old career in the world of mortgage broking. The recession had not been kind to that business and more than that, I hungered for something different.

It became clear that to pursue my passion from a business point of view, I would have to set up my own company. And if I was going to do that, I would need to give up refereeing.

It all added up. I was a highly ambitious individual and always set realistic targets. I wasn't sure that getting the World Cup final was on. There was no point continuing if that wasn't a viable goal.

Ironically, it was Lizzie who was most apprehensive about me jacking it in. She knew what it meant to me I suppose and feared that I would regret giving up while I was still capable of performing at world class level.

I pointed out the amount of time I was away because of refereeing, the holidays we couldn't have as a result. That summer, I was around for the first time in 10 years and it was wonderful. We have a mobile home in Wexford and the routine had always been that Lizzie and the gang would go down for July and August, with me commuting for a few days here and there.

But in 2013, I was there the whole time and it was a wonderful. Having all our weekends would mean we could replicate that and more, I reasoned. Lizzie would quite rightly laugh at that now because with the way the business has blossomed, I'm away just as much.

The decision was made to pack it in at the end of the season. I told Owen and he understood completely.

'Rollers, I think it's the right thing to do. Nobody's ever done it. Nobody ever left before their time was up.'

The next item on the agenda was when to announce it. We both agreed that it was better to do it at the start of the season. That way, if my refereeing did happen to deteriorate or I picked up an injury, it would not be perceived that I was being forced out. It was important to me that people knew I was leaving on my own terms. I also felt that it was only right to give the IRB two years notice that I wouldn't be involved at the next World Cup.

So I made the announcement in September and that last year was fabulous. Undoubtedly, there were players, coaches and supporters who would be glad to see the back of me. But largely, that last season was one big ego massage, as the nicest things were said to and about me.

I have mentioned the rivalry that existed between referees at the highest level but it was very healthy. Nigel and I are great mates and he wrote me a lovely note.

'It was an honour to work with you but it is an even bigger honour to be your friend.'

Craig dropped me a line too. I got on with all the guys. You had someone like Steve Walsh who has a really big personality that would be completely the opposite of mine but we worked together regularly so we learned to get on.

I was always a team player and I would like to think the lads appreciated that.

▐ █ ▌▐

I am proud of the fact that I refereed well in those last months. I did not slack off in any way and worked ferociously hard.

Owen made that point to the IRB and referee selectors immediately because I'm sure that was a concern, although it shouldn't have been to anyone who knew me. Some might have wondered if I would coast through that final campaign, feasting off the applause and presentations. Owen promised them that my levels would be off the charts because I wanted to leave a lasting impression.

For that reason, getting the Heineken Cup final was so gratifying. There were some detractors who argued that it was a sentimental appointment but I don't believe that for a minute.

There is no doubt Nigel was the man in possession going into the semi-finals. He was the top dog, doing the big New Zealand-South Africa Test, the elite games around the world. He would hold his hand up and say that he made a couple of mistakes in the semi-final though. While Saracens beat Clermont Auvergne by 40 points, the timing of some of those errors might have had a bearing on proceedings.

So the selectors appointed me to referee the final. They considered me the best man for that job on that day. I had proved it time and again. It was a dream to go out on such a stage but I would only have wanted it if I was good enough. I had no interest in sympathy.

Those that think it was a decision based on emotion are forgetting that I had also done the previous year's final between Clermont Auvergne and Toulon in the Aviva. That was one of the really good days, refereeing two French teams in Dublin. That was an encapsulation of my life really.

Clermont scored two tries to Toulon's one but not for the first time, Jonny Wilkinson proved the difference, slotting three penalties as well as the extras from Delon Armitage's try.

Jonny was an absolute gentleman and a true professional. The move to Toulon worked so well for him. It breathed new life into his career because I think he gained more perspective. I don't think Jonny had the right balance for a long time and that is very important.

Jonny learned to loosen up a little bit more. It was ironic that as he enjoyed himself more and grew to understand that rugby wasn't the be-all and end-all, he rediscovered his mojo and produced some of the best form of his career in the last few years.

▮▮▮▮

The ref cam was introduced for the first time in that final at the Aviva. It was the latest technological innovation and the latest step in media intrusion. So much money is coming into rugby from the broadcasters, they are calling the shots now and while some of their developments benefited the game, I would not agree that all of them have.

Getting mic'd up for the first time took some getting used to when you were as chatty as me. I had to cut out my running commentaries for a start.

Microphones can be dangerous as they pick up players' comments to each other or just general earthy language that is pretty common in a sport where guys are knocking the shit out of each other, but which can offend some poor soul watching at home who would probably be better served looking at the cricket.

The only humorous moment in the England-New Zealand Test in 2008 arrived in the second half, when Phil Vickery was getting treatment. I would know him quite well and I enjoyed refereeing him because he was honest.

'Phil, are you alright?'

'Some fucking cunt stuck his finger in my eye.'

I said nothing at the time and allowed him to be attended to by the medial staff. As we trotted back for a scrum, I turned to him and smiled.

'Phil, for the commentators and millions of viewers that missed it the first time, do you want to repeat what you said a second ago to the microphone again?'

The look of shock on his face was priceless. He declined the invitation unsurprisingly enough.

There is a protocol with regard to the mics. We normally went live while we were in the changing room. We are supposed to be cut off on the blow of half time then until the start of the second half. Off again then at the final whistle.

On one occasion, in a Heineken Cup game between Northampton and Ospreys, Ospreys head coach Steve Tandy challenged me at half time on the way in. On the Monday, I got an email from Donal Courtney, referee manager of the ERC, asking me what he'd said to me because the commentator had spoken about it at half time.

I played it down. Steve had felt that one or two decisions had gone against him and was venting his frustration but to me it was normal and had no effect on me. I was more pissed off about the conversation being aired when we had an agreement that the mic would be cut. It wasn't fair on me or Steve that it wasn't. So from then, I established a routine of asking were we off before saying another word.

TV has changed the game completely. All the televised Test, Heineken Cup, PRO12 matches cannot start until you get the nod from the floor manager. There was one Heineken Cup game where it was freezing and there was no signal coming. I had enough. Fuck this. Let's kick off.

Your man went apeshit. He lost the plot completely. They hadn't come back from their ad break yet. But you can't have players hanging around in the bitter cold that long and they shouldn't have brought us out if they weren't ready. I don't care how much they're paying.

It's bad enough that they have lengthened half time from 10 minutes to 15 so that they can fit in more analysis and rake in more revenue through advertising. It's too long. For AIL games it's four minutes. You have a quick word, turn around and go again.

The number of cameras and different angles have clearly improved the viewing experience for those watching from the sofa. That is critical in terms of the promotion of rugby. On the flip-side, you have an awful lot of armchair pundits now. They are sitting there with their remote control, pressing stop, rewind, and slow-motion play.

'Look, he's in front of the kicker if I pause it there now.'

I don't have a pause button out in the middle of the park. I don't have the luxury of taking five minutes to come to a decision.

The TMO came around as a result of the increase in cameras and they were clearly a benefit to the game. Ultimately, you want to arrive at the correct decision. It has gone too far now though. Because there is that safety net, referees are reluctant to make a decision.

TV is trying to take more and more control and at some point, you have to put the brakes on. Already, there is an agreement in PRO12 that they are going to have open mics between the touch judge and the referee as well as the TMO. That is not positive because it is going to change the officials' behaviour and how they speak to one other. That will have an impact on decision-making.

If a touch judge calls forward pass but the referee overrules him, that might place doubt on the credibility of the TJ, or indeed on the referee if the TJ was correct. It is fine to want transparency but you have to protect the key protagonists too and not prevent them from doing their jobs properly.

Broadcasters can be very naughty at times in the way they influence games. Take the Rugby Championship game between South Africa and New Zealand in Ellis Park in October 2014 as an example.

Liam Messam hit Schalk Burger high with his shoulder with about four minutes left but none of the officials picked up on it. Play went on for a number of phases before Wayne Barnes awarded a scrum to New Zealand.

Barnesy went to check on an injured player when the host broadcaster replayed the challenge on Burger in slow motion. The crowd responded as you would expect and the footage was replayed over and over.

The Springboks had been as unaware of what had happened as anyone but once they saw that, their skipper, former Munster man, Jean de Villiers went straight to Barnesy. It is only then, minutes after the offence, that the TMO was called in.

Between them, they decided that it was a penalty and Patrick Lambie slotted the 55 metres kick to inflict a first defeat in two years on the All Blacks.

In one sense, it was good that they came to the right decision but the TMO was only used because of the input of an outside agent that should have no impact on a game. I don't think that is where we want to be going.

Of course people are always unsure about new things. When citing commissioners were introduced initially, there was some concern amongst referees but it was explained that they were there not to undermine us but to pick up on anything afterwards that might not have been seen in live time.

There is so much physicality in rugby that some things can go unnoticed. On occasion, there are serious acts of foul play that haven't been picked up on and they should never go unpunished. We could all agree on that and so it made sense to introduce a mechanism that would address that.

The citing commissioner had the power to sanction a player, even if his transgression had been dealt with by the referee. There was no problem with upgrading a yellow card to a red. It has happened to me a couple of times. You might send a player to the bin for something but have missed a more serious act of foul play that kicked off the chain of events you adjudicated upon.

I had it once in a game between Wasps and Clermont. Jamie Cudmore was always an abrasive character in a similar mould to Bakkies Botha and Danny Grewcock. If there was a bit of mischief and he was in the vicinity, you always suspected that he might have something to do with it.

I saw him strike an opponent on the ground and issued a yellow card to give him a 10 minute cooling-off period in the bin. We didn't have access to the TMO at the time so I had to work with the touch judges and while we might have suspected that there was more to it, we could not give decisions on what we hadn't seen.

The citing commissioner had access to a reverse angle shot which showed a much worse transgression and increased the sanction to a red card. It was a decision I agreed with completely once I saw the same footage and the call I would have made had I observed it.

They may be saying that you got that one wrong but you can't take it personally. It's not like you are punishing someone and they are getting off. This is punishing serious foul play usually and the reason the process is there is to come to the right decision.

It isn't as if a referee's decisions are being overturned routinely. And if they are, it won't be long before he is removed from the panel. You have nothing to fear if you are a good referee.

We trialled a white card during the Super Rugby season in 2012. We used it if we weren't sure of the identity of a transgressor, which was fine, but also if we weren't sure that an incident deserved a red card. So again, we were just passing on making a decision, putting a guy on report for the citing commissioner to deal with.

You are the referee. If there's foul play you should deal with it. The citing commissioner only steps in if there's a sense that you haven't dealt strongly enough with it, or if you missed something completely. Of course if you went too hard, there is an appeals process too.

When the TMO was introduced first it was to determine whether a try had been scored or not but over time, the powers were extended to look back on such incidents, so that there could be no doubt about the level of transgression that took place or about the perpetrator's identity.

A white card was trialled again in South Africa's Varsity Cup this year but it had a different use. This time, it related to a team having a right to review a decision made or to refer an incident they felt might have gone unnoticed.

I would be in favour of a team challenge as used in cricket and American football now. You might not have three every set like you do in tennis but certainly there is a window for one per game or one each half. It gives coaches and captains some degree of input but would reduce the number of times captains approach referees looking to go back a number of phases in play to look at something they believe or hope occurred.

CHAPTER
TWENTY-FOUR

'When you play 16 against 15 it is not easy. I know he is an international referee but today he had a bad day.' – **Sale Sharks coach, Philippe Saint-André**

'Alain Rolland is one of the best referees in the world.' – **Ospreys coach, Lyn Jones**

These comments were made after a Heineken Cup tie between Sale and Ospreys early in 2007. Have a stab at guessing which team won.

I received many plaudits in my final season as a referee and they were very welcome indeed. They meant more because unlike the usual commentary, coaches were not trying to gain an edge, or were not governed by whether or not they won and lost. I think there was genuine positivity about the comments.

Generally, people think the referee has had a terrible game if their team has been beaten. That is an emotive reaction and I have total empathy with that. So you never take much notice. The statements made by Saint-André and Jones are the perfect indicator as to why you just can't read much into what players and coaches say.

In general, I think a lot of the coaches were nervous about me refereeing. They knew they had somebody that couldn't be influenced. Other referees might not be influenced by the coaches but the crowd, atmosphere, occasion and players talking to them during the course of the game can have a subconscious effect sometimes. I wasn't that type.

Other coaches liked that aspect to my game. Because what they saw was what they got and there was a consistency all the way through, they could prepare for that. They would have known I was very hot at the tackle area and worked hard on the breakdown.

The level of preparation by teams for referees is as deep as it is for any aspect of the game. Donncha O'Callaghan told me that the Munster players had a recording of my cadence for the four-step 'crouch, touch, pause, engage' on their iPods. The joke was that it was in fact a five-step sequence. 'Crouch, touch, pause, engage, collapse.' Bob Casey revealed another version of the five-step it in his *Irish Times* column as 'Crouch, touch, pause, have a cup of tea, engage.'

Suffice to say it was a bit of a mess. There had to be at least 1.75 seconds between pause and engage, in a bid to make the two packs settle before the engagement. You practised it. And packs tried to get a feel for your rhythm to gain an edge.

Coaches would also have known that I liked to play advantage wherever possible. It is one of the great laws within rugby union but how you interpret and apply it is everything. I couldn't give you the stats but I would hazard a guess that out of every 100 advantages I gave, around 80 or 90 of the teams played on. That shows an understanding of the game and what was on.

It is a difficult law. Some referees play advantage at every opportunity and end up having to come back for a higher percentage as a result. There are times when nothing is on and you might as well just award the penalty and save time.

▮▮▮▮

I tended to take every comment with a grain of salt although I wasn't one for reading newspapers. I wasn't wounded by criticism and wouldn't get a big head from any praise. It would be a lie to say that I didn't enjoy the last season though for all the positivity that surrounded it.

This was no armchair ride to the finish line though. I wanted to leave it all out there and I did. Far from a testimonial campaign, this was a hard-working one, full of incident.

The two most talked about games involved trips to what was almost my spiritual home in the Millennium Stadium.

It was here that I refereed my first Test between Wales and Romania. Where I presided over the sudden death shootout in the Heineken Cup semi-final between Cardiff and Leicester. In that swansong year, it was where I refereed my last Test between Wales and France, and my last ever game – the Heineken Cup final between Toulon and Saracens.

That last Test match of 68 was held on February 21, 2014. With the roof closed, the atmosphere was highly-charged and Wales won 27-6. It was a game in which I had to work hard and I doled out three yellow cards. Unusually for a match in which I was involved, the French got very frustrated and being able to speak to them in their own language could not rescue the situation.

In reality, it was their captain, Pascal Papé who could not be talked down. France were losing and he didn't deal well with it.

The first two yellow cards came at the scrum, when I binned Nicolas Mas and his opposite number, Gethin Jenkins. Neither was willing to change their behaviour after an attempt at management. A warning proved insufficient deterrent so I binned them.

'Get me some new props please.'

Later on, I sent Louis Picamoles to the bin. He applauded sarcastically as he left the field. I wasn't aware of it to be honest but he was to pay the price later by being dropped for the next France game.

Papé just seemed to be in a prickly mood from the start. It came to a head when Sam Warburton reached out to score a try for Wales in the second half that sealed the result in the home side's favour. I called for the TMO to adjudicate on whether or not the flanker had made it to the line. Papé approached.

'Look to see if Roberts, when he breaks through, if there's a knock on.' Demanding.

'Okay.'

'No, Alain. Look!' Aggressive.

'Okay!'

'Okay, thanks Alain.' Dismissive.

'Hey, come here. If you speak like that… if you continue to speak like that to me… hey, listen to me!'

'Alain, I'm sorry but you are not refereeing Wales the same as you did France just now.'

I said 'Non' and turned away. This was a situation that I did not want to escalate. I was attempting to get across to him that he could not speak to me in that manner but I was very careful in not saying I would take a specific course of action if he did. It's a fine line but it was important he understood that he should not be speaking to me that way.

I was taken aback completely by Papé's general attitude. It was the only time I had a real problem with a captain, apart from Steve Borthwick in 2008. I had reffed France 15 times before this. Titi Dusautoir had been captain for the previous few years, Fabien Pelous a number of times before that and I had a very good working relationship with them.

Titi's English wasn't very good but the fact that I could communicate with him in French made him very comfortable and we never had any issues. Even when New Zealand thumped France 30-0 eight months earlier, there were no problems.

This was the only time that it went wrong and I have to attribute that to Papé. He got the captaincy for the 2013 Six Nations as Dusautoir was coming back from injury. He got injured himself and Titi was restored to the position but it reverted to Papé again for the Six Nations in 2014. He just wasn't captaincy material. Part of his job is being able to communicate but he was unable to do so without his emotions getting the better of him. It is no surprise that Dusautoir was reinstated.

It was a pity that there were those kinds of issues. You want to get in and out of any game you ref and to have blended into the background. I put a lot of pressure on myself beforehand to have as good a match as possible. I wanted to show that I was as good as ever even though it would be my last Test. I wanted people to think that I could have stayed going another few years, although the locals were probably wishing I had departed three years earlier.

Philippe Saint-André came into the changing room afterwards and presented me with a jersey signed by all the team, which was nice. Clearly there were no hard feelings from this game or indeed that Heineken Cup game seven years previously that prompted his '16 against 15' remark. Later on, at the post-match reception, Wales presented me with a lovely crystal bowl.

Once the game was over, I thought no more of it but it really blew up in France, where the actions and words of both Picamoles and Papé were heavily criticised. Saint-André dropped Picamoles for one game, declaring his show of disrespect unacceptable.

He also criticised his skipper for his tone in dealing with me. It was the familiarity that was the big issue for the French media and supporters. He called me by my name a couple of times, which would be unusual. Apart from that, there was the use of the personal 'tu' as against the more formal or respectful 'vous' when saying 'you'.

It doesn't sound a big deal and it wasn't to me but in France, it is significant. After a previous game involving France, I was told by a performance reviewer that I should use 'vous' rather than 'tu' when speaking with players.

The next time I had them, I said 'vous' when talking to Titi and he got upset because he thought he had done something wrong for me to have switched from the personal to the informal. It is really subtle but a bit of a minefield. In France though, they would have argued that irrespective of how the game was going, Papé should not have spoken to a person of higher authority than him in a familiar fashion.

A discussion paper went into the IRB council afterwards suggesting that if there was ever an example of how a captain's challenge could work, it was this game. As Pascal continued to complain, if I could have turned around and asked him did he want to use his team challenge, that would have taken all the heat out of the situation.

If he didn't really believe there was a major issue, he would have decline because he wasn't going to waste it and he couldn't continue with his complaints then. Of course, if he felt he had a genuine grievance, he could accept and we could look at whatever he wanted.

I said it to Joël myself afterwards, that it was the perfect example of the potential benefits of a TMO team challenge. He agreed. However, with it being just a year out from the World Cup, it was deemed too close to begin experimenting with something that major.

▌▐■▐▌

You were into the stage now where nearly every game was going to be your last with a particular team or at a particular venue. I tried not get caught up in it because I wanted to be professional right down to the very last blast of my whistle. But I wanted to take it in too. There were numerous presentations, dinners and good wishes and each one was treasured.

There were a couple of big games as touch judge and I was delighted to be in the Aviva for Brian O'Driscoll's last home international. He is a legend of the game and it was so fitting that he got to end at home with victory, and finish his time in the green jersey with a championship.

Another icon of rugby retiring at the end of the season (BOD being the first, not me!) was Jonny Wilkinson. I have already written of my admiration for him. I rate him marginally ahead of Dan Carter, another out half of mesmeric quality. I just think Jonny had more individual influence.

New Zealand might have won a World Cup without Carter. England wouldn't have gotten close without Wilkinson. And I'm not sure that Toulon would have crossed the line in Europe without his experience and leadership either. So I was ecstatic to be involved in his last game too.

It was my last one as well of course and while that was personally a big deal, every good referee wants to be in the background. Jonny calling it a day ensured that was very much the case. Another reason to be thankful to him apart from the pleasure of seeing him play at close quarters so many times.

It was Toulon-Saracens, the Millennium Stadium, almost my spiritual home. May 24. My third Heineken Cup final. For a guy who wanted to go out on top, this was the perfect conclusion. As long as I didn't balls it up.

It went well thankfully. There was one stage where Bryan Habana, who is one of the most exciting players I have ever encountered, took a theatrical fall after a running into Owen Farrell. I gave him a bit of a ticking off for that and he accepted he'd been caught out. When you have empathy for players and the game, you understood that sort of situation when you see it, and you make sure you have noticed it. But with the ball in Saracens' possession, there was no need to do anything about it other than have a quiet word.

This was my 88th European game, having done 10 in the Amlin Challenge

Cup. It was my third Heineken Cup final. I missed out on a couple of more by virtue of that fantastic period of ascendancy enjoyed by Munster first and then Leinster.

There is no regret about that. In particular, as a former Leinster player and captain, I was delighted to see them flourish having suffered for so long with the tag of being soft.

Michael Cheika was the key man for Leinster. They developed subsequently and Joe Schmidt brought them to another level again but without Cheika, that success story might never have been written. He brought a ruthlessness to the team that hadn't been there. Bringing in the likes of Rocky Elsom was crucial in terms of establishing that culture. He was a colossus. Leo Cullen and Shane Jennings were important in that regard too when they came back from Leicester.

Felipe Contepomi complemented the flair of Drico and Gordon D'Arcy and the rest of that brilliant back division. But they needed the hardness to get over the line.

Cheika has been up in the dock more times than anyone else for the way he treats refs after he loses, but that's him. He sets very high standards and has a pathological hatred of losing. He was the perfect fit for Leinster, exactly what they needed.

The fact that it wasn't about money for him, being a hugely successful businessman, means he doesn't have to pander to anyone. He isn't worrying about keeping his job so he will do things his way. That takes the pressure off.

He was an inspirational choice by Australia to take over as head coach. In many ways, they replicated the Leinster he took over. It was a squad laced with attacking talent that tended to be bullied out of games. They had a bit of a soft underbelly, with the pack always targeted by the opposition.

It is no coincidence that this has improved since Cheika took over. The performances and results have improved gradually.

▎▐▌▎

It was a pretty amazing send-off. I could not have scripted it any better. As the end approached I joked with the TMO Simon McDowell that I would love to stop the clock so that it never hit 80. I wanted to keep it going. I actually said the same for my last Test. But of course I couldn't do that and I blew that whistle one last time. It was over.

There was no sadness. This was a happy feeling and there was a party vibe that helped. Will Greenwood said some nice things but it was Scott Quinnell who nearly got the waterworks going when he gave me a hug. I had refereed his shared testimonial with Rob Howley against a World XV at this very venue in 2005.

'Rollers, we'll really miss you. Thank you for everything.'

I began to tear up but thankfully the lights were dimmed as they were doing to presentation and I was able to compose myself. For those 15 or 20 seconds though, it hit home that it was all over.

So many thoughts go through your mind but at the nub of it all was that it was job done. I had embarked on an amazing odyssey, had so many wonderful memories and absolutely no regrets. I say that now with conviction. I would not change a thing because every experience is a learning experience.

It took ages to get inside with the presentations and photos but I was in no hurry. I was just soaking it all up. The extravaganza, the atmosphere, the pyrotechnics. One last time.

Sitting down in the dressing room, I was struck by how satisfied I felt. I didn't want it to stop but it had to. I had gotten more out of it than I could ever have imagined. People think refereeing is a thankless job but nobody puts a gun to our head and makes us go out there. I found it immensely satisfying. If you want to stay involved in rugby after your playing career is ended, there is no better way.

I was blessed.

CHAPTER
TWENTY-FIVE

People often ask me what meant more. Playing or refereeing. Representing my country or refereeing a World Cup final. The answer comes quickly but when you sit down and analyse it, the comparisons aren't so straightforward. They are different.

Nothing beats playing but refereeing is the next best thing.

I will never forget what it meant to play for Ireland, particularly on that first day when I was selected to start. I was the best scrum half in Ireland on that given day, picked ahead of the hundreds of people who played the position in the country at that time. That meant more.

I really wanted the World Cup final though and when you think about being the best referee on the planet on that given day, ahead of hundreds of thousands of other officials, it is incredibly humbling. Even getting to the World Cup was an achievement, being considered amongst a select elite group. But I always wanted to get better. To be the best.

So looking back on it now, I was as proud about being selected to do the World Cup final in Paris in 2007 as I was putting on the green jersey. And because I felt that I was representing Ireland anyway, in a sense, I was wearing a green jersey once more.

From an enormity point of view, the World Cup final is more significant because it is the biggest event in rugby. And you are a member of a very exclusive group. Before the 2015 event, only six people have refereed World Cup finals. Sadly, Kerry Fitzgerald, who refereed the inaugural decider, is no longer with us.

It was the pinnacle of my refereeing career but it was a different type of success. Winning my first international cap as a starter was the highlight of my entire rugby career because when you pare it back to your innermost being, from an emotional perspective, there's more involvement from within a team environment than you can get as a referee.

There is something different about going out as part of a team and knowing all those people in the stands, or a good portion of them are there to support you and your mates. When you are referee, even at the World Cup final, including family, friends and the selectors, there might be 15 or 20 people rooting for you out of 83,000. That's a different dynamic to 38,000 out of 40,000 on your side at Lansdowne Road, and you representing them.

That is how it should be. The game is about the players. It should never be about the guy in the middle. Spectators go to the games or switch on the TV to watch players. Not a referee being fussy and making himself star of the show.

A good referee can help the players to provide entertaining rugby by judging the materiality of an offence and not being trigger-happy. I was hard on the breakdown because you want that ball to get out quickly. That was my philosophy and I believe it was what most players and supporters wanted. For that reason, it was vital to understand the advantage law and apply it properly.

A good referee is able to communicate well, understood the game and empathised with the players. He is fit, physically and mentally. He prepares properly. He earns the players' trust.

A good referee facilitates the players from the shadows. Not an orchestrator but a helper.

I ∎ ∎ I

For a while I considered getting into the fitness side of things. It has always been an area of major interest and I had learned so much about nutrition, strength and conditioning and general fitness. I spoke to Karl Gilligan, who had been my personal trainer for around 10 years about what opportunities there might be.

In the end, I stuck to a more familiar theme to establish Alain Rolland Refereeing and Business Consultancy Ltd. There are a couple of strands to it.

I have a contract with World Rugby and a number of individual rugby unions to work on a consultancy basis with elite and developing referees, coaches and teams. I worked with the referees at the Women's World Cup in 2014 and was referee manager at the Junior World Trophy in 2015.

The national unions I am working with are the Tier 2 teams that have qualified for the 2015 World Cup: Georgia, Romania, Fiji, Samoa, Tonga, Japan, Canada, Namibia, USA and Uruguay. So there is a lot of travelling involved.

Generally my job in dealing with referees, players and coaches is to apply the principles that served me so well. Communication is the most important tool of all and trust comes when players and officials can talk to one another.

We are looking to eradicate unforced errors and to give referees and players the tools to manage their way through the high pressures of a game in the same way Owen Doyle did for me.

We are also looking at teaching players how to talk to referees. More Smit than Papé. There is a time and there is a way. We deal in interpretations of the laws, particularly at the breakdown and the scrum, the two areas that are responsible for the vast majority of penalties in rugby.

Another part of my work with World Rugby involves looking at TMO protocols. I have discussed that in previous chapters. This will ramp up after the 2015 World Cup because something needs to be done to return the majority of decision-making to the pitch and away from the booth.

As well as that, I have a separate contract to work with a couple of the Italian referees. That involves reviewing match tapes, advising on conditioning, fitness, time management and anything else that comes up. That has been very enjoyable and brings me back to the coaching I had always thought I would get into when I finished playing.

I felt I could offer more than just refereeing expertise though, given my years of experience in business management. So I teamed up with former referee, Brian MacNeice and James Bowen of renowned high performance business advisors Kotinos Partners, to launch a training programme focussing on critical skills for managers.

That has gone very well. So many of the principles of refereeing are applicable to managing a business and running a team.

It usually comes back to communication once more and establishing trust. I show clips and encourage dialogue. Just one example is the video of my exchanges with Steve Borthwick in 2008. You won't get somebody to work with you if your body language is as negative as mine was and you are getting snappy.

The importance of preparation, attention to detail, having a work-life balance, time management, discipline, being able to delegate and work within a team – these are all skills that are conducive to good supervision. Why go to a client and not know anything about them? If you're in business, and you have no knowledge, you cannot make an informed contribution to discussions.

As a result of this work, another company called AP Partners approached me to do similar work in France and I have done a few conferences. It is funny how much I enjoy talking in front of all these people, for someone who would be so quiet normally. I guess it is something I am passionate about and believe in, so public speaking has come very easily to me and is something I relish doing.

In addition to that I have companies who approach me to give motivational speeches. They give me a particular theme. A popular one is the characteristics of a good team and I never look any further than the All Black in that instance. As far as they are concerned, when it comes to setting standards, okay is not okay.

They also work at developing on-field leaders. Whether you have one cap or 130, if you have something to say you will be listened to. It is important to create that sort of an environment.

The most important thing about the All Blacks though is their culture. It is what being part of that team means to them. It is not about clocking in and clocking out to pay the bills. You will get much more out of your workplace if people want to be there, if they feel they can contribute in a meaningful way.

So thankfully, I have hit the ground running with the new business. Sometimes I sit in the World Rugby office with Joël Jutge and just smile, marvelling at the fact that we are being paid for doing something we love.

Lizzie made the very valid point that if I had been in Cornmarket on the Monday morning after the Heineken Cup final, with no rugby in my life, I would have found it very difficult to cope. The way things have worked out now, I don't miss refereeing because I am still involved in the game. I only got into refereeing as a means of staying in the game. I love rugby, I'm involved and I can still make an impact.

I will even be at the 2015 World Cup with the Tier 2 teams. It's perfect.

The one negative from a family viewpoint is that I am probably travelling as much if not more than I was as a referee. But when you are trying to establish a new business, you have to put in the hard yards. It will be worth it in the end.

As ever, Lizzie and the kids have been great and I cut as many corners as possible to get home as quickly as I can. I want to be a great husband and Dad too.

I am an exceptionally good time manager and there isn't a minute of the day that isn't accounted for. When I have to travel I will arrive as late as possible and leave as early as I can. If the rest of a team of officials were flying with me to games, they realised that it meant an early trip home. It is important to me.

You can't change the nature of the beast. Or maybe you can but I enjoy being competitive. It has made me who I am.

I want to do this work to the best of my ability. But then I want to train better than anyone still. I have done a number of charity cycles but I have no interest in a gentle stroll. I understand completely what the objective of the exercise is but if there's a group of us starting at the bottom of a hill, I want to be first to the top. And I get a kick from doing so.

▮▮▮▮

I still miss playing, much more than I miss refereeing. You cannot substitute the whole ball-in-hand experience, the physicality, weighing up the options.

Scoring tries and smashing someone in the tackle. You cannot replicate that.

Because my involvement at international level was so limited, operating in front of full stadiums of 15,000, 45,000 or 90,000 was not something I was accustomed to. As a referee at the elite level for 13 years, I got that most weeks. It was a different buzz to the anticipation of playing but a buzz nonetheless.

I had great fun refereeing and there were no initiation rites where I had to sing on a bus or take part in drinking games.

But I miss the changing room, seeing the jersey on the wall. I miss the motivational speeches, really ramping up the emotion in the dressing room before getting out there. Lads shouting, ready to kill and die for the rest of the lads.

As a ref, you know they're doing that across the corridor but it's your job to make sure that they don't kill or die, that they don't cross the line. But you recognise that they're willing to so if you see someone with that extra wild-eyed look, you have a word with his captain in a bid to cut off impending doom at the pass. You don't want to have to take drastic action.

Transitioning from being one of 20 guys going to war to the solitary existence of yourself in your own room with your own thoughts is quite stark and was one of the most difficult things to overcome initially. Being pretty well known made it easier for me than it was for some others because local club officials would want to talk about Ireland or 'Rock or something like that.

I've used the term a few times but as a ref, you have the best seat in the house. It is like sharing a stool with Elvis as he played the piano or walking the yard with Tim Robbins and Morgan Freeman in *Shawshank Redemption*.

Rugby has been a huge part of my life and I am so fortunate to be still involved.

On to the next chapter.